My 66 Years in the Big Leagues

Connie Mack

With a New Introduction by
Rich Westcott

DOVER PUBLICATIONS, INC.
Mineola, New York

Copyright

Bibliographical Note

This Dover edition, first published in 2009, is an unabridged republication of
the work originally published by The John C. Winston Company, Philadelphia,
in 1950. A new Introduction by Rich Westcott has been added to the Dover
edition.

Library of Congress Cataloging-in-Publication Data

Mack, Connie, 1862–1956.
    My 66 years in the big leagues / Connie Mack, with a new introduction by
Rich Westcott. — Dover ed.
       p. cm.
    Originally published: Philadelphia : Winston, [1950].
    Includes index.
    ISBN-13: 978-0-486-47184-6
    ISBN-10: 0-486-47184-5
    1. Mack, Connie, 1862-1956. 2. Baseball managers—Pennsylvania—
Philadelphia—Biography. 3. Baseball team owners—Pennsylvania—Phila-
delphia—Biography. 4. Baseball—United States—History. 5. Philadelphia
Athletics (Baseball team) —History. I. Title. II. Title: My sixty-six years in
the big leagues.

GV865.M27A3 2009
796.357092—dc22
[B]
                                          2008047118

Manufactured in the United States of America
Dover Publications, Inc., 31 East 2nd Street, Mineola, N.Y. 11501

INTRODUCTION TO THE DOVER EDITION

CONNIE MACK was originally born Cornelius McGillicuddy. Later, he was nicknamed the "Tall Tactician." Many simply addressed him as "Mr. Mack." Eventually, he was called, the "Grand Old Man of Baseball." By any name, it can be said without a degree of uncertainty that no one in baseball was ever comparable to Connie Mack.

Simultaneously, Mack was a manager, an owner, one of baseball's most influential participants, and a towering figure in the evolution of the game. Nobody in the history of baseball ever combined all those roles at once. Nor did anyone ever spend as many years in the game.

Elected to the Baseball Hall of Fame in 1937, Mack's illustrious career started in 1886 as a player and stretched through 1954 when his Philadelphia Athletics were sold and moved to Kansas City. He managed the A's for fifty of those years, extending from 1901 to 1950, guiding the club to nine American League pennants and five World Series victories. Counting a little more than two years with the Pittsburgh Pirates, Mack managed longer, won more games (3,731), and lost more games (3,948) than anyone in baseball history.

His job off the field, first as part owner of the Athletics, then as the team's sole proprietor, was equally noteworthy. A key figure in the origin of the American League, Mack helped to direct baseball from its low-level status of the late 1800s to a lofty ranking as the "national pastime."

With his partner Ben Shibe—ironically, also a partner of Phillies owner Al Reach in a sporting goods business—Mack had been awarded the Athletics' franchise and charged with the responsibility of forming a team and building a ballpark. Ultimately, Mack oversaw the construction of Columbia Park in the north section of Philadelphia. For the eight years that the A's played there, Connie lived in the neighborhood, local kids often following him from his house to the ballpark.

When Columbia Park was deemed too small for the Athletics' steadily increasing number of fans, Mack commissioned the construction of what would be named Shibe Park. There, at a stadium that became an icon among Philadelphia sports venues, the A's staged both their best and worst years.

Shibe Park, built at a cost of $315,248.69, was also the place where Mack made some of his most controversial moves. He raised the right field wall from twelve to thirty-four feet, thereby preventing fans sitting on rooftops across the street from viewing games for free. (Fans called the new barrier the "spite wall.") In 1939, he added lights to Shibe Park, making it the first American League stadium to hold night games. Neighborhood residents challenged both changes in court, although they lost each time.

With his office located high in a tower that dominated the front end of the ballpark, Mack governed an empire that had far-reaching effects on Philadelphia sports. For many years, the A's were the dominant sports team in the city, and whatever Mack said or did was usually accepted on merit. Connie hung out with local politicians, curried the favor of area newsmen, and hobnobbed with the city's upper-class residents.

He took in the Phillies as tenants at Shibe Park in 1938. In 1953, the Phillies renamed the ballpark Connie Mack Stadium. He provided the pro-football Philadelphia Eagles with a home for many years. He rented the field to Negro League baseball teams, giving them a spacious venue for huge crowds of their followers. And he provided a home for local high school and college football and baseball teams, major boxing matches, and a variety of other sporting and non-sporting events.

Mack was a master innovator. He was perhaps the first baseball executive to scout colleges and universities for talent, a process that resulted in his signing, among others, future Hall of Famers Eddie Collins, Eddie Plank, and Chief Bender. He had his former players primed to spot young talent, such as the case when Frank (Home Run) Baker sent him Jimmie Foxx and Ty Cobb recommended Sam Chapman. He was even one of the originators of the relief pitcher when he began stationing a hurler in a makeshift bullpen for use in case the starting pitcher faltered.

"Mr. Mack," Cobb once said, "knows more about baseball than anybody in the game."

Connie wore street clothes when he managed, a process that he began in the 1890s while piloting Milwaukee in the Western League. Around 1912, he began waving his scorecard to position his players. He was one of the early promoters of Ladies Day games, a practice he began in 1936. He joined with others, including Phillies owner Gerry Nugent and sports entrepreneur Eddie Gottlieb, to overturn Pennsylvania's "blue laws" which prevented professional teams from playing on Sundays. And he was one of the first owners to hire a publicity director, publish a team yearbook, and employ a public address announcer.

No one, of course, ever accused Mack of being perfect. He could have purchased a young pitcher named Babe Ruth from the minor league Baltimore Orioles for $23,000, but didn't. He had Christy Mathewson signed to a contract, but let him get away. Joe Jackson was a member of the A's before Connie traded him. He also swapped George Kell and Nellie Fox, getting little in return. All were young players on their way to glittering careers.

Mack's teams finished last in thiry-three percent of their seasons, a record unsurpassed by any other major league club. In 1915, the Athletics became the only team in baseball history to go from first place to last, plummeting from a berth in the 1914 World Series to a 43–109 record the following year.

That was because Mack had a penchant for selling off his best players, particularly after they had led his teams to a string of World Series appearances. In addition to needing the money that those deals brought, the often cash-strapped Connie claimed that fans would rather see a second-place team fighting for the pennant than a team that wins year after year. Dumping his top players satisfied that philosophy.

Yet despite shortcomings, not the least of which was his unwillingness to replace himself as manager when the A's were playing poorly, he was widely respected and liked by most of his players. He piloted the A's until the age of eight-seven. His career was only interrupted twice by illness. "You really admired him, and you learned a lot from playing for him," said outfielder Gus Zernial. Often, Mack helped strapped players, such as was the case when he loaned $2,000 to outfielder Whitey Witt for the down payment on a house.

Connie was strict, but a shrewd judge of talent. He knew when to farm out players and when to keep them. He knew to make young catcher Jimmie Foxx and shortstop Stuffy McInnis first basemen. He knew all the nuances of the game. And, as catcher and later coach, Ira Thomas once said, "He had the talent for bringing individuals together as a team."

In My 66 Years in the Big Leagues, which was originally published in 1950, Mack revealed many of these talents, as well as his rationale for operating the way he did. It is a book packed with special insights.

Sometimes writing philosophically, Mack, who died in 1956, discussed the game as it was when he was a major part of it. He did it in a way that was highly informative, straightforward, and sometimes humorous. A reader is exposed not only to the wisdom of the Tall Tactician, but also the thoughts behind what governed his actions.

Naturally, Mack emphasized his own successes and biases. He discussed the path he took from being an unknown catcher earning eighty dollars a month in his first season to one of the most powerful figures in baseball. He talked about forming the Athletics and luring players from the Phillies. He explained how he discovered and developed nine future Hall of Famers. And he cited his role in the construction of both Columbia Park and Shibe Park.

Mack didn't limit his book to a discussion of just himself and the Athletics. He provided glimpses of memorable games; top opposing players such as Babe Ruth, Ty Cobb, Christy Mathewson, Tris Speaker, and Lou Gehrig; the media; umpires; his friends and his foes; the Federal League; the role of women in baseball; and the game at high school and college levels. Connie even offered a look into the future, although his speculation fell far short of the reality of today.

The book was written before Mack's health deteriorated and before his sons, Roy and Earle, sold the team to a group led by Arnold Johnson, who shifted the franchise to Kansas City. It provides a special view of Connie Mack and the first fifty years of the team he ran. It is a book that makes a major contribution to the understanding and history of the game of baseball as it was played in the first half of the twentieth century.

RICH WESTCOTT

Rich Westcott is a leading authority on Philadelphia baseball and a long-time writer and historian. He is the author of nineteen sports books, twelve of which deal with baseball in the Philadelphia area.

INTRODUCTION TO THE 1950 EDITION

AMERICA hails with enthusiasm the historic year of 1950, which marks the close of the first half and the beginning of the second half of the twentieth century.

This year marks also two great American anniversaries: America's national game celebrates its seventy-fifth year or Diamond Jubilee of the National League, and the fiftieth year or Golden Jubilee of the American League.

Nationwide celebrations to be held in 1951 mark the beginning of the new era.

In commemoration of these historic events, the grand patriarch of America's national game, now in his eighty-eighth year, has written his autobiography relating his experiences and adventures during his "sixty-six years in the big leagues."

Known to all Americans as Connie Mack, he has been called "The Grand Old Man of Baseball," "The Noblest Sportsman of Them All," "Mr. Baseball," "A Great Champion, a Great Man, a Great Spirit," and the "Man with More Friends than Any Other Man in America." It is an important event for Connie Mack to give the world his memoirs, for he is the truest exemplification of the American spirit.

The national game to which he has given his long life is the truest exponent of the principles upon which our great nation have been founded and through which it has become the greatest nation in the world.

Baseball is democracy in action; in it all men are "free and equal," regardless of race, nationality, or creed. Every man is given the rightful opportunity to rise to the top on his own merits. The great democracy of fans in the grandstands and in the bleachers are given the right to cheer or jeer according to their own free will. It is the fullest expression of freedom of speech, freedom of press, and freedom of assembly in our national life.

Every baseball team and every baseball game is a United Nations in session, "of, by, and for the people." The peoples of all origins and from all nations gather in a unity of purpose on our baseball fields and in our stadiums. No one asks about the birth or the social or economic status of his fellow men. Here they gather, rich and poor, on absolute equality in human rights.

Wholesome competition, under our system of individual initiative and free enterprise, is the heritage of every American—the right of self-development.

The life of Connie Mack is proof positive of the American way of life. It is the wide-open door of opportunity for every American in every walk of life. Connie Mack started as a poor boy in a New England village, working for a few cents a day, and in his long and active life he has created a business property worth millions of dollars.

Erect, slender, alert, and in his eighty-eighth year, keen of vision and hearing, he is an impressive figure of dignity, courtesy, and graciousness. Although six feet two inches in height, he keeps his weight down to around 150 pounds. His penetrating Irish blue eyes look you straight in the face. He seldom raises his voice, but speaks with decision and friendliness. His features are aquiline, a perfect subject for a painter or a sculptor. His outstanding qualities are gentility, honesty, integrity. These, with justice and humanity, are the foundations of his strong character. He is a great American.

How he has conquered the years is a notable example of good living. His friends tell me that his daily habits are a model for any man. He does not indulge in tobacco, intoxicating beverages, or profanity. And he never worries, he leaves that to the other fellow. Moderation in all things is his motto, to live one day at a time.

Connie Mack has known and has been the friend of most of the great men of our times. Presidents, Senators, Congressmen, mayors, and leaders in all walks of life have held him in highest esteem. He is surrounded, as he sits in his executive offices, with trophies, loving cups, medals, and numerous tokens of the distinguished service he has rendered his country.

Tributes have come to him from all parts of the country. Among his thousands of treasured memories are the Philadelphia Award for distinguished service (1929); silver Buffalo Award from the National Council of Boy Scouts for Distinguished Service to Boyhood (1938); election to the Cooperstown Hall of Fame as "Builder of Baseball" (1939); appointment by the General Assembly of Pennsylvania and proclamation by the Governor of "Connie Mack Day" (1941); celebration of "Mack Day" at the Yankee Stadium in New York and the presentation of the keys to the city by Mayor William O'Dwyer before a large assembly at New York City Hall (1949); honorary degree, Doctor of Physical Education of Pennsylvania Military College; and the establishment of a vast circuit of juvenile baseball teams under the direction of the American Legion.

Memories dear to his great heart are the pennants won by his Philadelphia Athletics who, under his masterful leadership, have won nine American League pennants and five World Series.

The life of Connie Mack is an inspiration to every American. I believe it to be an American classic, one of the great autobiographies of our times. He never lost courage, he never lost faith. When forced by financial crises to rebuild his teams, he went to work with confidence and determination. We all admire his strong character and subscribe to his creed that our national game shall remain the true exponent of the American spirit.

—FRANCIS TREVELYAN MILLER

CONTENTS

CHAPTER 1

THE FIRST 100 YEARS ARE THE HARDEST

I HAVE had my share of cheers and jeers. They have called me Mr. Baseball, the Grand Old Man of Baseball, and many things unprintable. But if I were to write my own epitaph it would read, "He loved his God, his home, his country, his fellow men and baseball."

By the grace of God, if He so wills it, I enter my ninetieth year on December 23, 1952, with only ten years to go to cross the home plate of the century mark. Whether I make it depends on the decision of the Great Umpire who sooner or later calls us "out."

The scoreboard at the moment says: "Two strikes—three balls." Father Time is in the pitcher's box.

There is gratitude in my heart for having been privileged to take part in the development of America's national game. I have seen it rise from the cow pastures and sand lots into the greatest game in the world, a game "of, by, and for the people."

I was a boy in the typical American home town of East Brookfield, Massachusetts, a village of little more than 300 population, when the National League was formed seventy-five years ago. I was one of the fathers of the American League when it was organized fifty years ago.

Many happy memories are brought back to me as we celebrate the Diamond Jubilee of the National League, the

1

Golden Jubilee of the American League, and the Fiftieth Anniversary of the National Association of Professional Baseball Players. As baseball years are counted by seasons, these anniversaries all come at the close of the season of 1950.

The Power of Inspiration

Baseball is a powerful inspirational force in American life. It is a training ground for good citizenship. There need be no fear for the future of America so long as we maintain the high standards of good sportsmanship in our national game.

It seems significant to me that while the American people were celebrating the one-hundredth anniversary of our Declaration of Independence, and throngs were gathering at the Centennial Exposition in Philadelphia in 1876, the National League establishing America's national game was born.

It seems equally significant that the American League came in with the twentieth century and its amazing developments. With two great leagues under the American flag, and true to the American system of free enterprise, the natural result has been strong competition for supremacy.

We, however, have handled our problems much more intelligently than the nations who, in their fights for world supremacy, have engaged in two bloody world wars, settling their disputes on battlefields, while we in our national game have settled our disputes peacefully in our World Series.

When I was a young fellow of but seventy-three, my friends began to remind me that I had passed the allotted threescore and ten years and that the time had come for me to write my autobiography.

I succumbed to their entreaties to the extent of a series of personal reminiscences that appeared in *The Saturday Evening Post* under the title: "Life Begins at Seventy-Three." I now look back on these as the "follies of youth," for since that time I have reached, I hope, the discretion of maturity.

When a man is approaching his ninetieth year he begins to

gather wisdom. His opinions have taken on substantial form, and he is beginning to see the world as it is. As I look about me on the wonders of life, the magnitude of God's creation, I realize the infinite purpose behind it.

An old New England neighbor once declared: "The only improvement I could make on God would be to make good health instead of disease contagious." He too was shortsighted, for good health is contagious and disease is the exception. Millions of us are in perfect health, while a small percentage of us are in bad health.

I am more inclined to agree with the man who said: "The only change I would make in God's plan would be for us to grow younger each year rather than older. We waste too much of our youth in growing old."

We Live in a Marvelous Age

When I look around me and recall that I was here before most of our modern inventions, I begin to feel as old as Methuselah. I was here before the telephone, before electric lights, the talking machine, the typewriter, the automobile, motion pictures, the airplane, and long before the radio. I came when railroads and the telegraph were new.

It was in my first year of professional baseball that somebody invented the fountain pen, and it was then that the first electric trolley cars began to run. I was playing with the Washington Senators when somebody invented the adding machine and photographic films. I was with the Pittsburgh Pirates when somebody invented photo-engraving, and our newspapers first printed actual news photographs. Before that the only pictures we ever saw were old woodcuts or line drawings. It was quite a sensation to us when the horseless carriage came along.

We were just starting to win pennants with our Philadelphia Athletics when the Wright Brothers made their first successful flight in an airplane. It didn't create nearly so much excitement as our winning our first pennant. If anybody had suggested television to us then, we should have considered the person crazy.

It had never occurred to me at seventy-three, when I wrote the *Post* story, that I would ever be the author of a book. Well, here it is—believe it or not. When I heard about young people in their twenties writing their autobiographies, I decided that it was the duty of any man approaching his ninetieth year to tell how he did it.

In the vigor of youth as an octogenarian about to become a nonagenarian (and perhaps a centenarian) I am enjoying my debut as a young author. Moreover, as a man of Irish blood, I do it with a sense of humor.

If it is true that old men like to write about the follies of their youth to amuse us, then my recollections may not amuse you, for my follies, as follies are known, have been few. I have led a very exciting life without any false stimulations: I do not need and do not indulge in alcoholic stimulation; neither do I smoke or use profanity. I do not state this as a virtue, but as a fact. And I have known no dull moments. Certainly I have been in love, and I married both girls—but not at the same time!

Now nearing my eighty-ninth year I am still in love—in love with my family, in love with my country, and in love with baseball.

Announcement

For many years now my friends, the sports writers, have been speculating about when I will retire from baseball. I guess I should have done so many years ago but, being a man whose life is so absorbed by baseball, it has been hard for me to make this decision. I am still in fine health, I enjoy the work and up to now I would have been lost without the work on the bench.

But you have to make the break sometime and this 1950 season seems to be the most logical time. It will be a most strenuous year for me and, when it is over, I will consider that I have earned a rest from the vigorous activities of a long life.

I am therefore able to announce, here and now, my plans.

In complete accord, my associates in the Mack and Shibe families have begun to prepare the way for my retirement. While retaining the presidency for the time being, I have stepped out as treasurer, turning the financial tasks over to my son, Connie Mack, Jr., who has been assistant treasurer since 1938. My son Roy Mack remains as vice president. Our board of directors, with the exception of the late Robert J. Schroeder, remains unchanged: Roy, Earle, Connie, Jr., Benjamin Shibe Macfarland.

My Shibe partners are in active service. Benjamin Shibe Macfarland, grandson of our club's first president, who has been the senior road secretary in the American League in years of service, has been associated with the A's since boyhood. He is now secretary of our club, with his nephew, twenty-two-year-old Frank Macfarland, Jr., succeeding him as road secretary. Frank Macfarland, Sr., is now our assistant treasurer.

It is my desire always to have a Mack-Shibe combination in our national game. For this purpose I have trained my sons to keep the tradition going, and I hope they will train their sons to follow in the path of their grandfather—and so on all through the Mack line.

My son Earle will succeed me as manager of the Philadelphia Athletics. My sons Roy and Connie, Jr., will be associated in the business end and the financial operations. Earle Mack started about 1913 and played his first game as catcher with the A's when Coombs and Plank were pitching. At bat he got a single and a three-bagger and outhit any man in our club that day. And he was a good first baseman.

His managerial experience has covered many years as my assistant, and his previous experience was as manager of the Raleigh, North Carolina, club for three years, from 1913-1915. In 1917 he became manager of the Charlotte team in the North Carolina League; later the same year he was made manager of the Hanover team in the Blue Ridge League.

In 1920-22 he managed the Moline, Illinois, team, and went from there to the Martinsburg club in the Blue Ridge League, and won the championship. I called him to Philadelphia in 1924, and he has been the assistant manager of the A's for twenty-six years.

My son Roy never played baseball, but has become an expert in the business office. Connie, Jr., my youngest son, is interested in office administration. He played on his Germantown Academy team and then starred with Duke University but later became a coach. The Mack boys are all "chips off the old block."

Some people may charge me with forming a dynasty in our national game. Call it what you will, I assure you that the Macks and Shibes are imbued with the spirit of American democracy and will always remain true to the best traditions of American sportsmanship.

It's Great to Be Alive

Again let me say that it is grand to be alive on these Diamond and Golden Jubilees of our national game. Today baseball has reached tremendous proportions. Its future is assured on a sound financial basis. It offers unlimited opportunities to young men with athletic ability.

In 1949 more than 62,000,000 people paid admissions to witness the skill of the professional players. About 20,000,000 of these attended the games of the National and American Leagues, over 41,000,000 more attended games in the minor leagues.

Add to these millions more who eagerly followed the games

over radio and television, and you begin to appreciate what baseball is doing for the American people—millions of men, women, and children, finding recreation and exhilaration in our national game.

How many professional baseball games have been played throughout the country since I became manager of the Philadelphia Athletics? It has been conservatively estimated that more than 1,000,000 games have been played in organized baseball since baseball began.

We now have two major leagues and more than fifty minor leagues. These are playing some 60,000 games a year. That means that at the present rate they will play 3,000,000 games or more during the next fifty years.

Our yearly attendance will increase every year. At the present rate, the grand total during the next fifty years may reach 310,000,000—twice the present population of the United States.

This is a wonderful world, filled with wonderful people and, although I shall not be here to see if my predictions prove true, I shall stay here as long as the Great Commissioner of Time will renew my yearly contracts.

While these three-quarter century and half-century records are completed at the close of the 1950 playing season, the baseball world decided to hold year-long jubilee celebrations throughout 1951, starting the next great era in national baseball. The two major leagues, all the minor leagues, the American Legion Junior clubs, and the sand-lot teams will join in the festivities.

CHAPTER 2

BOYHOOD IN THE OLD HOME TOWN

My BOYHOOD in a typical American village was in itself a rich inheritance. It was there, close to the "good earth," that I learned what it means to be an American.

Fortunate indeed is the boy who is born in this land of freedom. My father and mother came here from Ireland in the days when Lincoln was reaffirming the principles of "equality and opportunity"; when he was declaring "God must have loved the common people—that's why He made so many of them."

My parents bid good-by to their beloved Emerald Isle to become Americans. And they were proud of it all the days of their lives.

My father, Michael McGillicuddy, came from McGillicuddy's Reek in County Kerry. My mother, Mary McKillop McGillicuddy, had an Irish heart big enough to hold the whole world.

Father and mother settled in their little home in the hills of New England, not far from Plymouth Rock, but nearer Lexington and Bunker Hill. Not far from here in the little village of East Brookfield, in Massachusetts, a hamlet of about 300 population, I was born around midnight on December 22, 1862.

My father was away in Lincoln's army, with the 51st Massachusetts Infantry, fighting for the preservation of the Union.

It was some time before he heard of me. I probably was intended as a Christmas present to my mother but I beat Santa Claus by a few days. My mother had me christened Cornelius McGillicuddy, but this soon was shortened to Connie Mack. And although you know me as Connie Mack, I am still a McGillicuddy all the way through.

I was only three years old when news of Lincoln's assassination reached our little town. Our family felt as if they had lost a personal friend, and my mother offered prayers for the repose of his soul.

At the end of the war, Father came home and returned to his job in the mill in East Brookfield. The McGillicuddy family grew and grew until there were seven children in the flock, five boys and two girls. And what a happy family we were!

This was in the days when my father, an honest, hard-working man, had to support a family of nine on wages of about ten dollars a week.

Personal Sorrow Comes to Everyone

The first personal sorrow I ever knew was when a contagious disease struck our community. Our home became isolated; no neighbor dared enter. Whether it was scarlet fever or diphtheria I do not know. But this memory can never be erased from my mind: My little sister, Mary Augusta, only a year old, died in my arms.

My sister, Nellie, who was about thirteen years old, also died during the epidemic. The hand of death had struck our home. Through it all my mother remained a woman of courage and character who gave her life to her home and family.

I am the last of the original McGillicuddys of East Brookfield. Gene, my youngest brother, who was ill much of the time, came to Philadelphia, but died here as a young man. Dennis also came to Philadelphia, where he was night watchman at the ball park. One time he was hit by a baseball bat, an injury from which he never fully recovered, and he too passed away. Another brother died of the flu in the epidemic of 1918. My oldest brother, Michael, lived to be eighty-nine.

My father, Michael McGillicuddy, passed away at fifty-two; but my mother lived to be seventy-five.

We were a happy family in our little home in East Brookfield. The house is gone now—it was burned to the ground.

Often I can still hear the voice of one of the East Brookfield gang yelling at me:

"Hey, Slats! Come on over and play four-o'cat!"

My friends used to tell me I was a pretty good "four-o-cat-ter" when I was nine years old. This is the way we played the game: With our bare toes we drew two rings thirty feet apart, with a batter in each ring. The pitcher stood outside the ring and tossed the ball to the batter so that he could hit it. When the batter hit it, he ran for the opposite ring.

If he got tagged with the ball between the circles, he was "out." If he was hit by a thrown ball he was out. If the ball was caught on the fly he was out. In those days our bat was flat and the homemade ball was soft, a cloth cover stuffed with cotton or rags.

It was not until I was older and bigger that I was permitted to graduate into the "big boys' game," where we had a big bat and a leather-covered ball, three bases and a home plate.

We kids were all industrious. I would pick vegetables at a neighbor's farm for about ten cents a week. When I was nine years old I worked summers in the cotton mill, where I received thirty-three cents a day for running errands, carrying stock, and operating an elevator.

My wages were paid monthly and averaged for the days I worked about six dollars a month—the exact amount of the monthly rent for our little home. I gave it to my mother, and she gave it to the landlord. It made me happy to know that I was helping to provide for my mother to this extent.

We were given an hour for lunch at the cotton mill. I split this valuable time into two parts: ten minutes for lunch and fifty minutes for "four-o'cat." Even when taking time off for fishing or swimming in Lake Lashaway, whose wooded shores were once inhabited by the Quabaug Indians, we were playing "pitch and catch" on the banks.

Life in the Country

The Brookfields, for which I have such fond memories, were a family of four villages. The mother town, Brookfield, originally called Quabaug, was founded in 1664, only forty-four years after the Pilgrims landed at Plymouth Rock. Its population now is only slightly over 1,300. In the village library, known as the Merrick Library, at the northeast corner of the Common, you will find the French writing desk that belonged to Louis XVI and Marie Antoinette, when she was guillotined. Not far away from the library is the famous Brookfield Inn, with its low-ceilinged taproom and sign bearing the date 1771.

East Brookfield, my birthplace, today, eighty-eight years later, has grown to about 1,000.

West Brookfield, with a population now of about 1,400, was' in the early years of the American nation the home of Ebenezer Merriam, whose sons opened a printing plant in Springfield, a few miles away, and began the publication of Noah Webster's dictionary.

Approaching the common in West Brookfield is a huge boulder from which George Whitefield, in 1741, preached his fiery sermon to more than 5,000 persons gathered by wagon and horseback from all the surrounding towns. Not far away may be seen Indian Rock, where King Philip's warriors from these natural breastworks in 1675 "one garrison house defended to the last."

North Brookfield stands in my memory not only for its tanneries and shoemaking establishments, but as the home town of my friend, George M. Cohan, the "Yankee Doodle Boy" who once lived here.

"Georgie" was not only a great trouper, but was also a great baseball fan and always carried a baseball bat, glove and ball in his baggage, ready for a game in any town where he stopped. He was always the loudest rooter in the grandstands along the big league circuits.

Reunion in the Old Home Town

Time turned back its flight when, at seventy-two years of age, I went back to the Brookfields with my pennant-winning Philadelphia Athletics, where George M. Cohan and I were guests of honor on Connie Mack Day in North Brookfield, July 10, 1934.

What a celebration that was! Our old friends were there to greet us with genuine small-town hospitality. We had our pictures taken with old-timers, such as Pat Carter, Joe Doyle, Janean Daniels, Frank Blair. Georgie and I relived the happiest days of our lives.

The great Cohan, the "Man Who Owns Broadway," exclaimed: "Gosh! It's great to be out here again as we were in the good old days. I'll never get over the wonderful memories I have of those good old days, the only smattering of real boyhood in my whole life."

I too was a boy again. "What a thrill I'm going to have," I remember saying, "when I step on the Old Common again reminding me of the great Fourth of July game of 1883—the year before I left the old home town to enter professional baseball."

All the Brookfields were famous for their baseball teams. I was the catcher for the East Brookfields. My last year with them we played the North Brookfields for the silver bat and championship of Central Massachusetts before a record crowd at the Oakland Gardens in Brookfield on September 19, 1883, and we East Brookfielders won by a score of 2-1.

Our reunion a half-century later was like turning back the clock.

I can see George M. Cohan now as he sat there and listened to the tales related about him. He was called everything from the leader of Cohan's gang in the village to the "Yankee Doodle Boy."

It was a great event when the "Four Cohans" (Jerry and Helen, Josephine and George) came to spend the summer in North Brookfield. They would give a show in the old Town Hall and every wide-awake Brookfielder was sure to be there. Georgie had a grudge against a local scribe and one time after inviting him to a front seat, lampooned him mercilessly in a topical song.

Some of Georgie's old baseball gang, located in the gallery, went into a wild ovation, in the midst of which Father Jerry Cohan rushed out from the wings and dragged his obstreperous offspring off the stage by the coat collar.

Cohan wrote his first song for one of these home-town performances. The fourteen-year-old lad, his hat rakishly set on the side of his head, a twirling cane in his hand, radiated his amazing personality over the footlights with a bang that started a chain reaction of Broadway hits.

At our reunion in North Brookfield a local historian reported in Cohan's own vivid words: " 'Life's a funny proposition after all!' Paraphrasing another of his famous couplets, we can assume he'll 'always leave us smiling when he says good-by' as he used to do in the good old days when the four Cohans left town for those nationwide tours, 'curtain raisers' of a career that was to make him America's best-known and best-loved man of the theater."

Although the theater was their profession, George M. Cohan and George Evans always had a ball team. Sam Harris played third base. George E. Brown was a player. Donald Brian, of *When I Was Twenty-One* and *Merry Widow* fame, was pitcher on Cohan's team.

I prize very highly a copy of the program for Connie Mack Day in North Brookfield. The good townsfolk went overboard in their praises of their East Brookfield country lad. It really embarrasses me to read their tributes, but I hope you will forgive me if I share some of them with you: "Six Feet and Two Inches of True American Manhood"; "His four-square honesty, his spirit of fair play, his high courage and ideals and his unfailing kindness and consideration for his fellow men."

You can't blame me if I pinch myself to see if I am alive. Such praises sound like eulogies at a funeral. But it's wonderful to hear your old neighbors say such things about you!

It is such home towns as the Brookfields that have given America many of its leading citizens, the American tradition of "the home-town boy makes good in the city." I could name scores of boys from the Brookfields who made their names in the world, who started from nothing and worked their way to the top.

I have told you that the Brookfields have been the nursery for baseball players. Three catchers in the big leagues learned the game on the village commons: Martin Bergen, brilliant catcher with the Boston Braves in the National League; Frank Bird, with the St. Louis Browns; and myself in both the National and American Leagues. Martin Bergen's brother, William, was first-string catcher for Brooklyn and held the major league record as a handler of foul balls.

My old friend, Frank Blair of West Brookfield, was captain of the Amherst College team; Bartholemew Howard was captain of the Williams College team; John Howe was pitcher and coach for Exeter; James Carter, pitcher in the New England League. Many other boys from the Brookfields were college players and semiprofessional stars.

The country town is the soil in which great athletes grow. The most famous sprinter of his time was William McCarthy, of North Brookfield, in the days of "Pooch" and "Piper" Donovan and "Stucky" Mike Murphy, who became famous as athletic coach at Yale University. Dennis O'Brien captained the Brown University track team. The Boland Brothers (Francis and Billy) were the speed kings at Holy Cross College on the cinder track. Anthony Lyons became a star at Amherst and was named on the All-American football team.

Life's First Big Adventure

The first big adventure in my boyhood was that day in 1883 when we young ball players in East Brookfield made a daring venture. Our manager wrote a letter to Pop Anson, inviting him to bring his Chicago Colts to East Brookfield on their way back from a series in Boston.

"We'll guarantee you $100," our offer read.

What do you think happened? Pop Anson accepted. We couldn't have been more pleased or surprised if we had fallen heir to the Rockefeller fortune.

We went out and looked over our sand lot where Pop Anson's Chicago Colts were to play an exhibition game. It was a vacant lot littered with what I once called Irish confetti: tin cans, plug-tobacco tags, and shoe-finding scraps.

Some of the others and I were working in the shoe factory at that time, and we used our lunch hours to dump the debris from the factory as far away as possible from what we called the diamond. We wanted to get it out of sight so that our Chicago visitors wouldn't stumble over it.

We had heard that the Colts were elaborate dressers, wearing white stockings and short dark Dutch pants; sometimes black tights, and loud-colored checkered bathrobes. One season they had appeared in dress suits with white-bosomed shirts, and they threw their spike-tailed coats as they walked onto the diamond. We also heard that they rode in state in open carriages, drawn by dapper white horses, four men in each carriage.

Imagine all that glamour coming to our little village of East Brookfield! Well, the players came, but left the glamour at home.

The gala day in East Brookfield found all the villagers trying to see the game. It was a bigger event to us than the inauguration of a President. We cheered ourselves hoarse as
Pop Anson and his Colts trotted onto our sand lot.

What a glorious sight it was! Pop Anson played first base. A
little fellow named Nicol played in right field. What a roar
he got from us East Brookfielders when he ran up behind the
great Anson and sneaked between his legs! Pop, who was a
born showman, appeared to be surprised and bewildered. We
nearly burst our buttons with laughter at the spectacle.

It was an exhibition game filled with exciting moments of
brilliant plays, daring base running, hard hitting, and hairbreadth outs. When it was over, we passed the hat to raise the
one-hundred-dollar guarantee for our visitors. Dimes, nickles,
and pennies fell into it. When we counted these, we found we
had just enough to turn over to Pop.

With a rousing ovation from old East Brookfield, we waved
our hats good-by as Pop Anson and his galloping Colts left
our home town.

My father, who also worked in the shoe factory, died when
I was in my teens. I consoled my mother, who by that time
had a big family of growing youngsters to feed, with the fact
that I would support the family. This placed the responsibility on me, a long, skinny Irish lad with hatrack shoulder
blades.

Do You Remember Your First Job?

My first man's job at sixteen years of age was to cut sole
leather. While my apprentice pay was meager, it somehow
helped to keep the family together. I first built the heels and
then I ran the machine that cut the soles. I worked myself up
to fifteen dollars a week. When times were dull, I took a job
during the winter for ten dollars a week, sorting half soles.

When I was twenty-one, I went into conference with my

mother and told her I could be of greater help to the family if I went somewhere else where I could make more money. I argued that the other boys were now getting big enough to help her at home.

"My son," she said, "your place is right here at home with us." Like all good mothers, she wanted to know what I had in mind, what I wanted to do in life. When I told her I wanted to become a big league baseball player she was shocked.

Nothing could dissuade me. I always knew I wanted to be a baseball player. The idea had been part of me ever since I was nine years old. The love of baseball had grown with me.

"I've got a chance to sign up with a professional team," I explained. "I don't want to spend my life in a shoe factory."

When my mother realized that my heart was so set, she reluctantly consented with secret misgivings.

"Promise me one thing," she said. "Promise me that you won't let them get you into bad habits. I've brought you up to be a good boy. Promise me that you won't drink."

I promised her, and that promise I shall keep to the end of my life.

When I told them at the shoe factory of my decision, they were greatly upset, not that I was so valuable to them, but because they thought I would never make good, that I'd be a failure. I know they really expected me to come back, hat in hand, and ask for my old job back.

When I walked out of my old home town in 1884, my sole worldly possessions were a pair of buckskin gloves with their fingers cut off to make catcher's mitts. I was on my way to fulfil my promise to myself. I was going to try to make the big leagues, and to make my dreams come true. For this was America, the land of opportunity.

Opportunity knocks at every man's door. Don't let any skeptic tell you it doesn't to everyone today, and here in America the opportunities are greater than ever before, if one has the good sense to seize them.

CHAPTER 3

I START ON THE LONG ROAD

"COME ALONG, Connie, we need a catcher." These cheerful words came to me when I was twenty-one years old from my boyhood friend, William Hogan. Bill had been the pitcher while I was the catcher on the old home team in East Brookfield. We had won the Central Massachusetts championship, and Bill had gone on to the Meriden team in the Connecticut State League.

Here was my opportunity! I lost no time in grasping it, and soon I was off to Meriden. This was in 1884 and there I got my first professional job. This, too, was the road to romance, for I had fallen in love with Bill's sister, Margaret Hogan, and later married her.

It was a big jump from East Brookfield in the horse-and-buggy days where we passed a hat at the games, instead of charging admissions, and held clambakes to help pay expenses, and yet it was only about sixty miles away.

I jumped into the professionals as a member of the Meriden team with the "stupendous" salary of ninety dollars a month. I was afraid to let the other boys on the team know what I was getting for fear they would think I was a plutocrat. Little did they know that I would have taken the job at half that salary!

I found Meriden quite a gay city, compared with the Brookfields. It was nationally known as the "Silver City" and supplied much of the silverware in the homes throughout the country. It practically lighted the country in the oil-lamp days when Edward Miller was building a great fortune on his Miller lamps.

Meriden, too, was the home of Big Ed Walsh, who later became the great right-hand pitcher for the Chicago Americans and is now one of the immortals in the National Baseball Hall of Fame. Ed and I held a reunion in Meriden in 1949.

When I started as a professional in the Silver City, the big man was Tom Reilly, a newspaper editor who became a distinguished member of Congress.

Working Your Way Up

After a year with the good old Meriden team I was signed up by Hartford, the home of Morgan Bulkeley, who had been the first president of the National League and who later became a United States Senator. The famous figures in Hartford in those days were Harriet Beecher Stowe, who had written *Uncle Tom's Cabin,* and Mark Twain, one of the most famous writers in America.

From Hartford I went to the New York Metropolitans in the old American Baseball Association. A year later, 1886, I was sold with four other players to the Washington Senators, then a National League team, for $3,500, five of us in the deal bringing $700 apiece. That was a high price in those days.

I was one of the first players to go south on a spring training trip in 1888. The manager in Washington was Old Ted Sullivan, and he conceived the idea that if he could get the jump on the other clubs by putting them in spring training, it would enhance his chances of winning the pennant. So he took all his players to Florida, a practice followed today.

A trip to Florida in the '80's was a big event. It took us three nights and two days to make the journey. We left at night and went from Washington to Charlotte, North Caro-

lina, in a Pullman, two big fellows in a berth. At seven o'clock
the next morning we were awakened in Charlotte, then had to
dress and go back to a day coach. We traveled on to Atlanta,
then to Savannah and on to Jacksonville, alternating between
day coaches and Pullman, two-in-a-berth at night.

When Hotels Barred "Senators"

I recall that we went to a hotel to register. The proprietor
received us cordially until he found out that we were baseball
players.

"Sorry," he said, "but we don't take baseball players."

The fact that we were the Washington Senators and came
from the nation's capital made no impression whatsoever on
hotel clerks.

We went from hotel to hotel. Ted Sullivan would leave us
outside and go in to register, but we always got the same
brush-off. Finally, the proprietor of a third-rate hotel agreed
to take us, but with this reservation:

"I'll take you in on one condition: We cannot let baseball
players mingle with the other guests."

We weren't even allowed to use the dining room, but were
given our meals in a special room. Ted would put a silver dollar on the table when we sat down, and say to the waiter:

"Now go ahead and feed my boys up right."

The waiter's eyes would bulge. He'd bring us fried chicken,
corn on the cob, sweet potatoes, corn muffins. When the meal
was over Sullivan would pick up the silver dollar and put it
back in his pocket. I saw that same silver dollar the whole time
we were in the South.

Other teams in those days apparently also ran into difficul-
ties on the road. Once the Cleveland team was quartered in
a hotel on a road trip. Ossie Schreck ordered a steak. When
it came, it was so tough that he couldn't cut it with a knife.

"Waiter," he said, "will you kindly bring me the porter?"

When the porter came hurrying in, Ossie smiled politely.

"Porter," he said, "will you kindly bring me a hammer and a nail?"

The porter, somewhat perplexed, brought Ossie the articles he had asked for. Ossie got up with considerable pomp, walked ceremoniously across the room and nailed the steak to the door. It wasn't long before the hotel manager came rushing in and threw the whole team out of the hotel.

Love and Marriage

While I was in Washington with the Senators, I was fêted by the fans and presented with a silver service at the end of 1887. Things were going so well with me at that time that I decided I should embark on another career. I was then twenty-six years of age, and my mind kept going back to a certain girl that I had left behind in New England when I left there in 1884.

As I told you, I fell in love with Margaret Hogan, but it wasn't until November 2, 1887 that I married her. We had five wonderful years together. Three children came to bless our union, and then Margaret died at the age of twenty-six. The loss was almost overwhelming. I was now a lone young father with three motherless babies, Marguerite, Roy, Earle.

My three children were brought up by my mother at our old home in East Brookfield. I went on alone for seventeen years before I fell in love again. Then in 1910 I married Katherine A. Hallahan, also a woman of high religious principles.

My three children in East Brookfield were now grown up, and I began raising another family. The second Mrs. Mack has presented me with five wonderful children, four girls and a son: Mary, Connie, Jr.; Ruth, Rita, and Elizabeth.

Again the McGillicuddys are a happy family. All but one of my eight children are living. My oldest daughter, Marguerite McGillicuddy McCambridge, died at forty years of age and left two sons.

I now have seven children living, three sons and four daughters; eighteen grandchildren; and five great-grandchildren. And I am proud of them all as they carry on the Mack strain of blood in America.

Old Days in Nation's Capital

I have told you how I was sold in the 1880's to Washington, in a bunch of five, for $3,500. About that same time Ed Delahanty (in the Hall of Fame) was sold for $1,900. The Pittsburgh Pirates sold Billy Sunday for $1,000. Today they'd both be worth a mint to any manager.

When I was catcher for the Washington Senators, the rule for major league batters was seven balls and three strikes. One year (1887) it was four strikes to make an out. Pitchers were using underhand delivery, fifty feet from the batting box. We were catching the ball on the bounce. Infielders and outfielders were catching them barehanded.

A batter was allowed to tell the pitcher what kind of ball he wanted pitched to him. A foul ball caught on the bounce was out until 1880. Back in 1887 we players were assessed thirty dollars for our uniforms and had to pay half a dollar a day for our board when away from home. A dollar a day was the usual price to pay for both room and board.

If you were injured, there were no extra players to take your place. You had to play as long as you could stand up.

The game was played with but one official, the umpire. He stood a safe distance behind the batter. When there was a man on base, the umpire walked out to the middle of the diamond and stood behind the pitcher.

These were the "good old days" before we had to worry about the cost of living. You could get a suit of clothes for ten dollars and a good dinner at a hotel for fifty cents. For twenty-five cents you could go to the ball game and sit in the bleachers. You could sit in the grandstand for fifty cents. When boxes came into style, you could be a plutocrat for seventy-five cents.

If there were 3,000 to 4,000 fans at a game in those days, we considered it a big crowd. A score of seventy to eighty runs was merely a "good game" in the early days. The first catchers to use the big mitt were called "softies."

The life of a baseball player was not a bed of roses. On one spring training trip after I had become a manager we arrived at midnight at the hotel where I had made reservations. The proprietor greeted us at the front door like long-lost brothers. He invited us all into the bar. When I told him my boys were not allowed to drink, a crestfallen look came over his face as he sputtered:

"My house is full. I have such a crowd of unexpected guests that I have no room left for you."

I took my boys on a midnight march to look for another hotel. At last we found a night clerk who evidently did not know that ball players were not supposed to be gentlemen. I offered him two dollars a day for food and lodging for each man, which he accepted.

When we were training in the South, I took my team to the hotel in which I had made reservations. I went to the clerk's desk to help the affable proprietor assign us rooms. He suddenly raised his eyes, glared at the doorway, and turned a violent red.

"Is that man with you?" he roared, pointing at the fellow in the doorway.

"Yes, sir," I said, "he's one of my men."

"I'm sorry," he said, as he closed the register with a bang. "I can't put your men up if he is one of them."

"My players are gentlemen," I said, "I'll vouch for their good behavior."

"I am not so sure as you are that all your men are gentlemen," he said. "But if you'll keep that fellow from doing what he did when he was here last year, I'll take one more chance with him. One bad move and out he goes—and all your team with him."

The gentleman in question was Ossie Schreck, who had nailed the tough steak to the door on his previous visit!

Quaint Customs of the Old Days

Baseball was thirty-eight years old before the first turnstile was introduced at the entrance of a ball park, sixty years before the present style of home plate was invented.

The first bases were not bags at all, but wooden posts standing four feet high. In 1876, the year the National League was organized, F. W. Thayer, of the Harvard Club, constructed the contraption of wires and leather that we call the catcher's mask. Allison, a catcher for the Cincinnati Reds, in 1869, had the first glove or mitt made by a saddle maker.

Before 1886, when a ball was lost, the umpire called a recess of five minutes while everybody searched for it. If, after five minutes, the lost ball was not found, the umpire was allowed to put a new ball into play.

When I entered the big leagues it was a mighty tough game, a cross between the mild cricket and the rough-and-tumble football, a sort of survival of the fittest.

After sixty-six years in the big leagues I can say with justifiable pride that baseball is now the cleanest, squarest, fairest game ever played. I'll proudly place its record beside that of any other sport. I'll go even farther: I'll match its integrity and honesty with any other profession, business, banking, law, medicine, or any of the other occupations in life.

True, there are moral lapses in all human pursuits. In every vocation we can find some black sheep. There are occasional embezzlers and defaulters in financial institutions, occasional disbarments in legal organizations, occasional indictments of men in high places in government, occasional unfrockings in the ministry, but these are of such a small percentage that they do not condemn the great professions which they represent.

The Fight Against the Gamblers

Scandal is so infrequent in baseball that when a player or team goes wrong this is magnified into sensational news. Why? Because such things happen so seldom. The first sensation over gambling occurred in 1877, one year after the National League was organized. The league officials dealt with it summarily and severely.

No big news of this kind occurred again for forty-two years. Then in 1919, just after the close of the First World War, in the first game of the 1919 World Series, six players were accused of selling out to a betting ring. They were indicted by the Grand Jury of Cook County, in Illinois, September 28, 1920. The trial took place in July, 1921, but the jury acquitted the players.

This celebrated trial created such a furor and the testimony was of such a nature, showing association with gamblers, that the players were never reinstated and were banned for life from professional baseball.

The result of this episode is an everlasting tribute to the honor of the national game, for immediately the National and American Leagues set up a system to protect it. It was agreed to appoint a High Commissioner of the highest character to preside over the game, who was to be invested with complete authority. Judge Kenesaw Mountain Landis, a distinguished jurist on the Federal Court, was made baseball's first High Commissioner in 1921 and ruled with an iron hand until his death in 1944.

Judge Landis ruled that baseball belongs to the American people and so must embody the high standard of American character. United States Senator Albert Chandler, from Kentucky, was selected as Judge Landis' successor, and he is maintaining the same high standards.

I was a party to these official transactions, and I feel that they attest the unimpeachable honor of our national game.

The 1919 sensation unwittingly performed a signal service to baseball. I shall not mention the names of the players who were accused, because I feel they have had sufficient blame poured on their heads. Two of them at least would be in the Hall of Fame today if they had not dishonored their names.

After three grand years with the Washington Senators, I went to Buffalo in the Brotherhood or Players League in 1890, then to the Pittsburgh Pirates under Ned Hanlon in 1891, becoming the manager of the Pirates in 1894. After six years in Pittsburgh, I became manager and part owner of the Milwaukee team in the Western League in 1897.

Things were now beginning to happen which were to revolutionize our national game.

CHAPTER 4

THE "PHILADELPHIA STORY"

M̲y "PHILADELPHIA STORY" begins in 1900 and continues through 1950, a half-century of glorious experiences.

A century and three-quarters after Benjamin Franklin came to Philadelphia, I arrived here too. I decided that if Ben could become famous here with his *Poor Richard's Almanack* I might stand a chance with Connie's Athletics.

It has been an inspiration to live in Philadelphia, where we may walk in the shadow of Independence Hall, where our Declaration of Independence and our Constitution were written. And to walk in the footsteps of George Washington, Thomas Jefferson, Alexander Hamilton, and the other fathers of the nation is a privilege we all respect.

There have been times when the sessions of our baseball league meetings were just as stormy as those which took place in the Convention that wrote the Constitution and in the convention halls where candidates for President of the United States were being nominated!

When the American League was being organized in 1900, we decided upon making it fifty-fifty between the West and the East—four Western teams, Chicago, Detroit, Cleveland, and Milwaukee; four Eastern teams, Philadelphia, Washington, Baltimore, and Boston. New York came in when Baltimore dropped out, and St. Louis later took the place of Milwaukee.

At the Birthplace of the Nation

I was awarded the Philadelphia franchise and hurried to the City of Brotherly Love in 1900 to dig up local capital. My friend, Ban Johnson, organizer of the league, told me to see Benjamin F. Shibe, one of the owners of the A. J. Reach Company, the manufacturers of baseball equipment.

I shall always be indebted to Ban Johnson for his good advice. I saw Mr. Shibe, who greeted me enthusiastically. We organized a corporation, and he was made president. He asked Charles Somers, a friend in Cleveland, to join us.

We now had our franchise, but we had no team and no park. What I know about Philadelphia I learned from walking the streets of the city, inspecting every vacant lot. We were in such a hurry to get started that we thought we might have to take a city playground. Finally we decided upon a site at Twenty-ninth and Oxford Streets, and got it on a ten-year lease.

Columbia Park was the name we gave it. We had just five weeks left after leasing the park to put up stands in order to keep the franchise. It didn't take us very long to construct a single-decked wooden grandstand, but what would we do for a team?

According to the custom of the times and considering the National League good game, I looked over our rivals, the Phillies, and began negotiations with four of their players. I signed up Napoleon Lajoie (now in the Hall of Fame) and pitchers Bernhard, Platt and Frazer.

I found a boy wonder at Gettysburg College who looked like a comer to me. His name was Eddie Plank. From Indianapolis I got Doc Powers, and in Pittsburgh another catcher named Harry Smith. After the start of the first season I got Harry Davis for first base, and added Socks Siebold, Lave Cross, and a few more live wires.

Our rivals, the Phillies, were not happy over our invasion of Philadelphia. They appealed to the court for an injunction, claiming we had stripped them of four of their players: Lajoie, Bernhard, Frazer, and later Duggleby. The plea was thrown out by the lower court. After that, two more Phillies' players came to us, Monte Cross and Elmer Flick.

The Phillies, now thoroughly aroused, appealed to a higher court. Our second season was just two days old when the State Supreme Court reversed the decision of the lower court and issued a permanent injunction against our using the ex-Phillies. You have heard the phrase "as smart as a Philadelphia lawyer." The lawyers for the Phillies lived up to the name. They staked their case on Lajoie, declaring him to be of such value that he was impossible to replace. And they won the case.

But the owners of the Phillies were not so wise as were their lawyers. They decided to establish their authority over their players and decreed a stiff fine on Lajoie, refusing to let him play until he paid it.

"I'll quit baseball before I'll pay it," was the rejoinder of the Big Napoleon.

We too had smart Philadelphia lawyers. We seized this opportunity to save Lajoie by sending him with Flick and Bernhard to the Cleveland team in the American League. The order of the Supreme Court applied only to the State of Pennsylvania, so Ohio was out of their jurisdiction.

Although we had lost the three players, they were saved for the American League. Because of injunctions granted by the state court, they could not play in Philadelphia until peace was established between the leagues in 1903. We never regained these players, although the great Lajoie returned to the Athletics to play his final two years in the big leagues in 1915 and 1916.

Discovering New Stars

Our Philadelphia A's, the name we had adopted, were now left flat. Soon we began to get help from American League

clubs. Fred Mitchell and Pete Husting were sent to us from
the Red Sox. Cleveland sent Ossie Schreck (Schreckengost).
There were still Eddie Plank, Monte Cross, Lave Cross,
Powers, Davis, and Siebold, around whom we could build a
team.

Hurrying to Norwich, Connecticut, following a tip, I found
a lad named Danny Murphy, who was playing second base.
Danny burst like a bombshell into the American League, five
hits in five times at bat in his first game.

Next I acquired Rube Waddell, great but eccentric pitcher
who had played for me at Milwaukee. Waddell was pitching
on the Coast and I sent him money for transportation, but
Rube hated to leave his friends out there and I finally had to
hire a couple of Pinkerton detectives to escort him East. Rube
was a carefree character with the mind of a child, but his
strong left arm helped us win the pennant in 1902.

The following year (1903) I made another great find. I
had decided to scout the schools and colleges for potential
material, and I brought to Philadelphia a Chippewa boy,
Chief Bender, from the Carlisle Indian School. This was
when the New York Highlanders were about to be transformed into the Yankees. Our American League extended
a hospitable hand, so I sent them Dave Fultz.

The insignia of our Philadelphia Athletics, as you know,
is the White Elephant. The story of acquiring it is an interesting one. In 1902 the Baltimore Club forfeited its franchise
in the newly formed American League. Its spot was filled by
the New York Highlanders, "the acorn from which sprung
the mighty Yankee oak."

The astute John McGraw took advantage of the opportunity and jumped from the crumbling Orioles to the New
York Giants, a leap to fame and fortune. When the sports
writers gathered around McGraw to fire a barrage of questions, one of the questions was: "What do you think of the
Philadelphia A's?"

"White elephants!" quickly retorted Mr. McGraw. "Mr. B. F. Shibe has a white elephant on his hands."

The press heralded the phrase. Cartoonists went to work on it. One of our local artists pictured a crowd in our old Columbia Park feeding peanuts to a white elephant.

Inasmuch as these were the days when the Republican Party was winning elections with the elephant, I was thankful that John McGraw's quick wit had not called us donkeys!

"Boys," I said, "we accept McGraw's appellation. We will name our Philadelphia A's the White Elephants"—White Elephants we have been ever since—White Elephants that stampeded into our national game and won nine pennants and five World Series.

I am a great believer in signs. As I once said, "If somebody called me Stumble Bum McGillicuddy, I would adopt the tag and do my utmost to parlay it into the name of the champion of the world."

When I came to Philadelphia my ambition was to make it the baseball capital of America. At times we succeeded in doing so by bringing pennants and World Series to Philadelphia. Then some other city would come along and take first place, just as New York and Washington had done when they took the national capital from Philadelphia after the nation was founded.

Some of you will remember that we opened Columbia Park in 1901; that we built the greatest team of the times and won our first pennant in 1902. We won our second pennant in 1905; finished second in 1907-09; opened Shibe Park at Twenty-first Street and Lehigh Avenue in 1909, and won our third pennant and first World Series in 1910.

Stampede of the White Elephants

Philadelphia was on top of the world. We won our fourth pennant and second World Series in 1911. For five years (from 1910-1914) the A's were almost unbeatable, winning four pennants and two World Series. We failed to get the pennant, only in 1912, when the Red Sox—with Speaker, Lewis and Hooper, the greatest outfield baseball had known—came in winner with 105 victories. Our 1912 A's were one of the great teams of all times.

There is one hazard that is hard to jump—that is over-confidence. Two straight pennants and two World Series victories made the boys feel they couldn't lose. Remember, we had vanquished the great Chance's Chicago Cubs four games to one, and the next year we conquered the New York Giants, who, with Christy Mathewson and Rube Marquard in the box, were beaten four games to two. This gave our boys a feeling of cocksureness that invariably results in a tumble.

But they quickly picked themselves up again and started out with a vengeance. They brought the pennant back to Shibe Park in 1913 and again in 1914.

Memories of my old teams are like family reunions. We have always been a happy family, winning or losing. Philadelphia has been home to us. When we won, the city gave us hearty ovations. When we lost, they looked at us sympathetically.

My method from the beginning of the A's was to find new material. We conducted nationwide searches in schools and colleges for potential players. I believe I was the first manager to send scouts out after them. Some of the other managers frowned at the idea, but it has paid us big dividends.

Among the boys we have found were Eddie Collins, who came to us when a junior at Columbia University. He played his early games at the age of nineteen under the name of Sullivan so as to retain his college eligibility. This was not uncommon at the time. Jack Barry became our shortstop when he was graduated from Holy Cross. John "Stuffy" McInnis, another scholastic star, came to us from Gloucester, Massachusetts. With John Franklin Baker, the home-run king of the times, they formed the greatest quartet in baseball.

These boys, who knew their Greek and Latin and their

algebra and geometry and trigonometry, put intelligence and scholarship into the game.

The Search for Talented Young Men

We found and brought to Philadelphia such boy wonders as Herb Pennock, a school lad only eighteen years old; Wally Schang from a Buffalo high school; Joe Bush, a nineteen-year-old lad, and many others who proved great finds. Pennock and Plank won their places in the Hall of Fame.

I considered Schang my greatest discovery of a catcher, until a few years later, when we acquired the one and only Mickey Cochrane, the peer of them all.

On their records, I think I have the right to feel proud of my discoveries. Look at Home-Run Baker. We brought him to Philadelphia when other managers were overlooking him on the Reading team. In my opinion he had everything. For four straight years (1911-14), he led the league.

It was a big event in those days of the dead ball when a batter made a home run. When Baker made two home runs in the 1911 World Series against the rugged New York Giants, it was more than an event; it was a sensation. It was a calamity for the Giants.

We had a pitching staff that was sensational: Chief Bender, the Chippewa Indian we had found in Carlisle College, Eddie Plank, Jack Coombs and Joe Bush. Three times the Chief led the league.

Baker played in 1,575 games, at bat 5,985 times, made 1,838 hits, 887 runs, with .308 as his lifetime batting average. Bender pitched 459 games, won 212, lost 128, with .624 as his lifetime winning average. Coombs pitched 355 games, won 158, lost 111, for a .587 lifetime average.

Meet a Great Scout

Ira Thomas has been a right-hand man with the A's for nearly forty years. He is the ablest scout I have ever known.

He believes in building on solid foundations. He keeps his eyes on the minor leagues and the schools and colleges, and tips me off on what he considers good material with promise.

It was Ira who brought in Grove and Earnshaw, two of the greatest pitchers in the game. What scout has a better record? Of course, some of the new material we get fails to come through. But Ira Thomas has never brought in a rookie who didn't have the stuff potentially. And he's out looking for them all the time.

Ira caught in the majors from 1906 through 1913, the last five seasons with the Athletics. He was one of my coaches from 1914 through 1917, and after managing in the minors, returned as a scout in 1925.

The A's are accustomed to being attacked for not winning the pennant every year. A sports writer as far back as 1924 said in his newspaper:

"As long as Connie Mack is connected with the A's they'll never get anywhere," but we finished second in the league the next year. Four years later we won our seventh pennant and fourth World Series. Then for good measure the next year we won our eighth pennant and fifth World Series, and a year later our ninth pennant.

In building winning teams one has to lay strong foundations. I had two catchers, Doc Powers of Holy Cross and Ossie Schreck of the College of Hard Knocks, both of whom were born to be stars.

Doc Powers caught the opening game in Shibe Park, but was taken ill during the game, and died shortly afterwards. Baseball lost one of its greatest potential players when it lost Doc.

I picked up Jack Knight, a sixteen-year-old Philadelphia boy in the Central High School. I found Amos Strunk in the Blaine Grammar School, and he made a mark for himself in the outfield.

In the postwar years of World War I, we began to come

back on the victory road. Then in the midst of the depression we went through precarious years, and I was forced to make retrenchments.

Philadelphia has been good to me, and I am going to take you into my confidence. We enjoyed together two magnificent eras when our Philadelphia A's were on top of the world. At the end of both of these eras I have broken up the great teams. Why? To meet urgent emergencies! The pressure of uncontrollable conditions created a crisis.

What Happened in 1914

I will try to give you a full accounting. The first of these breaks occurred in 1914, at the outbreak of World War I.

A third major league known as the Federals invaded the baseball field in 1914. With the bankroll of Harry F. Sinclair, the oil magnate, and money from Ball, the ice king, the Wards of the baking fortune and the Gilmore greenbacks, our players were being lured with big salary checks.

Our pennant winners were the targets of these financiers. They waved the "long green" in front of our players' eyes. Our team was divided into two factions: One for jumping to the rich Federal League, and the other for remaining loyal to the American League. Even with this split, we had won our sixth pennant. But during the World Series our team fell apart. The Boston Braves slaughtered us.

I felt this keenly, as I knew we could walk away with the series if only we had been united. It was the proof of the slogan: "United we stand, divided we fall." And we fell. I was especially hurt, as we were paying our players the highest salaries in our circuit.

Baseball fans throughout the country did not realize what was behind our collapse against Boston; neither did many of the sports writers. They said that the wonder team was taking it lying down. I knew that the "wonder team" was engaged in a civil war, fighting one another.

After giving the crisis much careful thought, I decided that the war had gone too far to stop it by trying to outbid the Federal moneybags. Nothing could be more disastrous at this time than a salary war.

There was but one thing to do: to refuse to be drawn into this bitter conflict, and to let those who wanted to risk their fate with the Federals go with the Federals.

The first to go were Bender and Plank. I didn't get a nickel for them. This was like being struck by a hurricane. Others followed. There was only one way to get out from under the catastrophe. I decided to sell out and start over again. When it became known that my players were for sale, the offers rolled into me.

If the players were going to "cash in" and leave me to hold the bag, there was nothing for me to do but to cash in too. So I sold the great Eddie Collins to the White Sox for $50,000 cash. I sold Home Run Baker to the Yankees. My shortstop, Jack Barry, told me he wanted to go to Boston, so I sold him to the Bostons for a song.

"Why didn't you hang on to the half of your team that was loyal and start to build up again?" This question has often been asked me.

My answer is that when a team starts to disintegrate it is like trying to plug up the hole in the dam to stop the flood. The boys who are left have lost their high spirits, and they want to go where they think the future looks brighter. It is only human for everyone to try to improve his opportunities.

Then the big blow came to the boys who had left us. The outlaw Federal League blew up in 1915. They had sunk their money and discovered there was no room for them in the baseball world.

Fight to Survive a Crisis

World War I was raising havoc with gate receipts in our ball parks. It took star players away from the game to send them to battlefronts. Spectators began to work in shipyards and factories to produce the goods necessary to win victories. I struggled along through seven lean years, establishing a record for remaining in the baseball cellar.

When the war was over, I formulated plans for recovery when the opportunity would come. I kept my eyes on prospective players. Aspiring youngsters flocked to Shibe Park. One year I tried out more than 300 of them.

The rumor got around that Connie Mack was going to build another great team. Farsighted owners, such as Ruppert and Huston, put their capital and brains behind a revival of baseball. I watched them cautiously before I began to plunge again. Baseball came back faster than I had expected and I had to put on speed to keep up with the procession.

If you think it is pleasant for a manager to be in the cellar, you have another guess coming. The first chance I saw to climb out was in 1921. We were successful in beating St. Louis, and I was hopeful we would be successful in Chicago, but they beat us four straight.

For three days after leaving Chicago I had the blues. On the third day I snapped out of it. I made up my mind that I must stop worrying! Worrying never got a fellow anywhere.

As soon as I stopped worrying, things began to look better. From that day I have never permitted myself to worry. I have had, as you well know, my ups and downs, and I have taken them both standing up, with a smile. I want it said of me that Connie Mack can *give it*—and he can *take it*.

While I was hard at work on my plans, I saw the Giants and the Yankees forge to the front. New York teams fought in the World Series for three years in succession. They were great teams with great managers, but the rest of the country began to wonder if New York had a monopoly on the game, just as they had wondered the same thing when Philadelphia was sweeping everything before them.

Starting to Rebuild from Ruins

The time had finally come to rebuild our team. This means, as it does in every line of business, heavy investments. I paid $75,000 to get Sammy Hale; then I paid $40,000 for Paul Strand. When they failed to produce, I bought other players for big prices. Ed Rommel was a good bet: he won twenty-seven games in 1922 with a team that finished next to last.

Jimmy Dykes, who today is one of my triumvirate of great coaches, offered himself at the gate back in 1918, and he proved to be a big bargain. Mickey Cochrane became a foundation stone upon whom I started to rebuild. Today he is another in my triumvirate of great coaches. Cy Perkins was another stand-by upon whom I could depend. He stayed long enough to cut in on two World Series purses, and he deserved them.

It costs money, as I have said, to build a winning team. I paid $300,000 for a combination of Lefty Grove, George Earnshaw, Mickey Cochrane, Max Bishop, and Joe Boley. My former star, Frank (Home Run) Baker sent Jimmy Foxx to me as a gift—the gift of a lifetime.

Do you remember the great Al Simmons? He wrote to me in 1921 that he was looking for a job and would come to Philadelphia if I would pay his train fare. That's when I missed the train. I didn't send him the carfare, and Al went to Milwaukee. As a result, I had to buy him after he had made good.

My new team was finally molded into winning shape, and we finished second in 1925. We were coming along fast in 1926 and for the next two years. We were twelve games behind the New York Yankees in July, 1928, but we forged our way to first place by September 8. On September 9 we met the Yankees in a double-header before the largest crowd that ever paid to see a game. More than 80,000 people were jammed into Yankee Stadium. Sad to relate, we lost both games.

But even defeat couldn't stop us. We came back with a

bang, and won the pennant in 1929 and also the World Series, the seventh pennant and fourth World Series for the White Elephants in the uniform of the Philadelphia A's. In 1930 we won the eighth pennant and fifth World Series. We did it again in 1931 when we won our ninth pennant, but we lost the World Series. In 1932 we finished in second place; in 1933 third place.

Happy Days

Our pennant teams of 1929, '30, '31 were world beaters. What a magnificent pitching staff we had: Lefty Grove, Big George Earnshaw, Rube Walberg. Grove is generally recognized as the fastest southpaw the game has ever known. Earnshaw, a master of the mound, became a Commander in the United States Navy in World War II.

What an aggregation of power hitters! Jimmy Foxx, our first baseman, was dynamite, second only to the great Ruth as the home-run king. Remember how he hit fifty-eight in one year? And don't forget that for four years Jimmy led the league in homers. Three times he was selected as the most valuable player in the American League.

In 1929 five of our A's were in the over .300 class. And Cochrane, Foxx, Miller, and Simmons were batting over .330. Al Simmons, whose real name was Aloysius Szymanski, was our first champion batsman. He led the league with .381 in 1930, and raised it to .390 in 1931.

The baseball world will probably never see a greater catcher than Mickey Cochrane. Mickey came out of Boston University. A great hitter, fast on bases, a throwing arm like a bolt of lightning, and a true American sportsman.

Here is a fact that may surprise you: Our Philadelphia Athletics in 1932 was the highest-priced ball team in the history of the game, not even barring the New York Yankees, with Babe Ruth's salary of $80,000 a season. Few people realize this.

Five men on the Philadelphia A's in 1932 were earning more than $100,000 as a group. I had twenty-one other players also in the higher bracket. On the other hand, the gate receipts were rapidly diminishing. During four years (1924-28) while we were only contenders, more people passed through the turnstiles each year than when we were world champions. Figure that out in terms of human nature.

Another great era had come and gone. The big depression was on. Attendances at ball games were dropping down. Another crisis loomed ahead.

The law of diminishing returns is unrelenting. No organization or business can stand the pressure long. No one can continue in business when operating at a loss.

I have been falsely accused many times of making a fortune by selling players. The truth is that half of my 1932 team cost me more money than I received by selling my entire pennant-winning team in 1914.

The profits in baseball come from the gate receipts. When people are paying to attend the game, the fans support it and keep the game going. When they stop coming, a manager has to sell some of his high-salaried players to meet the deficit. I have never sold my players to make a profit.

What Happened in the Big Depression

Our Philadelphia Athletics reached another pinnacle in the early 1930's just as the economic world around us was beginning to crash. We were going up when stocks were going down. The depression was sweeping the country; millions were out of work. We too were caught in the financial earthquake and, like most business houses, were forced to retrench.

I do not have to remind you of those dark days when the banks closed down, and it looked as if there would be a disastrous collapse of our economic system.

With our heavy investment and the expenses of building Shibe Park and operating the costliest team in our national game, we had to borrow $700,000 from one of our banks. The bank officers found that financial conditions throughout the country required them to tighten up on their loans. They asked us to repay the balance, $400,000, as promptly as possible. They did not like to press us, but their need for more liquid capital was pressing.

My partners and I sat down and faced the crisis with all the wisdom we could command. We asked ourselves the questions:

"What are our assets? How are we going to go on? What can we do?" And we answered with all the intelligence we could muster that our assets were our players, our real estate, and our credit. We had built a great ball park, and we had done it ourselves, without resorting to a bond issue. We had paid for it as a private investment. The depression had curtailed our credit. Banks were calling their loans. We'd have to sell players and try to stop the gap.

That is what we did, much to our discomfort. I pledged myself then that I'd never get myself into a position where I would have to do the same thing again. I made up my mind that I'd be prepared to meet any and every emergency. Every business at times has to make retrenchments, or it would go out of business.

A sports writer came to see me during that crisis with the story he had written about it. He asked me if I would like to see it before publication. I glanced at it and my eyes fell on these words:

"If Connie Mack sells the star members of his 1935 team, he ought to get out of baseball."

The sports writer saw that I noticed that statement.

"Have you anything to say about that?" he asked.

"I've never told a sports writer how to write his story," I replied, "and I'm not going to start now."

It costs money to win championships. You have twenty-five men on your team who feel they should advance, and deserve to get raises in salaries. If you can afford to reward them, it is the best investment you can make. If you can't afford it, there is only one thing to do—sell these players to someone who has the money to pay them what they are worth.

In Philadelphia we had spent a great deal of money to build a championship team, and we didn't have the bank roll of some of the financial magnates in New York and Boston and Chicago. Strange as it may seem, every city has its own psychology. Our Philadelphia fans are unlike those in New York. It is a curious fact, demonstrated over and over again that Philadelphians will turn out in greater numbers to see their home team fight to become champions than they will to see them fight to remain champions.

Why is this so? Honestly, I don't know. I can well understand why the late J. I. Rogers, owner of the Philadelphia Nationals, once said: "I have never wanted to win championships. I am fighting to get into second place. The crowds come back the next year to root harder than ever."

The big New York spenders, with Wall Street behind them, like to call Philadelphians tightwads. If they knew their baseball finance, they would realize that it was Philadelphia that put baseball and baseball players into the high brackets.

A Glance Into Private Bank Books

Let me give you a glance into my private cash books, for you might like to know what I paid for some of my men. I paid Baltimore $100,600 for Grove. Babe Ruth was sold to the Yankees for $100,000, so I raised the ante $600 for Grove.

I paid Baltimore $80,000 for Earnshaw, and $65,000 for Boley. Max Bishop cost me $25,000. I got Mickey Cochrane by purchasing an interest in the Portland Club for $132,000 and $50,000 cash for his services.

When the crash came and I was forced to unload my players, Tom Yawkey of Boston paid me $400,000 within three years for seven of my star players to pay off our obligations to the Philadelphia bank.

I have often been accused of being a financial wizard. This amuses me, as money has never been the objective in my life. Personally, I can sleep in only one bed, live in only one house, and eat three meals a day. The money that has come into my pocket always has been used to develop more players.

Greater than money is the satisfaction that our Philadelphia Athletics have won so many championships. Furthermore, I can claim that the A's have been the training school for more great players than any other city in the country. We have taken boys from schools and colleges and have made them world famous.

Hunting for "Gold" in Our Colleges

You'll pardon the pride of an octogenarian if he occasionally stresses some of the high spots of his team. We found Plank at Gettysburg College, Bender at Carlisle, Coombs at Colby, Eddie Collins at Columbia, Jack Barry at Holy Cross. Take our record as trainers of outstanding coaches.

We took Stuffy McInnis out of high school and now he is a coach at Harvard. Bender and Bishop became coaches at the United States Naval Academy at Annapolis, and McInnis at Exeter. Harry Davis came to the A's from Girard College. Coombs has been coach at Duke University for twenty-one years and has been given an honorary degree by Colby College, his alma mater. At the installation of the new president of Duke University in 1949, Jack Coombs sat on the platform with educators from 360 colleges and universities.

When we found Joe Jackson in Greenville, South Carolina, he was not able to read or write. We arranged for a more literate boy to join the team at the same time to be sure that Joe would always have a pal and to read to him the menus and also the reports of the games. When I let Joe go to my friend Charlie Somers, of Cleveland, I told him that Joe had the making of another great baseball player.

Talking about the salaries of players, and I think my friend

Ty Cobb will confirm this: I made an arrangement with Ty that would put him up around $80,000 for a season. He had progressive stipulations for his performances. If we won the World Series, he was to get $20,000 more over his season's earnings. We didn't win that year, but we did give him the extra amount anyway and I never regretted doing this.

The Shibe family, who are partners in the ownership of the Philadelphia Athletics, deserve a special tribute. Mrs. Thomas Shibe, a mother of our national game, still holds a large interest in the Shibe ball park. In my early partnership with the Shibes, I had a one-fourth interest in the club; then I bought out Jones, which gave me a one-half interest. In spite of the many business crises through which we have passed, we have worked along in a happy fifty-fifty partnership. Since Mr. Shibe passed away, the Macks have the majority ownership, but the two families still work together in perfect unity and accord.

Unless I have a winning team, I am very unhappy. I always want to win. There isn't enough money in the world to compensate me for the disappointment of landing even at the top of the second division. It hurts me more to break up great teams than it does the fans and this is something all too few people realize.

But I have never become discouraged. I start again at the bottom to build up another championship team. This requires time and patience, for it takes several years to build a winning team. The short cut is to go out and buy players, but I find deeper satisfaction in building them.

Crucial Days in World War II

The ranks of our teams were again depleted in 1941, when our country was plunged into the world conflict. Ball players in all leagues not only did heroic service along the battlefronts, but hundreds of others helped uphold the morale of our people on the home front.

Our national game survived the world crisis. With the end of the war in 1945, our victorious warriors came home. That was in my estimation the greatest World Series ever fought.

Since the close of the war, however, I have been persistently and consistently building what I feel sure will become another pennant and World Series team. My highest ambition is to do it again in 1950 before I retire, for I believe we have a team of stars in the making; we are building up another championship team.

CHAPTER 5

THRILLS AND DISAPPOINTMENTS

T HE BIGGEST THRILL I have ever had?" This is one of the questions often asked me. Another: "After sixty-six years in the big leagues, do you still get a thrill?" Every game I have ever seen played has had its thrills; and I've seen nearly 10,000 games in my lifetime.

Every time we have won a pennant has been an exciting moment. Every time we have won a World Series has been thrilling. And with nine pennants and five World Series to our credit, I think I've had my share of thrills.

I'll never forget the 1929 World Series. Lefty Grove, George Earnshaw, and Rube Walberg, three of the biggest names in baseball, were with me. The problem was in which order I should pitch them.

The Chicago Cubs, the National League pennant winners, feared Grove, Earnshaw, and Walberg because of their masterful work in winning the American League pennant. I knew that if they could lick one of these star pitchers they could break the spell and ride on to victory.

A major surprise at the offset would break their spirit, so my strategy was to nullify the Chicago plan of campaign at the start.

I was so heavily loaded with big pitchers at that time that sometime before the end of the regular season I found myself in a quandary. I arrived late at a clubhouse meeting and hesitated at the door. My eyes fell on Ehmke, a grand old-timer. I beckoned him to follow me. As we stood outside the locker-room door, I said to him:

"Howard, it looks as if I'll have to let you go."

Ehmke was a veteran for whom I had deep regard. This was a hard decision for me to make. It was a sort of professional death sentence.

"Mr. Mack," Ehmke replied, "I've always wanted to be on a pennant winner and in a World Series, and this is as close as I ever got to it."

"Do you believe you could win a game in the World Series, Howard?" I asked.

"Mr. Mack," he replied, shoving his pitching arm forward, "I've got one more good game in me, and I'd like to give it to you in October."

"Howard," I said, "I've changed my mind. You're going to pitch that game in the series. You stay home and work out here in Philadelphia. When the Cubs come here in their final games with the Phillies, go to every game and study their hitters carefully."

I asked Ehmke to tell no one, and he kept his pledge. The only man I let in on this confidential agreement was Eddie Collins, who had returned to the team as a coach.

Hero of the Day

When we arrived at the field in Chicago for the opening of the World Series, not one of the players knew the identity of our first pitcher. Our opponents were eager to get this information. The newspaper men were all speculating on whether it would be Grove or Earnshaw or Walberg, but I withheld it until the last minute.

Not until shortly before game time, when Ehmke took off his jacket and began to warm up, did the secret come out. The huge World Series crowd, the sports writers and the players of both teams were all taken by complete surprise.

Al Simmons was sitting next to me on the bench. He jumped up.

"Is he going to work?" he exclaimed.

"Yes," I said, "have you any objections?"

"Nope," Al replied, "If you think he can win, it's good enough for me."

Howard Ehmke proved that he was a great sportsman. He not only won the first game in the World Series against the Chicago Cubs by a score of 3-1, but he struck out thirteen Chicago hitters in one game and established a World Series record.

That beating administered by Ehmke shocked the Cubs: "If a has-been can strike out thirteen of our men," they said, "what can we hope to do against Grove, Earnshaw and Walberg?"

Here's the answer: We won that World Series four games to one. Ehmke took the first game, as you have seen, 3-1. Earnshaw won the second game 9-3; Earnshaw lost the third when Chicago won its only game 3-1. Rommel won the fourth game 10-8. Walberg won the fifth and final game 3-2.

The big surprise was: "What about Grove?" I answered that in the next World Series in 1930 in St. Louis, when Grove won two games, Earnshaw won two games, and we took the series 4-2.

In 1931 Grove again won two games in the World Series against St. Louis; Earnshaw won one game, and St. Louis with Grimes (2) and Hallahan (2) won four and captured the series 4-3.

It was one of the greatest thrills in my life to see Ehmke pitch that game and break a world's record. He smashed the record that Big Ed Walsh had held for twenty-three years when Ed struck out twelve men in a World Series. Ehmke raised the ante to thirteen.

Winning Against Great Odds

The fourth game of that series in 1929 developed into a terrific battle. We were trailing the Chicago Cubs 8-0, as we went into the seventh inning. It was a desperate situation.

"Get after them," I told the boys. "You can win it yet."

Al Simmons hit a home run. Jimmy Foxx singled. Bing Miller singled. Jimmy Dykes singled. Joe Boley singled. I sent George Burns to pinch-hit for the pitcher and he was out. Max Bishop singled. George ("Mule") Haas smashed into outfield. The sun got in Wilson's eyes and Haas went for a home run. Cochrane got a walk.

The team had batted around and Al Simmons came to bat again. He hit the first ball pitched for a single. Jimmy Foxx singled. Bing Miller was hit by a pitched ball.

Three men on bases and the score was tied 8-8 in the last half of the seventh inning, Jimmy Dykes smashed out a two-bagger against the wall that brought in two men. Boley and Burns struck out.

Ten runs in one inning! Coming from scratch we had passed the Chicago Cubs and snatched victory from defeat. I sent Grove to the mound to pitch the last two innings and he shut them out. We won by the score 10-8. What a game that was!

The fifth game of that World Series was another thriller. When our boys came to bat in the ninth inning, the score was 2-0 against us. We had made only two hits off Malone, the Chicago moundsman, in the entire game. Our pitcher, Walberg, was the first batter, and I sent Walter French in as pinch hitter—he struck out on four pitched balls. Max Bishop hit safe over third base. George Haas hit the second pitched ball over the wall and tied the score. Mickey Cochrane smashed out one to Rogers Hornsby. Two out! Here Simmons hit a double.

Jimmy Foxx was the next batter and was passed. Bing Miller, with two strikes and two balls, smashed the next pitch to the scoreboard. The winning run came in. We won the game 3-2, and the World Series.

My thrilling moments were not confined to the 1929 World Series; they began away back in the first years of our White Elephants. There is a saying that the customer is always right. Well, sometimes he can be wrong too. As long ago as 1909 I received a beautiful letter which read: "What a great thing it is to build such a grand building (Shibe Park) with such spacious accommodation and so much thought for the comfort of the public. But we fans would rather sit on a barbed-wire fence than to be looking at our present team." That "present team," however, became champions of the world the next season.

Sports writers began to talk about my "$100,000 infield," Baker, Barry, Collins, and Stuffy McInnis. I do not believe the game has ever seen anything better. Today any one of these men would bring far more than $100,000 on the open market; they might even be called a "Million Dollar Infield."

The 1911 season began with our trailing the Detroit Tigers, who won twenty of their first twenty-two games. They looked like sure winners. On the morning of the Fourth of July the Philadelphia A's came out in front by a nose. By the end of the season we were more than twelve games in the lead. We won our fourth pennant and second World Series, beating the "unbeatable" New York Giants.

The Ups and Downs of Life

My first great disappointment came in 1912. We had what I believed to be potentially the greatest team the game had yet known. Then misfortune struck us. Four or five of my stars broke training, and I had to suspend them. That year we didn't even finish second.

But in 1913 disappointments turned to joys. I had added Herb Pennock and Joe Bush to the pitching staff; I had also signed Wally Schang. Bender and Plank I used oftener than any manager had ever used two pitchers. I would put one of my youngsters in the box to start a game and then I would send Bender or Plank in to save it.

Sports writers began to predict that so-and-so would start the afternoon's game, and that either Bender or Plank would finish it. Coombs was ill, so we couldn't take chances. But by this jockeying, we won our fifth pennant and beat the New York Giants again, thus winning our third World Series.

We won our sixth pennant in 1914. Bob Shawkey, Chief Bender, Eddie Plank and Bush were with us. That World Series was the cause of one of the biggest surprises and one of the greatest disappointments I have ever had. We had won our third World Series the preceding year. The question now was: Who would win the National League pennant and meet us in the next World Series?

On the Fourth of July, George Stalling's Boston Braves were in last place. The New York Giants were fifteen games ahead, with the Braves far down in the cellar.

"My team is ready now and we'll win the pennant," announced the optimistic Stallings. I only smiled.

A miracle happened. By the first of September the Braves were but half a game behind the Giants. They had hit such a fast pace that nobody could stop them. They had three crack pitchers, George Tyler, Bill James, and Dick Rudolph. Hank Gowdy was catching; Johnny Evers was at second base; Rabbit Maranville was a whirlwind at shortstop. At the end of September the Braves were ten games in the lead in first place.

When the Crash Came

When our Philadelphia Athletics, as the American League champions, met the Braves they mowed us down four games straight, the first time in World Series history. We were beaten twice by James and twice by Rudolph. Hank Gowdy slugged our pitchers by batting .545.

Let me say here that I consider Chief Bender the greatest one-game pitcher, the greatest money pitcher baseball ever has known. There are crucial times when a pitcher doesn't get the breaks. And the breaks were against him and us in the 1914 World Series.

The human equation enters into the game when least expected. In 1935 I thought we looked like winners. We had the best outfield in the league; the infield was just as good. We had a fine young pitcher in Johnny Marcum and four other young hurlers—Benton, Dietrich, Cascarella, and Cain—who looked as if they would help us.

I tried out Benton in three innings each in two exhibition games. He struck out the nine men he faced on three pitched balls apiece in each game. My catchers were good, but they couldn't step to the plate in a pinch and slam out hits that would make winning runs. So I planned to put the slugging Jimmy Foxx back of the plate and give the fans and the rival teams a big surprise.

The set-up was great, but "the best-laid plans of mice and men often go awry." "Sugar" Cain went sour. When we were playing in Detroit, I heard for the first time that my pitcher wanted to go to some other team. I called him into my office and we had a confidential talk.

"Sit on that chair," I said, "until we reach an understanding, even if it takes all day."

"If you're going to trade me," he said, "go ahead and trade me."

I had had no idea whatsoever of trading him at that moment, but following a hunch that something was wrong, the next day I did trade him to St. Louis. When we played in St. Louis my friend, Rogers Hornsby, sent Cain in to pitch against us. He pitched as never before. Thirteen of our men were struck out.

I was sitting somewhat dispirited in my room after the game when Cain walked in.

"I got something that I want to get off my chest," he began. "Sit down, Sugar," I said, "and tell me about it."

"I just want you to know, Mr. Mack," he said, "that I haven't anything against you, or against the team."

"That's good," I replied. "What is your trouble?"

"Well," he said, "it was like this: We had another player and his wife living with us in Philadelphia. My wife was keeping their books for them. They got into an argument about the bookkeeping. I didn't like that, so I decided to break it up by leaving Philadelphia and taking my wife with me. That's the only reason I began putting out feelers for another job."

"Well, Sugar," I replied, "I don't blame you. I can understand how that would kind of get under your skin."

It is over such trivial things that the best of baseball teams can begin to break up. The computation of sums on household accounts had taken from me one of my good pitchers.

The Fall of the Mighty

The staff gradually began to crumble. We were playing in Boston, and Bill Dietrich, another good pitcher, was in the box. He had built up a nice lead, but he began to wabble. I told Cascarella to warm up. My son, Earle Mack, took him down to the bull pen. When Dietrich filled the bases and let in one run, my son Earle tipped his hat to me as a signal that Cascarella was ready. Earle told me afterwards that Cascarella had so much stuff, warming up, it almost knocked his glove off.

Cascarella came to the mound. He walked the first man to face him and forced in a run; he walked the second man and forced in another run. I signaled to him to pitch to them. If he let them hit, they might have run into a double play. He paid no attention to my signals.

My temper seldom reaches the breaking point, but that time my patience was exhausted. I called Cascarella in and with as much calmness as I could muster, ordered him to go inside and take off his uniform. "I don't know what I am going to do with you," I told him, "but I'll do something."

And I did do something: I sent him to Syracuse. He won so many games that Boston paid me $5,000 for my option on him. His first game for Boston was a crackerjack. Then he had to be taken out of the box for four or five games. His stuff began to show up again, and he pitched Syracuse into the International League championship, winning two games for them in the play-off.

The staff of four star pitchers was now down to two: only Benton and Dietrich were left. Benton, having struck out eighteen men in six innings in exhibition games, should have done great things. For some unknown reason he just couldn't compete with the big league batters. He was good one day and average on his next appearance, so I had to send him out on option. I felt sure that Benton had big stuff in him once he started.

Now it was up to Dietrich, the last of the four. We had a little heart-to-heart talk. I said to him:

"Bill, I've tried everything I know. I've tried you at starting your games and I've tried you at finishing games."

"Mr. Mack," he replied, as he kicked a clump of sod with his foot, "I'll tell you what's the matter with me. I've got a wife and baby. And I'm worried about my job."

"Is that all that's worrying you?" I asked.

"Yes," he answered.

"Well," I replied, "if that's all, you may rest easy. If I am here, your job is safe for the next three years."

"Start me right now, Mr. Mack," he exclaimed, shaking my hand vigorously. "Start me this afternoon."

I did, and he was knocked out of the box. But I kept my word to him because I had full confidence in him. I put him on the mound in Washington. In the first inning the Senators got five runs off him. In the second inning they got five more.

THE MACK MEN, probably baseball's best-known family, look over hundreds of
birthday telegrams sent to the boss, Connie Mack, in the Shibe Park office of the
Philadelphia Athletics. Sons Roy and Earle, at the right, beam approval as young
Connie Mack, Jr., reads some congratulatory messages aloud to his famous father.

SECOND GAME OF THE 1905 WORLD SERIES between the Athletics and the Giants at New York. Chief Bender pitching for the A's. This was the first era of Connie Mack's teams. They won pennants in 1902 and 1905, and in 1910 took their first World Series. Mack considers Bender, his Chippewa Indian discovery, "baseball's greatest money pitcher." Bender is now a scout for Phila. Athletics.
International-News Photo

Cornelius and Mrs. Margaret Hogan McGilli- Katherine Hallahan McGillicuddy, the present
cuddy, 1890, with sons Roy (standing) and Earle. "Mrs. Mack."

Photo by Bachrach

BIRTHPLACE OF MR. BASEBALL. This is the modest home in East Brookfield, Massachusetts, where
Cornelius McGillicuddy was born. Starting with the East Brookfield sand lots, young Cornelius
grew with the game to become the Connie Mack we know as one of the great names in baseball.

Courtesy of Roy Mack

MACKMEN OF 1894. The first team Mr. Baseball managed was the Pittsburgh Pirates. Connie Mack is in the center, in Pirate uniform. He was acting as a player-manager at the time of the picture.
Wide World Photo

With E. B. stitched on their shirts, East Brookfield's nine stand stiffly for their picture. All the Brookfields were famous for their baseball teams and these Massachusetts towns have contributed their share of players to the big leagues: Martin Bergen, the Braves' brilliant catcher, Frank Bird of the St. Louis Browns and "Mr. Baseball"—front row center—at the start of his career.
Courtesy Phila. Athletics

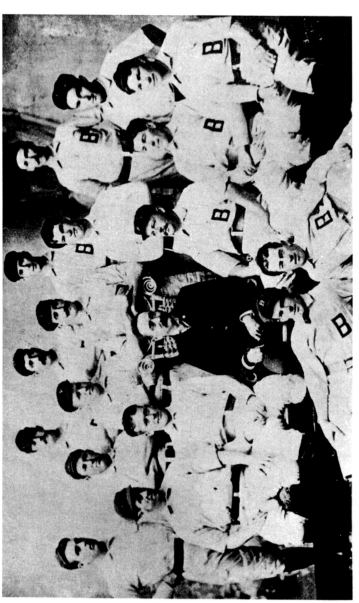

Whenever great teams are mentioned, first to come to mind is the Fighting Baltimore Orioles. John McGraw, manager of the N. Y. Giants for 30 years, was the scrappy third baseman. Willie Keeler, famous for "hitting them where they ain't" was right fielder. McGraw and Keeler lie on the floor in front. Ned Hanlon, the manager, ranked as the smartest of his time. Connie Mack says this old-time stellar aggregation slugged to victory like the ancient Roman gladiators.

International News Photo

HONUS "HANS" WAGNER. The highest-paid player in his day, 1897-1917, he started at $125 a month and worked up to $10,000 a season. In Hans' heyday, his salary created as much furor as Babe Ruth's $80,000. *International News Photo*

CY YOUNG. "He pitched more games than any other man in mound history and won more games than any man who ever entered a pitcher's box. His record remains unchallenged. It shows that he averaged twenty-five victories a year for over twenty years." — Connie Mack, evaluating all-time stars. *International News Photo*

EDDIE PLANK. "Gettysburg Eddie was one of our first big finds. He batted his way through seventeen years, 1901-1917, on our American diamonds. He stands with the greats of all times—one of few pitchers to win more than 300 games in the big leagues." — Connie Mack, in his evaluation of great players during his "66 years." *International News Photo*

Connie Mack watches batting practice. (1909)
Wide World Photo

Ty Cobb, the "Georgia Peach," takes a cut!
Wide World Photo

Tris Speaker pictured after joining Athletics.
Press Association, Inc.

Christy Mathewson, great N.Y. Giants' pitcher.
Wide World Photo

"OLD TIME" SHOTS

HOWARD EHMKE, who was Mack's surprise selection as opening pitcher in the 1929 World Series, getting the call over Grove, Earnshaw, and Walberg. Connie Mack says the success of this strategy gave him his greatest thrill of 66 years in big leagues.
Wide World Photo

GROVER CLEVELAND ALEXANDER of the St. Louis Cardinals, who struck out 2,184 men. Some think him the greatest control pitcher of all time. Only 8 pitchers in the big leagues have passed the 2,000 strike-out mark. He won 373, lost 208 games.
Wide World Photo

Rivals shake hands as Walter Johnson (left) of the Washington Senators greets Connie Mack in Washington, D. C., at the inauguration of the 1931 season. Their teams had been picked by experts as the two most likely to battle it out for that year's pennant.
Wide World Photo

EDDIE COLLINS, "discovery" of Connie Mack's from Columbia University; member of his famous "$100,000 infield." Mr. Mack sold him for $50,000 in the breakup of his great 1914 team.
International News Photo

CARL HUBBELL, Giants' pitcher. Known as the "Meal Ticket" because the Giants threw him into the game when a victory was needed. Known as "Long Pants" for obvious reasons.
Press Association, Inc.

RUBE WADDELL, pitcher in one of Mack's greatest batteries, 1902-1909. He gave his manager many an anxious moment with his wanderlust and screwball antics, but was a pitching genius.
International News Photo

FRANK BAKER, home-run king of his time, who led the league for four years (1911-14). Mack discovered Baker on the Reading, Pa., team, made him part of his famous "$100,000 infield."
International News Photo

Three scenes in the career of the late Babe Ruth. At left he is shown as a great pitcher for the Boston Red Sox early in his career. He takes a healthy swing at the ball (center) during an exhibition game in Florida while a member of the New York Yankees. At right he appears with team mate, the equally beloved and hard-hitting late Lou Gehrig.

Wide World Photo

Ten great baseball stars of other years gathered in August, 1944, to honor Connie Mack, then celebrating his 50th year as a major league team manager. From left to right: Al Simmons, Babe Ruth, Tris Speaker, Walter Johnson, Lefty Grove, Connie Mack, Bill Dickey, Honus Wagner, Frank (Home Run) Baker, Eddie Collins and George Sisler.

Press Association, Inc.

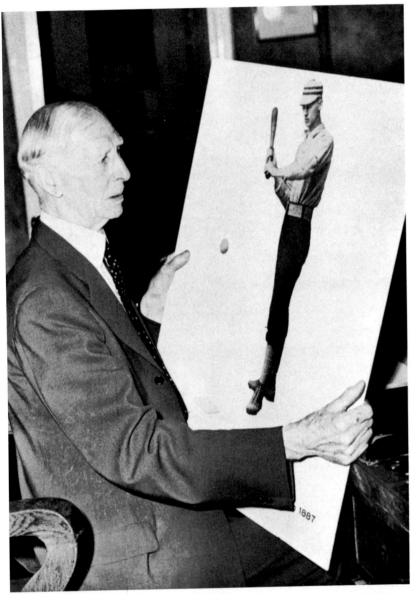

With this photo of himself, aged 26, Connie Mack recalls his days as catcher with the Washington Senators. In 1887, when this photograph was taken, young "Mr. Baseball" had been playing professional baseball for three years, and he received a silver service from the capital's enthusiastic fans.

Wide World Photo

ROGERS HORNSBY, whom Connie Mack labels "a great sportsman, a grand character. With Ty Cobb he is tops. Hornsby was the greatest second baseman of his time, while Cobb was the greatest outfielder."
Wide World Photo

THE MIGHTY MITE, Miller Huggins, manager of the New York Yankees in their heyday of the 1920's. Huggins' many differences with the great Yankee star slugger, Babe Ruth, made sporting page headlines.
Wide World Photo

JIMMY DYKES steals home in the third game of the 1929 World Series at Shibe Park between the Chicago Cubs and the Athletics. Though the Athletics lost this game, they took the series 4-1.

International News Photo

Opening play of the first game of the 1929 World Series at Wrigley Field between the A's and the Chicago Cubs shows Max Bishop grounding out to Charlie Grimm, Cubs' first baseman. Before 51,000 fans Ehmke pitched the Athletics to a 3-1 victory, striking out thirteen Chicago batters.

International News Photo

In National Baseball Hall of Fame are plaques of players, relics of early baseball days.
Wide World Photo

Entrance to National Baseball Hall of Fame, Cooperstown, N. Y.—birthplace of baseball.
Wide World Photo

Connie Mack Receives the Philadelphia Award in 1929. This $10,000 award is given annually from the Bok fund for "an act or service advancing the best and larger interests of Philadelphia."

Phila. Evening Bulletin

"Take him out! Take him out!" the fans in the stand began to yell.

I walked over from the dugout to the tier of boxes. "I'm going to keep Bill Dietrich in there until Washington gets twenty-one runs off him," I announced.

Bill heard my voice, that reassured him, and he settled down to work with a vengeance. The Senators were mowed down in rapid order. From that time on, they got only one more run.

Ty Cobb's First Game with the A's

I have found that it never pays to show favoritism to a player. And I have learned never to reprimand a player in front of his comrades, never to show strong dislike for any member of the team. Always treat them all as members of a family in a congenial household.

When Ty Cobb played his first game for the A's, I felt somewhat embarrassed. Here was the greatest player of his time, twenty-two years as the star fielder with Detroit and six years its able manager. He was noted as an expert on the strong and weak points of all the batters of all the other teams. I hesitated in giving orders to this great of the greats.

However, I realized that I was responsible for the strategy of the game. A rival batter came to the plate. I felt that Ty knew where to play him, but it seemed to me that he was playing too far to the right of the batter. I was about to signal my pitcher to put the ball where, if hit, it would go far to the left of where Ty was standing.

Standing up in the dugout, I waved to Ty with my score card to move over to the left. Everybody saw the signal. Even the pitcher turned and looked. What would the great Cobb do? Would he follow his own judgment or would he accept my decision? He saluted me as a soldier salutes a general and followed orders.

Now I was on the spot. If the batter hit the ball to where Ty had been standing, I'd certainly look silly. Ty had barely reached the position I had designated when the batter walloped the ball. Where did it go? Right into the hands of Ty Cobb! Did I feel relieved? I'll say I did.

When John McGraw retired from the game in 1932 I was greatly disappointed. He had won ten pennants for the Giants; I had won nine for the Philadelphia Athletics. I was anxious to get one more to tie McGraw, then he could retire, and I'd go on to try to beat his record.

I rate John McGraw's Giants of 1921 as his masterpiece. He had such top stars as Long George Kelly, Johnny Rawlings, Dave (Beauty) Bancroft and Frankie Frisch in the infield; Irish Meusel, George Burns and Ross Youngs in the outfield. Such a combination is hard to beat. On his pitching staff were such able men as Art Nehf, only pitcher to win games in four successive World Series; Fred Toney, Jesse Barnes and Phil Douglas.

John knew how to collect aggregations of great players through the years, such as Travis Jackson, famous shortstop and third baseman, with an arm that could throw a ball with the accuracy of a shot from a gun; Bill Terry, the first baseman, who hit .401 in 1930 and later became the manager of the Giants.

Every day was a thrill during the eight years I had Rube Waddell under my wing. With Rube one never knew what was going to happen next. He was the atom bomb in baseball long before the atom bomb was discovered, but his story will be told in another chapter.

Longest Games Ever Played

The greatest games in baseball were the two historic ones that went to twenty-four innings in the American League, finally to be topped by a twenty-six-inning game in the National League.

Our Philadelphia Athletics, in a terrific battle with Boston, played the first twenty-four-inning game on September 1,

1906. The game in Boston was tied at 1-1 until, in the twenty-fourth inning, Philadelphia scored three runs and won 4-1.

The game lasted 4 hours, 47 minutes. Our battery was Coombs and Powers; Boston's battery, Harris and Carrigan and Criger. Both Coombs and Harris went all the way.

Fourteen years later Brooklyn and the Boston Nationals broke this record with a twenty-six-inning game played in Boston on May 1, 1920. After 3 hours, 50 minutes, the game was called on account of darkness. Brooklyn's battery was Cadore and Krueger, Elliott, and Boston's Oeschger, O'Neill and Gowdy. The pitchers went all the way but both catchers needed relief.

Twenty-five years later, the Philadelphia Athletics engaged in another twenty-four-inning battle with the Detroit Tigers on July 21, 1945, in Shibe Park. We scored in the fourth inning, Detroit scored in the seventh inning and the breathtaking struggle continued, with neither side able to cross home plate during the next seventeen innings. This game, tied at 1-1, was called on account of darkness after 4 hours, 48 minutes, and was the longest game on record. The batteries were Mueller (19$\frac{2}{3}$ innings), Trout (4$\frac{1}{3}$) and Swift; Christopher (13), Berry (11) and Rosar.

The longest scoreless tie game was played between the Brooklyn Dodgers and the Cincinnati Reds in Brooklyn on September 11, 1946: nineteen innings, when the game was called on account of darkness after 4 hours, 40 minutes of play. Batteries, for Brooklyn, Gregg (10 innings), Casey (5), Herring (3), Behrman (1) and Edwards; for Cincinnati, Vander Meer (15), Gumbert (4) and Mueller.

The Pittsburgh Pirates and the Boston Braves played twenty scoreless innings in the National League on August 1, 1918, but the tie was broken in the twenty-first inning, when Pittsburgh scored two runs and won.

Those who witnessed these games got the excitement of a lifetime. But, as I have said before, one of my biggest thrills was the day when my pitcher Ehmke struck out thirteen men in one game and established a World Series record in 1929. And you would have risen out of your seat and thrown your hat in the air if you had been there on May 3, 1938, when Lefty Grove, then with Boston, struck out his 2,000th batter and gained his 260th victory when he fanned six Detroit Tigers. By 1941 he had won 300 victories and his strike-outs mounted high.

Eight pitchers in the major leagues have passed the 2,000 strike-out mark. Three of the eight record breakers had worn the Philadelphia A's uniform: Grove, Waddell, and Plank. Here's the record: Walter Johnson, 3,497; Cy Young, 2,836; Christy Mathewson, 2,447; Rube Waddell, 2,369; Grover Cleveland Alexander, 2,184; Dazzy Vance, 2,030. Lefty Grove (2,271) and Eddie Plank (2,257) also passed the 2,000 mark.

Historic Trip to Japan and Philippines

I'm going to tell you now about one of the greatest thrills I ever experienced in my career. It was when I was delegated to go with the first American baseball team to Japan and the Philippines in 1934 to demonstrate our national game.

Babe Ruth managed the all-star team, which was made up of players from both major leagues, and Judge Landis asked me to go along as good-will delegate. B. F. Shibe and my son, Earle, made the arrangements for the trip. Babe Ruth received $12,000 and all expenses, and he took his wife and daughter with him. Among the others who went were Lou Gehrig and Bing Miller.

The Japanese were literally crazy about the great national game of America and walked miles to see the great American athletes. We drew 209,000 people to the four games we played; every game was sold out at least three weeks in advance. Babe Ruth was their idol.

Tremendous parades welcomed us to each city. A Japanese

general walked thirty miles to present his sword to the first man who made a home run. He didn't seem to think it was possible to knock a ball so far that the batter could make a home run, but when Babe Ruth stepped to the plate and hit the ball out of the park, the august general fawningly presented his sword to the King of Swat.

Ambassador Grew, a master of Japanese psychology, was enthusiastic over our "diplomatic" mission. The Japanese even began to get up before daylight to play America's national game at sunrise. One day when we went out about twenty miles from the city to practice in a place where there were no houses, about 20,000 came to watch us. Where they came from no one knew, but they seemed to spring up from all directions.

Whenever they wanted to address the umpire, the Japanese always took off their hats! On one occasion they had twelve cameras to record our plays, so that they could imitate them later. No Japanese women were permitted to attend the games, however; quite a contrast to this country, where thousands of women fans enjoy the games.

While we were in Japan, we met four Senators, who accompanied us on our trip to Manila. Governor-General Frank Murphy, later a member of the United States Supreme Court, gave us a reception with the Senators as fellow guests. Governor Murphy was an ardent admirer of our national game and attended all the exhibitions.

At one game I sat beside him in the dugout and heard them calling for our battery, Whitehill and Hayes, to play a game with the Manila boys. It lasted one inning. The Filipinos were good fielders and good runners, but at that time they had not learned to hit.

They played the game differently than we do. When a pitcher went into the game he had to show that he was in good condition, so he would stand on the sideline and pitch to the catcher until the crowd was satisfied that he could finish the game. They consider it a dishonor to take a pitcher out of the box.

The Philippine pitcher was an excellent contortionist—but we made twenty-four runs (including several home runs) to their lone one run. Nevertheless, we congratulated them on their remarkable feat of making one run against what we considered the greatest ball players in the world.

Everywhere we went we had magnificent reception, and I know our boys did great honor to Uncle Sam. We played about twenty-seven games in Japan and the Philippines, for our tour took us about 800 miles from Tokyo. We were gone two months, and some of our boys later went around the world.

Since World War II, both the Japanese and the Filipinos have adopted baseball as their national game. General Douglas MacArthur, who was an excellent ball player in his youth, has given them great encouragement. With deep respect for their national traditions, he has performed epoch-making services in guiding them in the reconstruction of their devasted countries.

CHAPTER 6

HISTORIC EVENTS

I f i were to live one hundred years, I should not have time enough to tell you all the stories I remember about the historic events I have witnessed and experienced.

I have been an eyewitness to many of them; others have been described to me by people who saw them; others have been related by sports writers and have become the common property of the sports world, but I'd like to give you my own versions of these happenings.

I am not going to become involved in the argument of whether our national game was a version of "rounders" imported from England.

The word "baseball" was supposedly first used 176 years ago, when a quatrain was printed under the heading "Baseball" in 1774, two years before the Declaration of Independence was drafted. This is believed to be the first mention of the word in print.

> "The ball once struck off,
> Away flies the boy
> To the next destined post
> And then home with joy."

Our national game began on the sand lots of our country towns. When I began to play the game as a village boy, we had none of the modern equipment. All we had were our bare hands and our love for the game. But it is from these sand lots that many of our best players have come, so we owe a tremendous debt to these homemade diamonds.

There was no such thing as a called "strike" or base on balls in the early days of baseball. We swung at everything in sight, and after we missed three times we were out. The catcher stood far back and caught the ball on the bounce.

An old woodcut shows the game as it was played in the early 1830's. This was before the days of basemen. The batter hit the ball and ran around the bases. The player who fielded the ball "plugged" it at the runner. If he hit him, *the runner was out!*

Another quaint feature of the early game was that the runner ran in the opposite direction from the way we run today. First base was to the left of the catcher, and third base was in the position of our first base in the present game. There was no umpire in the game's early history. When a runner was hit by the ball, he knew he was out; he didn't need an umpire to tell him.

The umpire actually came into existence when the first game between two competing teams was played. This was the famous game between the Knickerbockers and the Excelsiors, played in Hoboken, New Jersey, on July 19, 1846. They played under new rules of their own laid down with the aid of Alexander Cartwright. Each team had nine men as we have today, on a diamond with flat bases ninety feet apart.

The umpire wore a high hat to distinguish him from the rest. Plugging, or throwing the ball at the base runner, was eliminated. The umpire was the sole judge on all outs. There was no appeal from his decision, except possibly to throw a ripe tomato at his high silk hat!

Beginning of Competitive Teams

That historic game in Hoboken really started the era of baseball. It soon leaped into popularity, and in a short time

twenty-five organized amateur teams in New York and New
Jersey entered into competition.

A team known as the Atlantics became one of the fastest
teams in the country before the outbreak of the Civil War.
The Knickerbockers, who had entered the rivalry as a gentleman's team of the upper social group, withdrew from the
scene when everybody began playing baseball.

Competitive teams were organized, especially in the East:
the Knickerbocker Baseball Club of New York; Jolly Young
Bachelors; Baseball Club; Gotham Club; Eagles; Putnams;
Eckfords; Empires; Atlantic Club; Excelsiors of Brooklyn;
the Unions, and many others.

Newly organized teams in various parts of the country
played under their own homemade rules. There was the New
York Game; the New England Game, frequently called the
Massachusetts Game; the Philadelphia Game. Finally, like
the states, the teams united on the national game.

Those early teams were frequently confined to neighbor-
hoods composed of men in the same occupation: The Man-
hattans, composed of New York policemen; Pocahontas Club,
composed of milkmen; Metropolitans, composed of school-
teachers; Phantoms, composed of barkeepers. The Knickerbockers was a "gentleman's club," composed of the socially
élite. From these origins have sprung our factory teams, school
teams, and town teams of today.

Ball players in the early days thought it was a sign of manhood to raise a beard. You couldn't be an athlete without
raising whiskers or at least a mustache. The beardless young
player was considered a sissy. In fact, most of the players on
the Washington Senators, when I was catcher back in 1887,
wore mustaches.

Clerks, business and professional men, and shop workers,
would get up at four o'clock in the morning to play the game
at sunrise so as not to interfere with their jobs in the ten-
twelve-fourteen hour days.

It was many years before the game was consolidated into uniform methods of play. The New Yorkers played it their way; the New Englanders stuck to their old method. The game in its early days in Massachusetts was played on an oblong, later on a square, and finally a diamond. Home plate was fourth base, running parallel with the catcher's position, not in front of it. The New Englanders continued to plug the runner between bases, and this custom did not entirely disappear until professional baseball had become a rage as far west as the Mississippi River.

First Western Trip a National Event

There was a team in Washington known as the Olympics, composed entirely of youths in Government offices. Their first Western tour was a national event. They rode through the streets of the capital en route to the station in carriages as if it were an inaugural parade, a brass band heading the procession. Red, white and blue plumes decorated the heads of the horses. The players wore spick-and-span linen dusters. Their cry was: "Westward Ho! Westward Ho! Here's to all who toss the ball."

At the railroad stations, women would present each player with a bouquet, and also shower them with flowers as the players stepped on the train. Those were the grand old days!

Wherever they stopped in their Western tour there were bands of music to greet them at the station. A speech of welcome was usually made by the mayor as he spoke with old-time eloquence from a flag-draped platform. The rival team, with military precision, lined up as a guard of honor, some of the teams in brilliant shirts and Zouave trousers. The citizens decorated the buildings along the streets of march with gaily colored bunting.

The question is often asked: How did the word "fan" originate? In the old days we referred to our rooters as "baseball cranks." The people brought fans to help keep themselves cool when the sun beat down on the bleachers. Those who did not bring fans, fanned themselves with their straw hats and later their score cards, until the spectators looked like a sea of fans. Thus it can be understood how the spectators in the stands may have become known as "fans."

Abe Lincoln a Baseball Fan

There are many stories about Lincoln's being a rabid baseball fan. It is said that when a delegation was waiting at his home in Springfield, Illinois, to inform him of his nomination for the Presidency, Lincoln remarked: "Tell them they'll have to wait until I make another hit!"

Some versions of the Lincoln story claim that Abe was playing ball in his back yard at the time, and that he took another good wallop at the ball before he went into the house to meet the distinguished delegation.

The fact remains, as A. G. Spalding, our noted baseball historian, records in his book, *America's National Game:* Lincoln did play ball. He was in Springfield when nominated as President by the Republican Convention in Chicago. At the moment of his nomination, according to some historians, Abe was in the Springfield railroad depot watching the telegraph ticker when the news from Chicago ticked over the wires. But certainly he had time to get back home and put in some baseball practice before the delegation reached him.

Strange as it may seem, the War Between the States started the first real momentum in making baseball our national game. Many a Union soldier carried a baseball in his haversack. Between battles, when the soldiers could relax, they would start the new game. Most of the soldiers from the Midwest had never seen it, but it didn't take them long to learn it in the army camps, and take it home with them after the war was over.

Yankee prisoners of war in Confederate prison camps taught it to the Confederate guards, who after the war took it home with them to all parts of the Southland. The game thus became nationwide.

In the 1860's the largest crowd that had ever witnessed any sports event in the United States gathered at Hilton Head, South Carolina, on Christmas Day, 1862, to see two Union Army teams fight a baseball battle. In this large Army camp, with its great concentration of soldiers, 40,000 men witnessed the game. The date of this event interests me, as I was born but three days before, in Massachusetts, while my father was with the Union Army in the South.

It was a big event when, in 1860, the Brooklyn Excelsiors went on tour. They were somewhat like a traveling show of barnstormers. After drawing crowds in Albany, Buffalo, and Rochester, winning every game in New York State, they continued on the road to Philadelphia, where a team known as the Athletics had been formed, and then on to Wilmington and Baltimore.

This first Brooklyn road team won fifteen games straight and cleaned up all opposition. A crowd of 3,000 was considered big in those days, and the excitement they created resulted in new baseball teams being formed along their route. Thus the Brooklyn Excelsiors have been termed the first missionaries in the game.

First Tragedy in Baseball

The first big star in the game was a nineteen-year-old boy wonder, James Creighton, who toured with the Brooklyn Excelsiors in 1860. Jimmy was like the first shot at Fort Sumter, for his achievements were heard round the world. He hurled the ball with a wrist throw that created speed. The sensation of his times, he became known as "Unbeatable Jimmy."

Young Pitcher Creighton was the first baseball casualty. While standing at the plate in a game of the Brooklyn Excelsiors *vs.* the Unions, on October 15, 1862, he was felled by a heart attack. Carried from the field, he passed away three days later, when only twenty-one years of age. This was baseball's first tragedy.

The first slide to base is supposed to have been developed by a player named Studley, of Washington, in the late 1860's. This was considered a circus stunt and created considerable excitement. It was never ruled out because it introduced more skill and excitement into the game, and it has since developed into a fine art.

The greatest impulse behind baseball was the organization of the National Association of Baseball Players in 1857. This gave the new game a professional standing. Baseball assumed formidable proportions with such rapidity that two years after the war the National Association had 237 member clubs. More than half of these teams were from the Middle West: Ohio, Indiana, Wisconsin, Illinois. These teams had not become professionals, as there was no league in existence to assure the players regular income. Semiprofessional baseball was simmering in on the edges. Some players were beginning to demand wages.

Sensation of the "Red Stockings"

The first professional team to pay regular salaries was organized in Cincinnati by George Ellard in 1869. The pros went on the road and captivated the people's imagination. Known as the "Red Stockings" (which they wore), the colorful aggregation that evolved into the present-day Cincinnati Reds met with unprecedented success. Other clubs entered the professional ranks and baseball was on its way.

Upon their arrival in Philadelphia to play the Athletics of that day, the Red Stockings rode to the ball grounds in a four-horse omnibus decorated with American flags. Some all-too-partisan fans met them with the cry: "You're going to get beat! You're going to get beat!" When Cincinnati won, the cry changed to a brief order to hie themselves to a warmer place!

When the Red Stockings returned home unbeaten, it was the occasion of what probably was the first home-coming celebration. Thousands cheered them wildly at the Cincinnati railroad station. The team headed a big parade through the streets to City Hall. As a token of the city's admiration a huge baseball bat, twenty-seven feet long, was presented to the victorious team.

Baseball drew its first big crowds in 1870 when Cincinnati went on the road for its second season. From Boston and Cleveland to New Orleans, they practically stopped business in every city they visited; and they won twenty-two straight victories. They aroused the populace with a new team song which began: "Hurrah! Hurrah! For the noble game, hurrah!"

The saga of this first professional team is filled with exciting episodes, for it was the first baseball team to play its way across the continent, from Boston to San Francisco, in 1869. Traveling 12,000 miles, the Cincinnati Red Stockings played fifty-seven games and won fifty-seven victories. One of their greatest victories was when they went to Washington and beat the Senators by a score of 24-8. Cincinnati then became the baseball capital of the United States.

Their first defeat, after building up a record of eighty straight victories, came on June 14, 1870, when they crossed bats with the Atlantics in Brooklyn before a crowd of 20,000 people, all standing, and all paying fifty cents apiece to see the game. It was a picturesque sight, the Reds in their knee breeches and the Brooklyn Atlantics in their long trousers. There were no such things at that time as chest protectors, masks, or gloves. As the catchers received most of the punishment, the game required more catchers than pitchers.

This historic game was tied 5-5 at the end of the ninth

inning. Extra innings were tense with excitement. The Red Stockings scored two runs in the eleventh inning. The Atlantics now had their chance at the bat. With a rally heretofore unheard of, the Brooklynites smashed out three runs and won by a score of 8-7.

This was really big news throughout the country. Baseball had hit the jackpot.

It is interesting to compare the salaries of these first professionals with the money that ball players are getting today. The top man on the salary pay roll then was George Wright, who, with his older brother Harry, built up the team. They became famous as the "Wright Brothers" long before the famous Wright Brothers of airplane history came into prominence. George Wright, the greatest shortstop of his time (now in the Hall of Fame), received $1,400 for the season. He hit 59 home runs in one year, with a batting average of .518.

The salary of Harry Wright, manager and captain of the first professional team, who played center field, was $1,200. He is the man who engaged a seamstress, Mrs. Bertram, of Cincinnati, to make the uniforms for the Red Stockings, knee-length pants, which set the pattern for the baseball uniforms used today. The salaries of the other members of that team ranged from $1,000 down to $800.

America's National Game Invades England

The first transoceanic trip in baseball was made in 1874 when Al Spalding, the greatest pitcher of his time, took the Bostons and the Athletics to England to show the Britishers the new American game. The Englishmen, who were wedded to cricket, looked askance at the "blasted confusion."

The two American teams gave fourteen exhibition baseball games in England. There was no applause from the stands. But when the Americans accepted their challenge to "play cricket" there was much enthusiasm. England's greatest experts met the Americans in seven cricket matches, and the Americans won them all.

It should be said that the Wright Brothers, who had joined the Bostons by this time, were expert cricket players and had coached the American athletes. Because of their training in alertness and quickness and accuracy in action, they quickly mastered the English game. Al Spalding was a hero in America, the first ball player to be followed by groups of admirers when he appeared on the streets.

The National League Is Born

I was fourteen years old when the news came that baseball had become big stuff. A National League came into existence on February 2, 1876, and baseball became established as our national game. Its first president was the Honorable Morgan Bulkeley, of Hartford, Connecticut. But the "Father of the National League" was William A. Hulbert, who succeeded Mr. Bulkeley as president.

Hulbert was a businessman who had become president of the Chicago club. He insisted that the game be run on a strictly business basis. He set up playing schedules and contracts that must be lived up to, such as a staff of trained umpires assigned by the leagues; rigid rules of conduct; uniforms of specific color for each team; and he established fifty cents as the uniform price of admission to all National League games. Written contracts for players became mandatory. Franchises were to be granted only to cities of 75,000 or more population.

Baseball had been threatened by loose management and gambling. It was in danger of being taken over by professional gamblers. Liquor was being sold on the grounds, and brawls and fist fights were common. Hulbert stopped all this and established law and order. These were the first great achievements of the organized baseball under the National League when baseball was put on a sound business basis.

William Hulbert died suddenly at fifty years of age, six years after the League was organized. Our national game is a lasting memorial to his name. In the Graceland Cemetery in Chicago there stands a monument in his honor. His grave is marked by a big stone baseball erected on a stone base. The names of the eight National League Clubs of that time are chiseled on the ball. There could be no more appropriate memorial to the man who gave the last years of his life to establish our national game.

CHAPTER 7

RECOLLECTIONS OF GREAT PLAYERS

M̲Y̲ MEMORY goes back at this moment to old "Cap" Anson, also known as "Pop," whom I first met during my boyhood in New England. He was the greatest player of the nineteenth century. Starting as a third baseman, he could play any position infield or outfield. As first baseman he was the greatest of his times; as catcher he was tops.

Anson came to the Chicago White Stockings as an Ohio farm boy in 1876, the year of the birth of the National League. The White Stockings won the first pennant for the League. The records show that Anson hit over .400 two seasons and over .390 two other seasons.

The White Stockings under "Cap" Anson was a veritable team of Samsons, an aggregation of six-footers. Up to 1886 they had won five championships; they were known as the strong men of baseball. In this group were Mike Kelly, King of the Diamond, and the mighty Jim McCormick. The Chicago crowds called the infield the "Stone Wall," and the team was known as the Heroic Legion of Baseball.

Among the players on Cap Anson's team was the famous Billy Sunday, the 100-yard champion sprinter, who played outfield, and who became later the most famous evangelist preacher in America.

Mike Kelly, after his playing days were over, opened a saloon in partnership with the famous umpire, Honest John

Kelly, in New York. While he was on a train going to Boston for a vaudeville performance, he caught pneumonia. When carried to the Boston Emergency Hospital, he whispered: "This is me last ride." And it was, for he died a few hours later.

The name of the mighty Dan Brouthers brings back a flood of recollections. Big Dan came into the majors in 1878, when I was a young boy. He was the great first baseman and a mighty slugger of his times. Dan was a huge, quiet man, with temperate habits and kindly manner, unless he became aroused by something he thought was an injustice.

Boyhood Heroes of the Diamond

Al Spalding was another of my boyhood heroes. From the time I was a youngster until I reached voting age, there was no bigger man in the game in my estimation. Later the ball we used was called the Spalding ball, and it continues to be the official ball in our major leagues.

Acclaimed the greatest pitcher during the 1860's and the 1870's, Spalding became a noted manager in the 1880's, then a league magnate. He was a famous sporting goods manufacturer, publisher of official baseball guides, the national game's leading historian, and when he died he left a big fortune. One writer described him as a man with the "appearance of a Greek god and the manner of a bishop."

Exciting Moments in the Old Days

I recall the first championship games, long before the World Series were inaugurated. The first was played in 1885, when I was with the New York Metropolitans of the old American Association, between the Chicago White Stockings of the National League and the St. Louis Browns of the American Association. Both teams claimed the victory, which ended in a squabble.

In the following year, 1886, while I was with the Washington Senators, then a National League team, Cris Von der Ahe, one of the most fabulous baseball owners in history, who owned the St. Louis Browns, challenged Al Spalding's Chicago White Stockings to another series.

"I'll play only under one consideration," Spalding replied. "The winner take all!"

"I'll take you up," Von der Ahe quickly retorted. A pot of $15,000 was to go to the victor.

Sporting history had never heard of anything like this. Baseball fans around the country were aroused to fever heat.

Four victories for one team were to decide the World Championship. As they entered what proved to be the final game, the St. Louis Browns had already won three games. The Chicago White Stockings had won two games and were making a live-or-die effort to tie the series at 3-3 and force a grand finale for the championship. Each team had scored a shutout.

Excitement was tense as the teams met in St. Louis. Men in plug hats and high-crowned derbies filled the grandstand. Ladies in crinoline and bustles genteelly waved their kerchiefs from the stands.

For the Chicagoes, Cap Anson was on first base. John Clarkson, famous as a speed king, was in the box. Mike Kelly was behind the bat. For the St. Louis Browns, Bobby Carruthers was in the box, with Doc Bushong, a playing dentist, behind the bat. Arlie Latham, St. Louis' pride, was on third base.

Cap Anson's men were leading 3-1 when a sudden shower caused Captain Comiskey of the Browns to demand Umpire Dickey Pearce to grant time out. Anson vigorously protested.

The spectators poured onto the field, some demanding the game be stopped and others that it be continued. During the tumult, the decision was taken out of Umpire Pearce's hands, for the rain stopped.

The game had reached the eighth inning when the big

moments came. St. Louis was at the bat. Curt Welch, their center fielder, stood at the plate. Chicago Clarkson shot over one of his fast balls. Welch bunted. A wild throw to first, and Welch raced on to second base.

The next hitter flied out; the man who followed him flied out. Two out with Bushong up. Clarkson walked him. The tying run was now on first. Curt Welch was on second. Arlie Latham came to the plate. Catcher Mike Kelly, of the Chicagoes, put up a loud howl and declared that Arlie had a flat bat. Umpire Pearce examined it, found it had been whittled on one side, and ordered another bat be used.

Arlie, standing at the plate, raised his hand to Doc Bushong and shouted, "Stay there, Doc, I'll bring you both in."

Left-fielder Dalrymple, of the Chicagoes, moved down toward third base where Arlie was noted for hitting the ball. Arlie spotted the move instantly.

Clarkson shot one of his sizzlers over the plate. Arlie stood motionless. The St. Louis rooters became impatient. Arlie held up one hand and called out, "Don't get nervous, folks. I'll bring them both in!"

Again Clarkson shot a fast ball over the plate. Arlie smashed it over Dalrymple's head. As he ran back desperately to his old position, the ball grazed his finger tips and sped into the deep grass. If Dalrymple had been standing in his usual position, it would have been an easy catch, right into his hands.

Welch scored—Doc Bushong scored—and Arlie landed on third base. The score was tied. The crowd was in an uproar. Like the famous Babe Ruth in later years in Chicago, Arlie had kept his promise.

But St. Louis was unable to get Arlie home with the winning run. The next man went out and the game moved into the ninth inning. It was now a battle of the "giants." Pitchers for both teams became powerhouses. Neither side scored in the ninth.

When the "Great Von" Became a Hero

It was the tenth inning and Curt Welch was up again. Clarkson put on steam. The ball grazed Welch, and he went to first base. Umpire Pearce, believing the batter had edged in front of the ball, called Welch back to the bat.

Welch, enraged by the decision, smashed Clarkson's next pitch straight at him, and it slipped over second base. Welch landed safely on first.

The next man up was Foutz. He hit a ground ball that looked like a double play. Chicago fumbled it. Welch got to second base, and Foutz got to first.

Robinson came to the plate. St. Louis fans were going wild by this time. Robby dumped a ball right in front of the plate and was out at first base, but the runners advanced to second and third. Manager Comiskey had ordered a bunt. He was playing the percentages, there was only one man out and he now had the winning run plated on third base.

Doc Bushong at the plate! Clarkson glared at the runners on bases and shot a high ball that Bushong had to dodge. As Clarkson was winding up, Curt Welch leaped from third base and started for home.

Clarkson shot the ball at home plate, high but inside. Catcher Kelly jumped to grab it, but it bounded from his finger tips.

Welch slid across home plate with the winning run in a hairbreadth finish. The St. Louis Browns had won the World Championship and the $15,000 pot of gold.

Cris Von der Ahe was in his glory. He could have had anything in St. Louis that he wanted. Standing there on the field with his top hat and flaming colored vest, he was cheered to the echo by the crowds. In celebration, he ordered champagne for everybody, his team, the newspaper men, and the fans.

He had a commanding personality, a bristling mustache and a red, bulbous nose. He was proud of the "Von" in his name and proud of St. Louis. Everybody knew him as the millionaire sportsman. Apartment houses were named after members of his team. The name "St. Louis Browns" was the trade-mark on crockery and linens and blankets in St. Louis homes. Von ordered a sculptor to make a life-size statue of himself, and when he died, bankrupt through the prodigal use of his fortune, his monument was placed over his grave.

Our National Game Tours the World

We were all excited when we heard at the end of the 1888 season that Al Spalding had decided to tour the leading nations of the world with the White Stockings and a team of star players from the other seven clubs in the National League.

I was with the Washington Senators at that time and was not a member of that round-the-world group. The exponents of America's national game left Chicago in October, 1888, and after a memorable journey around the globe, returned to the United States in April, 1889.

After playing exhibition games in our Mountain States, they sailed from San Francisco. Their first stop was at Hawaii. They arrived on Sunday, a day late, so the game was canceled. Living in Hawaii, where he had been for fifty years, was Alexander Cartwright, today an immortal in the Hall of Fame, whose bronze tablet calls him the "Father of Modern Baseball." It being the Lord's Day, he did not meet the boys from America on their one-day stop.

Al Spalding, in his history of America's national game, vividly describes their adventures on this trip. They played exhibition games in New Zealand, Australia, and India. Passing through the Red Sea, they went to Egypt, where they played at the foot of the Sphinx.

A cherished memento of this incident is a photograph showing the globe-trotting American baseball stars climbing the Sphinx and huddling together under its chin. The Sphinx and the ancient pyramids seem to have taken no notice of their distinguished visitors, however! King Tut did not rise from his tomb. The Pharaohs did not deign to speak to them, and even Cleopatra refrained from smiling at them.

But they did conquer Italy. The land of the Cæsars seemed to realize that new Cæsars from the New World had arrived. Rome greeted them with outstretched arms and all Italy met them with jubilant throngs. And indeed she should, for many of our baseball players are of Italian origin.

France, too, took the players to its heart. Paris threw its arms around them. Here they were looked upon as new Napoleons out to conquer not only Europe but the entire world.

England's hospitality was rather strained, on the other hand. She remembered that on a previous visit an American ball team had beaten her players at their national game of cricket. A cartoon in an English humorous weekly took sly gibes at America's national game.

The Famous Brotherhood War

In 1888-89 I joined some friends in the organization of the Baseball Players Brotherhood. We plunged headlong into the powerful Spalding, John T. Brush, the rich Indianapolis owner, and such magnates as A. H. Soden, president of the Boston Club.

We had in the brotherhood such men as John K. Tener, later Governor of Pennsylvania, and Charles Comiskey, who was soon to become the millionaire owner of the Chicago team in the American League. The purpose of our brotherhood was to protect the players. The group which vigorously opposed us was interested in protecting the magnates.

The Brotherhood and the National League broke into open warfare in 1889, while I was with the Buffalo Brotherhood team. It threw a bombshell at the big fellows by stating that their new Players' League, with teams in every major city, would be operated in the interest of the players. Players from National League teams lost no time in rushing to us for protection.

The National League appealed to the courts that players were breaking their contracts and joining the new league. Litigation followed, but the National League contracts were held inequitable.

The baseball war of 1890 threatened to throw both the National League and the Brotherhood League into bankruptcy. The magnates had dropped about $4,000,000 in their desperate attempt to break the Brotherhood by offering big prices for their team franchises.

Owners of Brotherhood teams, seizing the opportunity to cash in, sold out. Players began to scramble back to their old magnates. They had been suspended for life, but they were received with open arms when they came back as prodigal sons.

It was during this war that the Pittsburgh Pirates received their name. They had signed two players from the American Association, which immediately charged them with a "piece of piracy." Since that day the name "Pirates" has stuck to the Pittsburgh team.

But the Brotherhood, although it retired, had started a new era in baseball. Club owners had awakened to the realization that ball players are human and must be given a fair deal or they will rebel. By the same token, the magnates had discovered that contracts must be equitable if they were to stand court tests.

CHAPTER 8

GAY BLADES IN THE GAY NINETIES

THE NINETEENTH CENTURY slipped away like a tired old man. Father Time stroked his long white beard, gathered up his scythe and hourglass, and shambled through the rear door, with the bow of a departing guest. I am not so sure that he didn't take a baseball bat along with him as a souvenir.

The last decade of the nineteenth century was the passing of the plush age, the horse and buggy, the oil-wick lamps, the stovepipe hat, and whiskers.

Through the gay nineties gentlemen in Prince Alberts and silk hats, ladies in bonnets and bustles, rode in barouches and hansom cabs to the ball parks.

These, too, were the days when "Me and Mollie O'Rourke danced the light fantastic on the sidewalks of New York," when we were singing, "There'll Be a Hot Time in the Old Town Tonight" and "Take Me Out to the Ball Game."

These were turbulent times in baseball as well as in world events. Famous Castle Garden at the entrance to Manhattan Island closed its doors; the electric chair was set up at Sing Sing; a crank threw a bomb at Russell Sage, the eminent banker; the Homestead strike near Pittsburgh stole the spotlight from the Pittsburgh Pirates, and an anarchist tried to assassinate Henry C. Frick, the steel magnate. I was with the Pittsburgh Pirates at that time and witnessed the riots that followed.

80

We played to record-breaking crowds during the season of 1892, when we were celebrating the four hundredth anniversary of the discovery of America.

At the opening of the League season in Washington in 1894 the national capital was invaded by Coxey's Army with some 20,000 unemployed from the Midwest.

The blowing up of the *Maine* in Havana harbor exploded us into the war for Cuban liberation and its extension to the liberation of the Philippines in 1898-99. Many of our ball players entered these conflicts.

The Era of the Orioles

The gay nineties was the era of the famous Baltimore Orioles, flamboyant birds, who swooped through baseball history more like bold American eagles than modest little orioles.

I knew these "birds." I had met them in deadly combat when I was a catcher for the old Washington Senators and the Pittsburgh Pirates and later when I became manager of the Pirates. I could say without hesitation that they were "tough birds." Hundreds of stories are told about them.

The Orioles played the game like gladiators in ancient Roman arenas. Full speed ahead, they slugged their way through to score their victories.

Good old Ned Hanlon, who was my boss when I was with the Pittsburghs, went to Baltimore to manage the Orioles and led them to three National League pennants in succession, 1894-95-96.

The Baltimore Orioles were the past masters of infield strategy. They developed the bunt, the hit and run, the double steal, and the squeeze into both an art and a science. On that championship team in one year were four who are today in the Hall of Fame: The irrepressible John McGraw, "Wee Willie" Keeler, "Uncle" Robbie Robinson, and the mighty Hughie Jennings.

Later McGraw began bagging pennants as manager of the

Giants. Uncle Robbie became manager of the Brooklyn
Dodgers and started them on the pennant road. Hughie Jennings, as manager for the Detroit Tigers, carried them to
three pennants. Gleason, another Oriole, became manager of
the White Sox.

It was a team of past, present, and future greats. When
the Orioles pulled thirteen hit-and-run plays, winning four
straight against the Giants, John Ward, then the Giants'
manager, entered vigorous complaint. He declared that Ned
Hanlon was teaching his team new tricks that threatened to
demolish the game.

"We Orioles used to stay up nights thinking up new plays,"
John McGraw once confessed. "Sure, we were scrappy; they
called me 'Muggsy.' Perhaps we were roughnecks, but we
were in there to win. And the crowds loved it."

John was a pal of Wee Willie Keeler and gloated over
the little outfielder who "chased 'em and caught 'em," until
he became known as the "bushel basket." Willie was a wizard
at the bat and as a base stealer. In one season he stole seventy-
three bases.

In later years, when Babe Ruth was the home-run king,
McGraw remarked: "The Babe's okay, but Wee Willie
Keeler's lifetime batting average beat the Babe's. And remember that Wee Willie was doing it when we played with a
dead ball."

With the Beaneaters

The 1890's was a turbulent decade of the so-called rough-
house days in baseball. The Boston Beaneaters were ready for
any fray, ever willing to take on the pugnacious Baltimore
Orioles and give them a dose of their own medicine. I had
left the Pittsburgh Pirates and had become manager and part
owner of the Milwaukee team in the Western League, but
many stories came to us of what was going on in the big
circuits.

One story is told of a typical fracas in Philadelphia in 1894, when the Boston Beaneaters came to town. Boston was leading in the eighth inning. In the last half of the inning Philadelphia began a rally. Rain was threatening.

The Beaneaters knew all the tricks of the trade. They began a systematic stall. They railed at the umpire for not calling the game. They held up play with an assortment of clever schemes to kill them.

"Play ball or forfeit the game," the umpire persistently warned. The Beaneaters remained stubborn, and the game was forfeited to Philadelphia. Crowds of Philadelphians, jubilant over their victory, surged upon the diamond and taunted the Boston Beaneaters with barbed gibes.

Tommy Tucker, the huge Boston first baseman, always on the lookout for a man who could lick him, found himself in the midst of the mêlée. The police rescued him, but not before the fist of a Philadelphian hit him in the jaw and broke a cheekbone.

It required all the policemen in the ball park to protect the other members of the chagrined Bostonians. They were loaded, under guard, onto a coach to take them from the field to their hotel, but the exuberant kids pelted them with balls of mud.

Officer Walker, the Philadelphia policeman who was riding on the coach to protect the out-of-town players, jumped from the vehicle just as a mudball hit him in the face. One of our best chroniclers records:

"Within a few minutes his helmet was down over his eyes and ears, his billy was rolling in the gutter, his badge was half torn off his coat."

With fond memories I also recall Amos Rusie back in the 1890's. He was generally recognized by sports authorities as the great pitcher of his day. I also remember Hugh Duffy, outfielder for Boston, who startled baseball by attaining a batting average of .438; and Ted Breitenstein, who made a comeback and stayed on the mound and the water wagon as well until he was past fifty years of age.

The Famous Delahanty Mystery

There are many stories about Ed Delahanty, known as the "Wild Irishman." In one game he hit a ball with such power that it split in two. In another game he hit one so hard that it broke the ankle of a third baseman. In a game in Chicago in 1896 he got five hits, four of them home runs, in five times at bat. This Atlas, who for a time carried the baseball world on his shoulders, met a tragic death. His mangled body was found against a wharf, twenty miles below Niagara Falls.

The mystery of his death was not solved until a witness stated he had seen a strange man in the darkness of the night fall off the bridge into the tumultuous waters of Horseshoe Falls. The body picked up at the wharf twenty miles away was identified as the great Delahanty. This was the end of the man who had led the National League batters in 1899 with an average of .408 for the Philadelphia Phillies.

I have seen baseball heroes come and go for nearly three-quarters of a century since I started playing town ball in my old New England home town. I have known most of them, and many have been intimate friends.

The Indian from the Maine Woods

You may have heard of the Penobscot Indian from Maine, whose name was Sockalexis. He was a huge fellow who looked like an Indian on the warpath and who scalped the great pitchers of his day. He swung his bat with the power of a tomahawk.

Rumors spread from Maine that an Indian was on the rampage on the baseball diamonds there. Holy Cross College heard of him and brought him down to give him an education and to utilize his skill on their baseball team. The roaming Indian stayed one season, made a batting average of .444, and was quickly signed up by Pat Tebeau for the Cleveland Indians.

Sockalexis was the first full-blooded Indian to play in the major leagues. When he appeared at the bat the fans broke out in vociferous war whoops. His throwing arm was the wonder of the times. Standing erect in deep center field, he could throw a ball like a shot from a gun—straight over home plate as perfect as a strike. His feet were as fleet as those of a Maine deer. He could do a 100-yard dash in ten seconds.

Sockalexis caused a sensation when he came to New York. The first time he stood up against the Great Amos Rusie, whose blazing curve frightened the batters, Sockalexis smashed it far out into center field for a home run. That first year for Cleveland he made a batting average of .331.

The stolid young Indian's future seemed assured, until fire-water struck him out. It wasn't long before he found himself on the down road. He drank himself out of the big league, wandered to the Connecticut state teams, played a while in such cities as Hartford, Meriden, Bristol, until he found himself begging on the streets for a few pennies to buy more fire-water. The trail ended back in the woods of Maine where a heart attack felled him. And that was the end of the great Sockalexis!

The Tale of the Iron Man

I wish I could tell you about all the players and managers I have known, but I can only give you flashes here and there as they crowd into my memory. If I fail to mention some of the old-time favorites, it is only because there are too many to gather on these limited pages.

I remember Iron Man McGinnity. It is doubtful if the Iron Man was as great a moundsman as Amos Rusie, but he had a fine record as a winning pitcher.

McGinnity was a magician in the box. It was difficult for
a batter to get his measure. Sometimes his fingers would
almost scrape the ground as he hurled the ball. He knew all
the tricks for putting a batter on the hot spot. He pitched and
won five games in six days in his first season with Brooklyn.
When he was with the Giants, he won three double-headers
in one month and collected eleven victories in twelve days.

Time takes its toll, but the Iron Man refused to grow old.
After his remarkable records in the big leagues, he continued
to pitch in the minor leagues until he was fifty-two years
of age.

"Casey at the Bat"

The gay nineties produced many picturesque personalities
and scenes. Those of us who have heard DeWolf Hopper, the
old-time Broadway star, will never forget his dramatic rendi-
tion of the hit of the last century: "Casey at the Bat." In a
very short time the whole nation began to recite it. Famous
in Gilbert and Sullivan operas, a great actor and a baseball
fan, DeWolf Hopper held us all spellbound with the melo-
dramatic lines written by Ernest Lawrence Thayer:

The outlook wasn't brilliant for the Mudville nine that day;
The score stood four to two, with but one inning more to play;
And so, when Cooney died at first, and Burrows did the same,
A sickly silence fell upon the patrons of the game.

A straggling few got up to go in deep despair. The rest
Clung to the hope which springs eternal in the human breast;
They thought, if only Casey could but get a whack, at that,
They'd put up even money now, with Casey at the bat.

But Flynn preceded Casey, as did also Jimmy Blake,
And the former was a pudding and the latter was a fake;
So upon that stricken multitude grim melancholy sat,
For there seemed but little chance of Casey's getting to the bat.

But Flynn let drive a single, to the wonderment of all,
And Blake, the much despisèd, tore the cover off the ball;
And when the dust had lifted, and they saw what had occurred,
There was Jimmy safe on second, and Flynn a-hugging third.

Then from the gladdened multitude went up a joyous yell,
It bounded from the mountaintop, and rattled in the dell;
It struck upon the hillside, and recoiled upon the flat;
For Casey, mighty Casey, was advancing to the bat.

There was ease in Casey's manner as he stepped into his place,
There was pride in Casey's bearing, and a smile on Casey's face;
And when, responding to the cheers, he lightly doffed his hat,
No stranger in the crowd could doubt 'twas Casey at the bat.

Ten thousand eyes were on him as he rubbed his hands with dirt,
Five thousand tongues applauded when he wiped them on his shirt;
Then while the writhing pitcher ground the ball into his hip,
Defiance gleamed in Casey's eye, a sneer curled Casey's lip.

And now the leather-covered sphere came hurtling through the air,
And Casey stood a-watching it in haughty grandeur there;
Close by the sturdy batsman the ball unheeded sped.
"That ain't my style," said Casey. "Strike one," the umpire said.

From the benches, black with people, there went up a muffled roar,
Like the beating of the storm-waves on a stern and distant shore;
"Kill him! kill the umpire!" shouted someone on the stand,
And it's likely they'd have killed him had not Casey raised his hand.

With a smile of Christian charity great Casey's visage shone;
He stilled the rising tumult; he bade the game go on;
He signaled to the pitcher, and once more the spheroid flew,
But Casey still ignored it, and the umpire said, "Strike two."

"Fraud!" cried the maddened thousands, and echo answered, "Fraud!"
But a scornful look from Casey, and the audience was awed;
They saw his face grow stern and cold, they saw his muscles strain,
And they knew that Casey wouldn't let that ball go by again.

The sneer is gone from Casey's lips, his teeth are clenched in hate,
He pounds with cruel violence his bat upon the plate;
And now the pitcher holds the ball, and now he lets it go,
And now the air is shattered by the force of Casey's blow.

Oh! somewhere in this favored land the sun is shining bright,
The band is playing somewhere, and somewhere hearts are light;
And somewhere men are laughing, and somewhere children shout,
But there is no joy in Mudville—mighty Casey has struck out!

CHAPTER 9

THE BIG PARADE

THE GREATEST event in our national game at the dawn of the twentieth century was the organization of the American League, which was to revolutionize baseball and start it on its tremendous half-century of expansion with the coming of the World Series.

The "big parade" of famous teams and famous players could go on for volumes, but here I can mention only a few high spots.

The question often arises: Who was the greatest player the game has ever known?

It is generally agreed that Hans Wagner was the "greatest shortstop," and many believe him to be the "greatest player of all time." John McGraw and Ed Barrow have entered this claim.

"Wagner was the best shortstop I ever saw," McGraw declared. "He was a fine catcher, as good a third baseman as I ever saw, one of the best outfielders, and one of the greatest hitters."

There isn't much more that could be said about any player. I agree that Wagner was "great" and would not dispute McGraw's and Barrow's claims, but you will understand if I call attention to the record of Ty Cobb. Ty played more games (3,033) than Wagner (2,785); Ty was at the bat more times (11,429) than Hans (10,427). Ty made more hits (4,191) than

Hans (3,430). Ty made more home runs (118) than Hans (100). Ty had a higher batting average (.367) than Hans (.329). In fact, Ty Cobb had the highest batting average in the records of the Hall of Fame.

Who Was Our Greatest Player?

It has been a rule of my life never to enter into controversies, and I'm willing to leave this paramount question to the records, but my hat's off to both Ty Cobb and Hans Wagner, and to every other man in the Hall of Fame.

Wagner was a grand sportsman all the way through. He honored the Pirates' uniform, which he wore for eighteen years. For eight years he led the National League in batting. His record of 720 stolen bases is exceeded only by Ty Cobb, Max Carey, and Eddie Collins.

One of our leading baseball historians says that Hans was the link connecting the old barehanded days to the modern school of sluggers. He played from the old days of the Wrights to the modern era when Babe Ruth became the idol of the nation.

Hans Wagner, too, was the highest paid ball player of his day. He started at $125 a month and worked his way up to $10,000 a season. This was before the times that salaries skyrocketed, until Babe Ruth got $80,000 a season. But in Hans' heyday his salary created about as much excitement as the Babe's $80,000.

Ed Barrow tells how he found Wagner: "I was out on a search in 1905 for young fellows who looked good. I heard about a Dutchman with tremendous power in his arms. I found him betting all comers that he could throw a rock farther than any other man in the crowd. He would easily throw a rock a hundred yards and then collect the bet. I signed him on the spot for thirty dollars a week as promising baseball material, and he quickly proved himself to be the greatest slugger of the times."

Who Was Our Greatest Pitcher?

This question opens another nationwide controversy—who was the greatest pitcher? The leading contenders seem to me to be Christy Mathewson and Walter Johnson, with several other mound champions right on their heels. Johnson had terrific speed. Mathewson had a magnificent change of pace. Christy's winning record (.665) excels Johnson's (.596). Johnson's shutouts (113) excel Mathewson's (83).

But before you make your choice, let's look at the records of some of the other great pitchers. Here's Cy Young, who pitched more games than any other man in mound history (906) and won more games (511) than any man who ever entered a pitcher's box. His record remains unchallenged. It shows that he averaged twenty-five victories a year for over twenty years.

Cy entered the baseball world with a victory. From then on he hung up the fabulous string of victories that made him famous. In his first game he allowed but three hits—he even struck out Cap Anson twice.

I find Cy had three no-hitters in the record book. He had a fast ball, a curve, and a spitter that almost hypnotized the batter. One of his great records is a perfect game—only two men have done it since 1880. Not a man reached first base; twenty-seven batters went down in perfect order.

Cy Young had his picture taken with Bob Feller in 1941. Bob, a speed-ball wizard himself, looked at the baseball patriarch with admiration. The Old Master stayed on the pitcher's mound until he was forty-four years old. Shortly before his retirement he pitched twenty-one victories for the Red Sox.

Cy, in his retirement, often spoke with reverence of the players of the past. He doesn't think they have ever been surpassed, and he truly believes that he lived in the golden age. And who can say that he didn't?

Wagner had great admiration for Cy Young. "Walter

Johnson," he said, "was fast, but no faster than Rusie. And Rusie was no faster than Johnson. But," he added, "Young was faster than both of 'em!"

My memory now goes back to Rube Waddell. His gangling figure, towering well over six feet, and his bony face and long arms, reminded me of Abe Lincoln.

When Rube trotted to the pitcher's box as if he were walking over a plowed field, the fans would greet him vociferously with: "Hey, Rube!" He always acknowledged the salutations with a courtly bow, not the usual, "Hi, fellows," or "Thanks, boys."

Some Memories of the "Great Rube"

There are many who claim to have discovered the Great Rube, but I'd like to put in my claim for a share of the honors. Rube began to play in his teens in his home town, Butler, Pennsylvania, where he was born. Later he began to play in near-by towns, and first appeared as a professional in Oil City. Scouts discovered him and signed him up with Louisville in the National League on a salary said to be five hundred dollars a season.

The wanderings of Rube soon became baseball lore. Like many of the early players, he liked his cups. When he was reprimanded for drinking, he would remark: "Well, I guess I'll go fishin'. I'd rather fish than play baseball anyhow."

Rube's wanderings took him to Detroit, then in the Western League; to semi-pro games in Canada; back to the professionals in Columbus; then to Grand Rapids; back to the Louisvilles, and on to Pittsburgh.

A crowd had gathered in Brooklyn one day in 1900 to witness a game against Pittsburgh, with the Great Rube in the box for the Pirates. When the time came for the game to start, it was discovered that Rube had wandered out of the park. Immediately a frantic search was made for him.

After many anxious moments the missing celebrity was

found. The Great Rube was under the stands, playing "miggles" with adoring small boys. He objected to having his game of marbles rudely interrupted; but when persuaded that the crowd was waiting for him, he strode back to the field and the box and pitched a shutout against the Brooklyns, allowed only three hits, and struck out ten men.

Not long after this he wandered away from Pittsburgh, without saying good-by, and was found in Punxsutawney, Pennsylvania, where he was pitching in his old haunts.

I was then manager of the Milwaukee Club, in the newly born American League. I believed that Rube, a kindly fellow, could be persuaded to concentrate his great abilities on the game. The big left-hander appealed to me—I was always fond of left-handers.

My experiences with the Great Rube were many and varied. I recall that on one occasion I made a bargain with him. "Rube," I said, "you've just won the first game of a doubleheader. If you'll pitch the second game, I'll let you go on a fishing trip."

Rube's eyes lighted up with joy. He pitched the second game too, grabbed his fishing rod and hurried off to the river. The string of catches he brought home was even larger than his string of baseball victories.

Wanderlust soon got hold of him again. Barney Dreyfuss claimed prior rights on Rube in an old contract when he jumped the Pittsburghs. Rube went back to the Pirates, but was soon traded to Chicago. From there he found himself in California with an "outlaw" league. He liked Los Angeles and Los Angeles liked him; in fact, the whole Pacific Coast was captivated by him.

The Waddell Detective Story

I had become manager of the Philadelphia Athletics in the new American League in 1900. I still had a warm place in my heart for the Great Rube and I wanted him on my team. Getting into communication with him, I made him agree to come to Philadelphia, and I sent him the railroad fare.

Even though Rube was on the railroad train to come East, the Los Angeles fans appealed to him to stay in California. Deeply impressed by their loyalty, he stepped off the train and joined them in a grand celebration, and of course the train went on without him!

When I heard this, I hired two Pinkerton detectives to go to the coast. They finally persuaded Rube "to come home to Pennsylvania." That was in 1902, and that first year we started the season in last place. We climbed up the ladder, however, to first place and won our first pennant. Rube Waddell struck out 210 men and won 23 games. Waddell and Schreckengost (we called him Schreck) was the greatest battery of those pennant-winning times.

Yes, we had our anxious moments with Rube, but he was worth it. When he wandered away from a game we usually found him fishing or playing with the kids. We once found him in a show window, posing as an automaton. Another time we learned that he had joined the fire department. "So I can ride on the fire engines," he said. Another time we found him leading a parade.

I remember one spring training season in Florida when Rube decided he wanted to be an alligator wrestler. When he saw a man making his living wrestling alligators, Rube jumped into the pool, engaged in combat with a 'gator and dragged it out victoriously. We had difficulty in keeping him out of alligator pools from that time on.

We were paying Rube $3,000 a season, and he felt like a rich man. If he could be kept under control, we told him, he would get a much larger figure, but Rube wasn't interested in money. I venture to say that if Rube were playing the game today and were concentrating on winning pennants, he would be getting about fifty thousand dollars a season.

On one occasion in Washington he rushed into a burning

building and safely carried to the street the victims who were trapped in flame and smoke. While on a Philadelphia-Camden ferryboat one afternoon somebody shouted, "Woman overboard!" Rube dove into the river to rescue her, only to find it was a hoax.

Rube stayed with me six years, the longest time he ever spent in any one place. All baseball historians agree he was the most famous pitcher of the day.

Rube seemed to be getting the wanderlust again, and so I decided to let him go to St. Louis. When our Philadelphia Athletics appeared in St. Louis, Rube threatened to get revenge. "I promise you a beating," he said. Then he proceeded to strike out sixteen of our men.

Tragic End of a Great Pitcher

He wasn't destined to stay in St. Louis long, for the urge to travel again overcame him, and his wanderings were quickly resumed. From St. Louis he went to Newark, then to Minneapolis, where he won twenty games in 1911 and twelve in 1912.

There are several versions of what happened to him after that. I have been told that Manager Joe Cantillon took Rube home with him to Kentucky for the winter. Here he is said to have become very fond of the geese that followed him around on the Cantillon farm. He taught them to jump rope, Rube holding one end and a goose the other end. It is said that he also taught one goose to do sums, but I've never found anyone who can verify that story.

In the midst of his big plans to go into vaudeville with an animal act, the Reelfoot levee, near the Cantillon farm, broke loose in angry rage. Neighbors of the Cantillons in the town of Hickman were marooned on housetops and in trees. They were rescued and crowded on the hastily built rafts with other families in the same predicament.

Rube Waddell was the hero of the flood as he had been

on many baseball fields. With other volunteers, he stood in the roaring waters up to his armpits through perilous hours in a desperate attempt to plug the sixty-foot gap that had been torn in the levee when the river burst its banks.

There are those who claim this incident happened in Minnesota. Wherever it was, Rube contracted a severe cold. His serious illness worried Cantillon. Rube insisted on keeping on playing. He joined Virginia in the Northern League, but after a few games collapsed. Cantillon had him removed to a ranch in Texas, and from there he was taken to a hospital in San Antonio. Ball players who had known Rube in his great days came to cheer him up, for he was a true sportsman to the last.

On the hospital bed lay the shrunken figure of the once powerful athlete, who now weighed less than one hundred and twenty pounds. His face was haggard. He could hardly speak above a whisper.

"I'll be over there tomorrow and show you guys how to run," he whispered with effort. "I've got my weight down now."

A few days later the Great Rube passed away. Tuberculosis had struck him out. He had played his last game—and lost.

CHAPTER 10

THE FAMOUS MARCH ON

An almost endless procession marches before me as I salute the veterans of our baseball army from this reviewing stand. Coming down the line, farther than you can see, are thousands more young Americans hoping to join the ranks of baseball.

I have already told you about the veterans of pennants and World Series who have been with the Philadelphia Athletics, so now I shall describe some of the adversaries we met in combat.

Perhaps the most outstanding figure in the procession is Christy Mathewson, a fine type of American manhood. I never had the honor of having him on my team; he was the private property of John McGraw, but I shall always revere Christy's memory.

Christy was a son of Pennsylvania, and began as a pitcher for his home town, Factoryville, when he was fourteen years old. A story about him is told there: The Factoryville team was to play a rival team in a town ten miles away. The school-mates of Husk Mathewson were eager to have him go with the team, but its bewhiskered and mustached members exclaimed:

"What, a kid? He's too young to play with men."

"Give him a chance, try him out," the boys pleaded.

The town team finally relented. On the Main Street of

97

Factoryville the town boy was given a tryout. Neighbors lined the sidewalks; others watched him from wagons and buggies. For two solid hours Husk Mathewson showed them his stuff—he struck out every man on the home team at least once, and this included the captain who had doubted Christy's ability up to that time.

"Well," conceded the captain, "you'll do; come along, we'll take you."

Husk Mathewson pitched his first big game that day. His two hours of pitching in the tryout had not tired him. He not only pitched a winning game, but made the hit that clinched the game; Factoryville won by a score of 19-17. There was great rejoicing in that town that night as Husk Mathewson and his conquering heroes came home victorious.

Mathewson's parents wanted Christy to get an education before he was won over to baseball. He went to Keystone Academy, where he became captain of the school team, and, strangely enough, he played second base there. Not until Keystone found itself up against a powerful rival did Mathewson take the box. With his roundhouse curve and his fast ball, he soon became known as the greatest schoolboy pitcher in Pennsylvania.

During the summer vacation Christy offered his services to a small-town team for one dollar a game. Honesdale, another Pennsylvania town, lured him with an offer of twenty dollars a month and bed and board. Here he developed his famous fadeaway pitch.

The desire for an education still possessed Christy, and he went to Bucknell University, where he became an all-round athlete. Here he pitched winning games for his university and also became a star on the football team.

Story of the Great Mathewson

Here was a college man gaining fame as a baseball-football champion. His masterful pitching for Norfolk raised the eyebrows of the big league managers, and as a result three major league offers came to him.

It was at this time that I almost procured Mathewson for the Philadelphia Athletics. I bought him from Norfolk, only to find that the Giants and Cincinnati also had bought him. All of us were so eager to get him that we appealed to the courts for a decision. The Giants won the case—Mathewson went to New York. It was one of my early disappointments that we never had Mathewson on our Philadelphia team.

Christy was 6 feet 2 inches and weighed 195 pounds—a powerful giant. He was a model in clean living, a youth of high principles, integrity and honesty, and an example to boys throughout the country. He advised young men against all forms of dissipation. He made it a point never to play ball on Sunday, for he was a truly religious person.

There is no doubt that Mathewson set a high moral code for our national game. He was lauded by the churches, ministers used his career as sermon topics; he gave dignity and character to baseball. But he was never mollycoddle; he was the essence of good sportsmanship. He played to win, and he won.

Mathewson's genius was not wholly confined to baseball, for he was also an able businessman. He was highly esteemed in insurance circles and was a top-ranking agent during the winters when he wasn't playing ball, and he knew how to invest his earnings. As a winter recreation he became an expert checker player; he was so skilled that he could play blindfolded against a dozen other experts at the same time.

Few knew that Mathewson turned down offers as high as $65,000 a year, with three-year provisions, in his loyalty to the New York Giants.

He Made Baseball a Science

Christy studied the potentialities of every batter and figured them out in percentages. He knew the kind of balls they could hit and those they could not hit. He was not so much interested in strike-outs as he was in placing the ball where it would be hit into fielders' hands for an out. He did not waste his strength; he conserved it for moments when the game was in danger, then he put on overwhelming speed.

In one of our 1911 World Series games we had Collins, Baker and Barry, known as our "$100,000 infield." We were playing against the Giants when Baker came to the bat in the ninth inning of the third game. Mathewson thought he had him figured in percentages. One strike—two strikes—the ball came over the plate where the percentages said Baker couldn't hit it.

Mathewson let go one of his great puzzlers. Baker smashed it into the right-field stands for the home run that won the game. From that minute Baker the infielder became known as Home Run Baker.

After sixteen years with the Giants, Mathewson's arm began to wear out. In 1916 the idol of New York was traded to Cincinnati. It was said he eventually would become a manager. Giant fans were shocked; Cincinnati fans were thrilled. Then came the announcement that brought sorrow to the whole baseball world.

"I am through as a pitcher," Christy said. "I will never pitch again for any team except the New York Giants." Once more he pitched in the Giants' uniform against the Chicago Cubs. It was his last game, and he won it, 10-8.

During World War I, Mathewson managed the Cincinnati club; but before its close he entered the Army. After the Armistice he was sent to Europe to join the Army of Occupation in Germany. While on the transport in mid-ocean he became violently seasick. After his arrival in Europe he was felled by escaping gas in a trench. There was little realization then that Christy was gassed and would never entirely recover.

On his return home, not realizing his own condition, he became coach for his beloved Giants. Later he was made president of the Boston Braves. But the earlier lung infection crept up on him; the great Mathewson died of tuberculosis. His perfect physique, his flawless habits, his strong constitution were undermined by that dread plague.

Most Beloved Player That Ever Lived

Another man whose memory I shall always esteem was the great Babe Ruth. He was never on the A's, but he was its most powerful adversary when we played against the New York Yankees. I estimate that the Athletics entered more than 300 combats against the Babe.

We all know about Babe's boyhood in Baltimore and how he became the Great Babe, King of Swat, but few think of him as a pitcher. Back in 1914 when he was on the mound for Baltimore, Providence and the Red Sox, he captured twenty-four victories for the three clubs. He was a fast-ball pitcher, not a curve pitcher. He led the league in 1915 with the highest pitching percentage, and he pitched twenty-nine consecutive scoreless innings in World Series, a record that has never yet been broken.

Why was the winning Babe taken out of the box? Because he was such a mighty batsman that he was needed in the game every day. His managers solved this problem by putting him in the field; and there again he proved himself a master of the game.

When Colonel Jacob Ruppert bought the Babe, in 1920, he proved such a tremendous drawing card that Ruppert erected the world's largest baseball stadium, which became known as the "House That Ruth Built." He became the best baseball investment ever made, and brought millions in gate receipts.

There were times when Babe's boyish pranks were in danger of wiping out those millions. When he went on a barnstorming tour in defiance of the orders of Judge Landis at the end of 1921, he was suspended for the first six weeks in the 1922 season. When he came back, he drew even larger crowds as he batted his way to the top of the league—.393 in 1923 and .378 in 1924.

Then, having risen to the pinnacle of popularity, he was knocked out in 1925—not by a baseball but by hot dogs! He stuffed himself with this typical American delicacy, and developed a mighty stomach-ache. An ambulance rushed him to a hospital in Asheville, North Carolina, where the Yankees were stopping on their way north from spring training. Newspaper headlines throughout the country treated his illness as a national crisis.

The big blowup came in St. Louis during the 1925 season when Babe was back in the lineup. He got into disputes with Miller Huggins, the Yankee manager. Finally, Huggins suspended Babe indefinitely and fined him $5,000 for failure to keep training rules.

"Huggins must be fired! That fine must be recalled, or I'll quit!" the Great Ruth shouted as he roared into the office of Colonel Ruppert in the Yankee Stadium.

The Colonel glared at the big fellow in whom he had made such a large investment and then retorted calmly, but decisively, "That fine stands and Huggins stays!"

Babe Ruth—"King of Swat"

The "King of Swat" really was good-natured in spite of his temper. Realizing that his tantrum was striking him out, he turned right-about face, made up his mind to behave himself, and became a model for the boys of the country. His obedience from then on was perfect!

The two biggest drawing cards in the history of the game, in my opinion, were Babe Ruth and the mighty Lou Gehrig. Later Joe DiMaggio began to bring the fans to their feet in the Yankee Stadium. It has been aptly said that while Ruth was the Home-Run King, Lou Gehrig was the "Crown Prince" in the royal family. Joe DiMaggio must therefore have been heir apparent. The Yankees became almost invincible as they won pennants year after year.

It was in 1927 that Babe made his world record: sixty home runs in one season. His life record, as stated elsewhere, was 714, and Gehrig's reached 494. There never has been anything like these two records either before or since on the same team.

My admiration for the New York Yankees has been fully justified throughout the years. They've set a fast pace for baseball. My hat is off again to big-little Miller Huggins, who captured six pennants in eight years. When complimented on his genius he remarked:

"Great players make great managers!"

Huggins' career proved also that great managers make great players. It's like the age-old question: "Which comes first, the chicken or the egg?"

I agree with those who say that the greatest of all Yankee teams was in the big show in 1927. It was a great season for every member of the champion Yankees. Their amazing slaughters at the bat gained for them the epithet: "Murderers' Row."

Those Yankees really murdered the ball. They practically assassinated rival pitchers. Babe Ruth slugged out 60 homers; Lou Gehrig made 47. The batting average that season for the Babe was .356. Combs, too, got .356. Bob Meusel made .337. Still more remarkable, the batting average for the eight regulars on the Yankee team was .320.

The Cardinals in Flight

The most colorful team since the days of the flaming Baltimore Orioles has been the St. Louis Cardinals. Their fighting spirit earned for them the name of "Gas House Gang." But don't let that name fool you—they came right out of the West and plunged their way into league pennants and World Series. The insignia of the bird on their uniforms is a misnomer.

Rogers Hornsby was the one who started the Cardinals on their winning stampedes, Gabby Street and Frank Frisch, the "Fordham Flash," were their managers in the 1930's.

Frisch's champions in the stampede were the Dean Brothers, Dizzy and Paul, who fascinated the crowds with their brilliant antics. These two prizes came from the Arkansas cotton fields to put the Cardinal pitching staff in the front of the line. Dizzy and Paul won forty-nine spectacular games in 1934, and the Cards finished in first place that year.

"Who won the pennant?" Dizzy would ask. Before anyone could have a chance to reply, he would answer himself, "Me and Paul!"

"Who's going to win the World Series?" Again Dizzy would give his own answer: "Me and Paul!" And me and Paul did it.

The Dean brothers liked nothing better than to play the Brooklyn Dodgers. They considered that pugnacious team a fair rival. In a double-header, the first game was won by Dizzy, who pitched a three-hitter. Paul pitched the second game and made it a no-hitter.

"I wish I'd known that kid brother of mine was going to pitch a no-hitter," Dizzy exclaimed, rubbing his head. "If I'd known, I'd have done it too."

When the Cards went on a rampage, they were frequently led by spicy Pepper Martin, sometimes called the "Wild Horse of the Osage." When the Athletics were trying to lasso him in the 1931 World Series, the "Wild Horse" ran away with five stolen bases from our astute Mickey Cochrane. Anybody who could steal one base on Mickey was a seven days' wonder.

Dazzy Vance and Tex Carleton were the other mound wizards. And there was Joe Medwick in the outfield with Pepper Martin. Rip Collins at first base lived up to his name. And Lippy Durocher as shortstop put an end to many batters.

Great Cardinals have come and gone through the years. They always have been and always will be a threat to rival teams. During World War II the Cards were as victorious as our American armies: they won three pennants and two World Series in four years.

Among their outstanding players have been Stan Musial, one of the best all-round players in the game; Slats Marion, a shortstop of all shortstops; Country Slaughter, the slaughtering right fielder; and "The Cat" Brecheen, whose clutch ball scratched out the eyes of rival batters.

My Selection of the Greatest All-Round Player

I am not taking issue with the sports writers, neither do I dispute their reasons for selecting Babe Ruth over Ty Cobb as the greatest baseball player in the last fifty years. But for my money, Cobb was the greatest who ever lived and we may never again see his equal.

Ruth was a great gate attraction, no doubt the most outstanding crowd pleaser, but based on a player's value to his team alone, the honor must go to Ty Cobb. Cobb was the greatest competitor I ever saw, a fiery and fearless player.

Winning and winning alone was all Cobb ever thought of and never gave his own personal safety much concern. Never have I seen a player so intent on winning that he would bring harm to himself if it was necessary.

Certainly, Ruth hit the home runs and glamorized the game, but Cobb's record in winning the batting championship nine straight years, missing a year and then coming back to win it the next three, is one of the outstanding feats of baseball.

This was the controversy at the close of the first half of the twentieth century. There have been controversies such as this since baseball began. The life records of these players should help to settle the issue, but even then the controversy will continue, as it does about the great pitchers, Christy Mathewson and Walter Johnson, and the A's own Lefty Grove.

Everyone knows what I think of Ty Cobb, for I talk about him every chance I get. I don't think anyone has ever sur-

passed him as an all-round player, either in fielding, hitting
or base running. I'd like to put Tris Speaker up in that top
rank too. Tris was everywhere in the outfield; he could grab
a ball up against the fence and net a ball off his shoes directly
behind second base.

The instant a batter hit a ball, Tris could gauge the spot
where it was headed. He could sprint with his back to the
stand, and the ball would generally land in his hands, so accurate was his judgment of speed and distance. His greatest
days were with the Red Sox and the Cleveland Indians.

The Cleveland Indians have given me many a hard battle,
but everybody who knows me knows how I admire them. I
have been entranced by Franklin (Whitey) Lewis' stories of
this able team. Whitey tells about the Indians back in 1869
when Forest City played the famous Cincinnati Red Stockings
in the first intercity ball game. He describes how the Cleve-
lands, then known as the Spiders, played their first postseason
games with Selee's Bostons in 1892—and later against the Baltimore Orioles in the National League Temple Cup Series
in 1895. This series, started in 1894, antedated the famous
World Series by nine years.

The big parade of famous players and teams is endless, for
every year new players are coming over the horizon, as those
which have passed in procession march on.

CHAPTER 11

A VISIT TO THE HALL OF FAME

IN THE LITTLE community of Cooperstown, New York, on the shores of beautiful Otsego Lake, is located the American shrine known as the National Baseball Hall of Fame and Museum.

Every time I go to Cooperstown I am filled with patriotic fervor, for here is enshrined the American spirit which has made us a great nation. I feel sorry for the man who is so sophisticated or hard-hearted that he is ashamed to express his emotions. And I thank God that even as I approach ninety years of age, my heart beats faster when I hear the words of "The Star-Spangled Banner."

In the Hall of Fame and Museum, which was opened on June 12, 1939, is the largest collection of baseball souvenirs and historical data in existence. We learn how and where the national game developed, and we can see the uniforms of famous players such as Cy Young and Babe Ruth, who helped to develop it.

Here are treasured trophies, historic baseballs, pictures of old-time clubs, paintings and lithographs of early games and famous events, pictures of the winners and souvenirs of all the World Series. There are nearly 4,000 items in this collection.

There is also a valuable library of books and records covering every phase of baseball, in which may be found the answers to the thousands of questions asked by fans from every part of the United States as well as from all parts of the world.

A few of the notable exhibits and historic facts about them should be mentioned here. In a place of honor, on an artistic standard, we see an ancient baseball which, as the guidebook says, is unlike anything seen today. "It is undersized, misshapen, and obviously homemade." It is stuffed with cloth and has none of the compactness of the tightly wound cord and the solidity that give carrying power and makes home runs possible with our modern "live" baseballs. The bronze plaque identifying this antique memento bears this inscription:

THE ABNER DOUBLEDAY BASEBALL

*This Baseball was Preserved in the Family of
Abner Graves, a Schoolmate of Abner Doubleday,
until presented to the National Baseball Museum.*

The mystery about this ancient ball is an American classic in itself. In the little village of Fly Creek, on the crossroads near Cooperstown, a farmer was searching through his attic in 1935. He found a dilapidated, musty old trunk that had gathered dust for generations.

He delved into the trunk, and one by one inspected the curious mementos he found there. He looked through the many old books and family pictures. Finally he pulled out of the mysterious trunk a strange, crude, homemade ball. What was it? Where did it come from?

A Sherlock Holmes Search

The discovery of the relic started a Sherlock Holmes search. Perhaps this was *the* ball that would help support the claims that baseball started in Cooperstown. All the evidence substantiated the theory that this ball once belonged to Abner Graves, a schoolmate of Abner Doubleday.

It was recalled that during an investigation started in 1908, when a commission was set up to establish the place of origin of our national game, many material facts were weighed. The investigators included the leading baseball executives of the times.

The commission's findings confirmed the Cooperstown claims, which had passed down through generations by word of mouth. The chief witness was Abner Graves, then an elderly man, who presented, in a series of documentary letters, evidence that his boyhood friend, Abner Doubleday, invented the game of baseball in Cooperstown in 1839, by marking out a diamond on the turf and explaining the rules of his "new ball and bat game."

Graves said he was one of the village boys who were taught the new game by Doubleday himself, who was then a young cadet in a military school in Cooperstown. In later life he became a general in the Union forces in the Civil war and made a notable record in many decisive battles.

There were counterclaims from many parts of the country, but in running them down it was found they were either the old games of "Rounders," "One O'Cat," "Two O'Cat," or those games which came later than the Abner Doubleday occurrences in Cooperstown. The links in the chain of evidence supported the claims of Graves and the findings of the commission officially sanctioned by organized baseball.

The discovery of the century-old ball further supported the commission's decision. The ball was officially declared to be the "Abner Doubleday Baseball."

The ball itself has had an interesting career in its old age. Stephen C. Clark purchased it in 1935, and began to exhibit it, together with other baseball mementos, in a room in the Village Club in Cooperstown. Alexander Cleland joined him in the project. The exhibit attracted such wide attention that the idea of a national baseball museum was conceived.

Cleland became so enthusiastic over the plan that he communicated with or visited the leading baseball people throughout the country. Among these, the most responsive was Ford

Frick, president of the National League. He helped Cleland
to get the coöperation of Judge Kenesaw Mountain Landis,
then baseball's high commissioner, and William Harridge,
president of the American League.

The Ball Begins to Roll

Through the activities of Ford Frick and others, the officials
of organized baseball fell into line. The whole baseball world
rallied around the idea developed from the Abner Doubleday
ball. Majors and minors, universities and colleges, high schools
and preparatory schools, even libraries, endorsed the project.

America's first museum devoted to sports began to take on
substantial form. Treasured relics and documents and con-
tributions came rolling in. They came in such numbers that
soon a building was required to house the collection growing
around the Abner Doubleday baseball.

On the one-hundredth anniversary of the beginning of baseball in America, the National Baseball Hall of Fame and Museum was dedicated. It is a monument to the vision and
energy of Ford Frick. The famous players of the past and baseball's highest executives attended the ceremonies, along with
many other distinguished guests.

Today it is a national institution; its official brochure correctly calls it "not only a sanctuary for rarest trophies but also
a haven for scholars and historians."

The Exhibits in This Museum

Dominating the museum is what might be called a national
statue to America's national game. It is a towering replica of
the United States Capitol in Washington. On its dome rests
a huge baseball. The entire structure is supported by sixteen
regulation-sized baseball bats, each bat representing a major
team in the National and American Leagues.

The huge ball crowning the Capitol bears the autographs
of the governors of the forty-eight states, Judges of the

Supreme Court of the United States, high church dignitaries, leaders in the baseball world, and leading sports broadcasters. This national memorial was presented to the Hall of Fame by the alumni of St. Mary's Hospital, of Cincinnati, one of the most historic cities in baseball annals.

The bronze bust at which we are now looking is that of the great Christy Mathewson, which occupies a place of honor on the main floor of the museum. It is interesting to note that the sculptor was a woman, Gertrude Boyle. An ardent woman baseball fan, she watched the famous pitcher for many seasons from the grandstands at the Polo Grounds, and then created this memorial to his memory.

Here, among the many curios, are two bronze statuettes of an old-time pitcher and batsman in long trousers fastened at the ankles. This was the attire before the debut of knee-length pants, which first appeared with the uniform worn by the Cincinnati Red Stockings in 1869.

Here we see a pair of the skin-tight fingerless double gloves worn by players in the 1870's. Here, too, are the first catcher's mitt, the first factory-made mask, and many of the other "firsts" in the game. The bat used by George Wright when the Cincinnati Reds became the first team to turn professional in 1869 is in a prominent place.

The most prized bat in the world, the famous bat with which Babe Ruth hit his record-breaking sixtieth home run off Zachary of Washington on September 30, 1927, is likewise exhibited. Babe autographed the bat and gave it to the sports writer James M. Kahn the day following the game in the Yankee Stadium. When the Hall of Fame was opened, Kahn presented the bat to the museum.

Another display is known as the "Babe Ruth case." This contains his uniform and equipment, the famous No. 3 which the King of Swat made famous. Youngsters and their elders gather around this historic case in admiration of the home-run king.

Treasures for Every Baseball Fan

The three-story building is filled with treasures telling the whole story of baseball. We see the uniforms, bats, gloves and shoes belonging to heroes of the diamond: Ty Cobb, Christy Mathewson, Walter Johnson, Larry Lajoie, Lou Gehrig, and many others. Here's the glove worn by George Sisler at first base; gloves worn today are much bigger than this one. In the early days players wore tight, small gloves on both hands.

Among the prizes in the museum is the autographed ball used by Cy Young when he pitched his five-hundredth victorious game. Another curio is the ball used on June 29, 1867, in a famous old-time game when the New York Mutuals defeated the Independents by a score of 28-26.

Here are baseballs used in no-hit games; balls used in World Series and all-star contests; balls from all parts of the world. One with unraised seams from the Australian League creates attention. It is not unlike the official ball used in the National League in the 1880's. Then there is a ball made of sealskin that was used in Newfoundland and the Far North.

It is easy to visualize the whole history of baseball in the prints, etchings, photographs, and paintings hanging on the walls of the museum. The first games with Abner Doubleday in 1839 were played on a cow pasture, with a brook running through it. The pasture was transformed into a modern baseball field as a memorial to Doubleday by the townspeople of Cooperstown, who contributed more than $40,000 to drain and fill in the old cow pasture and erect modern wood and concrete stands.

At the entrance of the field is a marker erected by the State of New York. It reads: "Doubleday Field. Where baseball was invented and first played in 1839." The stands which completely encircle it hold 9,000 spectators, "nearly three times the population of Cooperstown." The field is now laid out according to major league dimensions, and the diamond is rated as one of the finest in the country.

During the Centennial celebration, before the Abner Doubleday Field had been developed to its present perfection, two teams played a game according to the rules of 1850. The annual Hall of Fame game draws an overflow crowd as large again as its seating capacity, when two major league teams, one from each league, meet in combat. Babe Ruth played here at one time, with a record-breaking crowd.

We View the Historic Mementos

Another high point in the museum is the last photograph of Babe Ruth in uniform, wearing the uniform that is now on display in the museum. It was taken at his last appearance at the Yankee Stadium when he waved good-by to the cheering throngs. His widow and his executors have donated many mementos to the museum, and eventually there will be a "Babe Ruth Room" when the building is enlarged.

A picture that attracts special attention is the Babe standing before a huge crowd and pointing at the far-away fence in the third game of the World Series in Chicago in 1932. The rooters for the National League were taunting him. The Babe, always good-natured, pointed at the fence and proceeded to knock a home run over the very spot at which he had pointed. George Magerkurth, the umpire behind Babe Ruth at the home plate, confirms this spectacular event. And the Babe himself admitted it.

We stop with deep interest before a painting of the First Formal Match Game ever played between men's teams. It took place at Hoboken, New Jersey, June 19, 1846, and bears the inscription: "Knickerbockers *vs.* New York."

On the second floor of the museum is a collection of photographs of the Presidents of the United States who have followed the custom of tossing out the first ball on opening day in Washington.

In the museum's library is housed the most complete collection of books on baseball in the world. Here are the year-by-year records of every major leaguer in history, and complete box scores covering every game in the majors since 1876, when the National League was founded.

The first newspaper to report the game regularly was the *New York Clipper,* and we find bound volumes of this in the library. The first official record book was *Beadle's Guide* in the 1860's; many others, including Spalding's, have since followed. These are all preserved in the library.

Able Executives of the Hall of Fame

The Hall of Fame owes much to the able staff executives in charge of its public service. Its first director was William Beattoe, of Cooperstown, a baseball sportsman and enthusiast greatly loved by the public. The director from 1946 to 1948 was Ernest L. Lanigan, a great baseball statistician, now the historian of the Hall of Fame.

The present director is J. A. Robert (Bob) Quinn, formerly one of the most popular players and one-time owner of the Boston Red Sox and Braves. The president this year is Stephen C. Clark; vice president-treasurer, Paul S. Kerr; vice president, Rowan D. Spraker; secretary, Walter R. Littell.

The administrative committee in 1950 consists of: Stephen C. Clark, Chairman of the committee; Paul S. Kerr, secretary of the committee; Director Robert J. Quinn; Edward G. Barrow, former president of the New York Yankees; Grantland Rice, dean of American sports writers; Melville E. Webb, veteran baseball authority on the Boston *Globe.* I consider it a high honor that my name is also included on this committee.

CHAPTER 12

A TRIBUTE TO THE IMMORTALS

O<small>N THIS DIAMOND</small> jubilee of America's national game there are fifty-five bronze tablets in the Hall of Fame, erected in honor of the men who have been elected to this baseball academy of immortals.

It would be impossible in this limited space to pay tribute to all of them, despite the fact that I consider each and every one a noteworthy player. Many were my friends in the early days of the game; others were my own "boys."

The Hall of Fame Committee controls the policy of the national institution and elects to the gallery of immortals the players and builders who were active in the era prior to those elected by the balloting of the Baseball Writers' Association of America.

First Players in Hall of Fame

I was invited to the dedication and considered it a great honor to be there. Taps were blown in honor of the living and the dead, and more than 10,000 people bowed their heads in silence.

The first players elected to the Hall of Fame numbered a fateful thirteen. But when the doors were officially opened that dedication day, only eleven passed through its portals. Two were missing—Christy Mathewson and Wee Willie Keeler, who had passed away before the event took place.

The ceremony of cutting the ribbons at the entrance gates was performed by Ford Frick. Beside him stood Judge Kenesaw Mountain Landis, William Harridge, president of the American League, and the late W. G. Bramham, who performed valuable service as president of the minor leagues.

As the gates swung open the crowd of onlookers broke into cheers. There stood the three greatest outfielders of all times: Ty Cobb, Babe Ruth, and Tris Speaker.

I was privileged to go through the open bronze doors first, because I was the oldest, no doubt. Each of us, as we were presented to the throng, tried to express our gratitude in a few words. The records say that I "choked up and moved on with tear-filled eyes."

In the true American style, photographers were on hand to snap our pictures. When we sat down, Eddie Collins, the smiling Babe Ruth, Connie Mack (still stage-struck), and Cy Young were in the front row. Ty Cobb, however, failed to appear in time to have his photograph taken. Someone was heard to say, "Ty's late—just as he always was for spring training."

Standing behind us was a row of immortals: Hans Wagner, Grover Cleveland Alexander, Tris Speaker, Napoleon Lajoie, George Sisler, and Walter Johnson.

We then went to Doubleday Field, which was filled to capacity, where three thrilling exhibition games were played during the day. The first game was an old-fashioned "town ball," the kind I used to play as a boy in the old Brookfields.

The crowd was fascinated by a two-inning game of early baseball, the kind played by the New York Knickerbockers in the 1850's. The pitcher, called the thrower in those days, stood only forty-five feet from the batter, who was then called the striker. The catcher stood back at a safe distance, as was the custom in the days before masks and chest protectors and shin guards and catcher's mitts.

The centennial exhibitions closed with a modern nine-

inning game between two major league mixed teams. Lefty
Grove, Dizzy Dean, Ducky Medwick, Hank Greenberg, and
Mel Ott were among the stars. This anniversary day brought
back to me many happy memories.

Bronze Tablets to the Immortals

Today I am revisiting these historic scenes with you in
memory. I can mention but a few of the tablets as we quickly
pass along.

We stand before the bronze plaque bearing the portrait of
Grover Cleveland Alexander. Under it are these lines: "Great
National League pitcher for two decades with Phillies, Cubs
and Cardinals starting in 1911. Won 1926 World Championship for Cardinals by striking out Lazzeri with bases full
in final crisis at Yankee Stadium."

Those who remember this game will never forget the exciting moment as Alexander the Great, 6 feet, 1 inch tall,
hurled the winning ball. In his twenty years in the pitcher's
box he played 696 games with 90 shutouts, 373 victories and
208 defeats, percentage .642. He was in the majors twenty
years, from 1911-1930.

There is the tablet honoring Adrian Constantine Anson,
known and beloved as "Cap" and "Pop." It bears this tribute:
"Greatest hitter and greatest National League player-manager
of nineteenth century. Started with Chicagos in National
League's first year, 1876. Chicago manager from 1879 to 1897,
winning 5 pennants. Was .300 class hitter twenty years, batting champion 4 times."

"Pop" Anson, the famous first baseman, was in the majors
twenty-two years, 1876-1897. He was truly a striking figure,
6 feet, 1 inch and weighing 220 pounds, the heaviest man in
the Hall of Fame. He played 2,253 games, at bat 9,084 times
and made 3,081 hits, a lifetime average of .339.

There is Dan Brouthers, whose Christian name was Dennis,
the heaviest hitter of all the first basemen, with a lifetime rec-

ord of .348. He was a star in the major leagues for seventeen years, 1879-1896, a towering fellow of 6 feet, 2 inches, weighing 200 pounds, a left-hander at bat and in throwing. Dan played 1,668 games, at bat 6,788 times, and made 2,365 hits.

And here is Mordecai Peter Brown (Three-Fingered), first major leaguer to pitch four consecutive shutouts, achieving this feat on June 13, June 25, July 2, and July 4 in 1908. How well I remember him! This "three-finger" pitcher was in the majors for fourteen years, from 1903-1916. He pitched 480 games; won 239; lost 130; a .648 percentage.

What Records These Men Made!

We move along to a plaque with this description: "Jesse C. Burkett: Batting star who played outfield for the New York, Cleveland and St. Louis N. L. teams and the St. Louis and Boston A. L. teams. Shares with Rogers Hornsby and Ty Cobb the record of hitting .400 or better the most times. Accomplished this on three occasions. Topped the N. L. in hitting three times, batting over .400 to gain the championship in 1895 and 1896." Burkett's lifetime batting average was .342, equaling that of Babe Ruth's record in later years, although Burkett was not a home-run hitter, like the Babe.

In its place of honor is a bronze bearing the name: "Frank Leroy Chance. Famous Leader of Chicago Cubs. Won pennant with Cubs in first full season as manager in 1906. That team compiled 116 victories, unequaled in major league history—also won pennants in 1907, 1908, and 1910 and World Series Winner in 1907 and 1908. Started with Chicago in 1898; also manager New York A. L. and Boston A. L."

Here is the master of them all—the great and only Ty Cobb! His memorial in this Hall of Fame reads: "Tyrus Raymond Cobb, Detroit-Philadelphia A. L. 1905-1928. Led American League in batting twelve times and created or equaled more major league records than any other player. Retired with 4,191 major league hits."

During his twenty-four eventful years in the majors he played 3,033 games, a world record. He was at bat 11,429 times; that too is a world record. He made 4,191 hits; that's another world record. His lifetime batting average was .367, and that has never been beaten. I'm proud to be able to say that Ty Cobb was one of my boys and has been a lifelong friend.

This Hall of Fame seems to be full of "my boys." On the bronze tablet at which we are now looking is Mickey Cochrane. The inscription says: "Gordon 'Mickey' Cochrane, Philadelphia A. L. 1925-1933, Detroit A. L. 1934-1937." It pays this tribute to him: "As a fiery catcher compiled a notable record both as a player and manager. The spark of the Athletics' championship teams of 1929, '30, '31, had an average batting mark of .346 for those three years. Led Detroit to two league championships and a World Series title in 1935."

Mickey is a master of baseball strategy. He left the Detroit Tigers in 1938 after thirteen active years, 1925-1937, in the majors, where he was one of the great catchers of his time. In 1,482 games, 5,169 times at bat, he made 1,652 hits, 119 home runs, and established a batting average of .320.

Mickey Cochrane is back with the Philadelphia Athletics as a coach for 1950, along with Jimmy Dykes and Bing Miller, other stars on the championship A's of the early thirties. This combination is the best coaching staff in baseball. It should prove a spark plug for the Athletics in another battle for the pennant.

Old Masters of Years Gone By

When I look at the bronzes erected in honor of these old-timers, they bring back many happy memories. Here is another of my champions. The tablet reads: "Edward Trowbridge Collins, Philadelphia-Chicago, Philadelphia A. L. 1906-1930. Famed as batsman, base runner, and second baseman, and also as field captain. Batted .333 during major league career. Second only to Ty Cobb in modern base stealing. Made 3,313 hits in 2,826 games."

Another great Collins has a niche in the Hall of Fame. His bronze tablet says: "James Collins, considered by many the game's greatest third baseman. He revolutionized style of play at that bag. Led Boston Red Sox to first world championship in 1903. A consistent batter, his defensive play thrilled fans of both major leagues."

Everybody knows the name Comiskey, famed throughout the nation. The bronze tablet in his memory tells his story: "Charles A. Comiskey, 'the Old Roman.'" There could be no finer tribute to him. The legend reads: "Started 50 years of baseball as St. Louis Browns' first-baseman in 1882 and was first man at this position to play away from the bag for batters. As Browns' manager-captain-player won 4 straight American Association pennants starting 1885, world champions first 2 years. Owner and president Chicago White Sox 1900 to 1931."

A famous name to conjure: Ed Delahanty. His tablet calls him "One of the game's greatest sluggers. Led National League hitters in 1899 with an average of .408 for Philadelphia; American League batters in 1902 with a mark of .376 for Washington. Made 6 hits in 6 times at bat twice during career and once hit four home runs in a game." Delahanty played in 1,825 games, 7,493 times at bat, he made 2,593 hits with a lifetime batting average of .346—four percentage fractions higher than Babe Ruth.

We must remember these old-timers when we're talking about our modern heroes of the diamond. Other tablets include one to "Hugh Duffy, brilliant as a defensive outfielder for the Boston Nationals. He compiled a batting average in 1894 which was not to be challenged in his lifetime—.438."

Miracle Men on the Diamonds

Another magic name, the miracle man, Johnny Evers. His bronze memorial reads: "John Joseph Evers, 'the Trojan.'"

He was rightly named, for the tablet tells us he was "middle-man of the famous double-play combination of Tinker to Evers to Chance. With the pennant-winning Chicago Cubs of 1906, '07, '08, '10, and with the Boston Braves' miracle team of 1914. Voted most valuable player in National League in 1914. Served as player, coach, and manager in big leagues and as a scout from 1902 through 1934. Shares record for making most singles in four-game World Series." He played in some of the most spectacular games the diamond has ever seen.

"Buck" Ewing. Here's another magic name. The tablet records: "Wm. B. 'Buck' Ewing, greatest nineteenth century catcher. Giant in stature and Giant captain of New York's first National League champions 1888 and 1889. Was genius as field leader, unsurpassed in throwing to bases, great long-range hitter." Buck Ewing was baseball's hero for eighteen years. He starred in 1,280 games, at bat 5,348 times, and made 1,663 hits, with a lifetime .311 batting average.

At this moment we are looking at a bronze tablet erected in honor of "Frank Frisch, New York N. L. 1919-1926, St. Louis N. L. 1927-1938, Pittsburgh N. L. 1940-1946. Jumping from college to the majors, the Fordham Flash was an outstanding infielder, baserunner and batter. Had a lifetime batting mark of .316. Holds many records. Played in fifty World Series games. Managed St. Louis from 1933 through 1938 and won World Series in 1934. Managed Pittsburgh from 1940 through 1946." A brilliant second baseman, he played nineteen years in the majors in 2,311 games; 9,112 times at bat, made 2,880 hits and 105 home runs, with a .316 batting average.

Memories That Warm Your Heart

Your heart is warmed as you look at this memorial to Lou Gehrig, who passed on in the height of his fame: "Henry Louis Gehrig, New York Yankees 1923-1939, holder of more than a score of major and American League records, includ-

ing that of playing 2,130 consecutive games. When he retired
in 1939, he had a lifetime batting average of .340."

Lou Gehrig, at first base, standing 6 feet, 1 inch and weighing 205 pounds, was another of the many college men playing
in baseball. His friends called him "Columbia Lou." As we
have already seen, he was a notable example of character, intelligence, and manhood, the highest qualities of good sportsmanship. During seventeen years he played in a total of 2,164
major games, at bat 8,001 times, making 2,721 hits and 494
home runs, with his .340 batting average.

In this group of famous American athletes we are glad to
see a tablet inscribed to : "Charles L. Gehringer, second baseman with Detroit A. L. from 1923 through 1941 and coach in
1942. Compiled lifetime batting average of .321. In 2,323
games collected 2,839 hits. Named most valuable player in
A. L. in 1937. Batted .321 in World Series competition and
had a .500 average for six all-star games."

Here's an old warrior who brought honor to our national
game: "Clark C. Griffith, associated with major league baseball for more than fifty years as a pitcher, manager and executive. Served as a member of the Chicago and Cincinnati teams
in the N. L. and the Chicago, New York, and Washington
clubs in the A. L. Compiled more than 200 victories as a
pitcher. Manager of the Cincinnati N. L. and Chicago, New
York, and Washington A. L. teams for twenty years."

Famous Pitchers and Famous Batters

Stop for a moment to pay tribute to another of my "boys."
This is the bronze tablet to "Robert Moses Grove, Philadelphia A. L. 1925-1933, Boston A. L. 1934-1941. Winner of 300
games in the majors over a span of seventeen years. Led A. L.
in strike-outs seven consecutive seasons. Won twenty or more
games eight seasons. In 1931, while winning thirty-one games
and losing four, compiled a winning streak of sixteen straight.

Won seventy-nine games for the three-time pennant-winning Athletics team of 1929, 30, 31."

"Lefty" Grove was one of the greatest of greats. He established many records that have not been broken up to this time. His skill in the box will long be an American legend. Standing 6 feet, 3 inches, weighing 204 pounds, he was master of his art. Pitching 616 games he won 300, lost 141, with 33 shut-outs, establishing a lifetime .680 percentage, the record for the past seventy-three years.

We are now looking at the greatest batter the National League has ever known, the great Rogers Hornsby, whose record is exceeded only by Ty Cobb in the American League. The honor roll reads: "Rogers Hornsby, National League batting champion 7 years, 1920 to 1925, 1928. Lifetime batting average .358, highest in National League history. Hit .424 in 1924, 20th century major league record. Manager 1926 world champion St. Louis Cardinals. Most-valuable-player, 1925 and 1929."

Rogers Hornsby is a great sportsman and a grand character. With Ty Cobb he is tops in baseball. Rogers, in twenty-three years in the majors, 1915-1937, established his .358 batting record against Ty Cobb's record of .367, but he made 302 home runs against Ty's 118 home runs. Hornsby was the great second baseman of his time while Cobb was the greatest outfielder. Hornsby played in 2,259 games, at bat 8,173 times and made 2,930 hits.

The ace pitcher, Carl O. Hubbell, well deserves the tribute given to him. It reads: "Carl Hubbell, New York N. L. 1928-1943. Hailed for impressive performance in 1934 all-star game when he struck out Ruth, Gehrig, Foxx, Simmons and Cronin in succession. Nicknamed 'Giant's Mealticket.' Won 253 games in majors, scoring sixteen straight in 1936. Compiled streak of 46⅓ scoreless innings in 1933. Holder of many records."

Hughie Jennings' tablet reads: "Hughie Jennings of Baltimore's famous old Orioles. He was one of the game's mighty mites. A star shortstop, he was a constant threat at the plate. Once hit .397. Piloted Detroit to three championships." At bat 4,840 times he made 1,520 hits, with .314 as his lifetime batting average.

We are in front of a memorial that commands our highest respect. On the bronze plaque we see the strong features of a great man. The inscription below it reads: "Byron Bancroft Johnson, organizer of the American League and its president from its organization in 1900 until his resignation because of ill health in 1927. A Great Executive."

I'll never forget Ban. He was not only my friend but my adviser when I came into the American League.

CHAPTER 13

STARS OF YESTERDAY AND TODAY

W<small>E ARE SURROUNDED</small> by famous men, among them the great Walter Johnson. The inscription on his bronze tablet reads: "Walter Perry Johnson, Washington, 1907-1927. Conceded to be fastest ball pitcher in history of game. Won 414 games . . . Holder of strike-out and shutout records."

Johnson shattered records for twenty-one years. Standing 6 feet, 1 inch, weighing 200 pounds, the master right-hander pitched 802 games with 113 shutouts, a world record.

"King" Kelly! How well I remember him! His tablet reads: "Mike J. (King) Kelly, colorful player and audacious base-runner. In 1887, for Boston he hit .394 and stole 84 bases. His sale for $10,000 was one of the biggest deals of baseball's early history."

Here is another of my "boys," a Napoleon of baseball. The tablet reads: "Napoleon (Larry) Lajoie, Philadelphia (N) 1896-1900, Philadelphia (A) 1901, Cleveland (A) 1902-14, Philadelphia (A) 1915-16. Great hitter and most graceful and effective second-baseman of his era. Managed Cleveland 4 years. League batting champion 1901-03-04."

Big Napoleon Lajoie could have carried the famous little Napoleon under his arm. Nap was 6 feet, 1 inch and weighed 195 pounds, whereas the Napoleon beaten at Waterloo was a little five-footer. Lajoie was rightly named the Napoleon of baseball. During twenty-one years, 1896-1916, he fought gallantly in 2,475 diamond battles. On the firing line 9,589 times, he made 3,242 hits and 71 home runs with .338 as his lifetime record.

The inscription on the bronze tablet bearing Judge Landis' portrait reads: "Kenesaw Mountain Landis, baseball's first commissioner, elected, 1920—Died in office, 1944. His integrity and leadership established baseball in the respect, esteem and affection of the American people."

Judge Landis, after seventeen years as a Federal Judge in the United States District Court of Northern Illinois, resigned to serve the rest of his life as first commissioner for the American and National Leagues of Professional Baseball Clubs and the National Association of Professional Leagues. The entire nation is indebted to him for the magnificent service he rendered to this great American sport.

I feel quite humble as I look at the next tablet, and it is only as a matter of record that I mention it. It reads: "Connie Mack, a star catcher, but famed more as manager of the Philadelphia Athletics since 1901. Winner of 9 pennants and 5 World Championships. Received the Bok Award in Philadelphia, 1929."

Brilliant Stars Gleam in the Past

The next tablet is erected to the champion of champions: "Christy Mathewson, New York N. L. 1900-1916, Cincinnati N. L. 1916. Born Factoryville, Pa., August 12, 1880. Greatest of all the great pitchers in the 20th century's first quarter. Pitched 3 shutouts in 1905 World Series. First pitcher of the century ever to win 30 games in 3 successive years. Won 37 games in 1907. 'Matty was master of them all.'"

Christy Mathewson should have a big place in the hearts of the American people. A towering fellow, 6 feet, 2 inches, weighing 195 pounds, he dominated our baseball diamonds for seventeen historic years, 1900-1916. With marvelous control of the ball and unexpected change of speed and curves, he pitched 634 masterful games with eighty-three shutouts. Victorious in 373 pitcher's battles; he lost, generally by slight margins, 188 games, leaving a lifetime record of .665, exceeded in the second quarter of the century by Lefty Grove when the latter established his record at .680.

Who, do you think, is this keen Irish face glowering at us from the bronze? It is none other than "John J. McGraw, star third-baseman of the great Baltimore Orioles, National League Champions in the '90's. For 30 years manager of the New York Giants starting in 1902. Under his leadership the Giants won 10 pennants and 3 world championships."

John McGraw, with whom we all fought and whom we all loved, completed fifty eventful and stirring years in baseball. For sixteen years he was the life of the party in action on the diamond; and for the remaining thirty-four years of his life he was the life of the party from the managerial bench. There never was a dull moment with McGraw.

During his energetic years on third base, 1891-1906, the little 5 foot, 7 inch giant, weight 150 pounds, was dynamite in 1,082 games. At the bat 3,919 times, he slugged out 1,307 hits with a lifetime batting average of .334, and set that as the goal for his players all the rest of his life. When baseball lost John McGraw, it lost a personality that could never be replaced.

Iron Man McGinnity! His tablet reads: "Joseph Jerome McGinnity, 'Iron Man.' Distinguished as the pitcher who hurled two games on one day the most times. Did this on five occasions. Won both games three times. Played with Baltimore, Brooklyn, and New York teams in N. L. and Baltimore in A. L. Gained more than 200 victories during career. Recorded twenty or more victories seven times. In two successive seasons won at least 30 games."

Can These Aces Ever Be Excelled?

Here's another of my "boys." The bronze tablet reads:
"Herbert J. (Herb) Pennock, outstanding left-handed pitcher
in the A. L. and executive of Philadelphia N. L. club. Among
rare few who made jump from prep school to majors. Saw
twenty-two years' service with Philadelphia, Boston, and New
York teams in A. L. Recorded 240 victories, 161 defeats. Never
lost a World Series game, winning five. In 1927 pitched 7⅓
innings without allowing hit in third game of series."

Six-footer men dominate the Hall of Fame. Here's "Edward
S. Plank, 'Gettysburg Eddie,' one of the greatest left-handed
pitchers of major leagues. Never pitched for a minor league
team, going from Gettysburg College to the Philadelphia
A. L. team with which he served from 1901 through 1914.
Member of St. Louis F. L. in 1915 and St. Louis A. L. in
1916, '17. One of few pitchers to win more than 300 games in
big leagues. In eight of 17 seasons won 20 or more games."

"Gettysburg Eddie" was one of our first big finds. He bat-
tled his way through seventeen great years, 1901-1917, on our
American diamonds. He stands with the great mound generals
of all times. Eddie was 175 pounds of greased lightning. Pitching 623 games, he won 325, lost 190, with .631 as his lifetime
percentage.

Another old friend of mine, known and loved as "Uncle
Robbie," is honored by a tablet which reads: "Wilbert Robinson, 'Uncle Robbie,' star catcher for the famous Baltimore
Orioles on pennant clubs of 1894, '95, and '96. He later won
fame as manager of the Brooklyn Dodgers from 1914 through
1931. Set a record of 7 hits in 7 times at bat in single game."

We are now standing before the tablet inscribed: "George
Herman (Babe) Ruth, Boston-New York A. L., Boston N. L.
1915-1935. Greatest drawing card in history of baseball.
Holder of many home run and other batting records. Gathered 714 home runs in addition to fifteen in World Series."

This lad from a Baltimore orphanage won an everlasting place in the hearts of the American people. The Yankee Stadium, known as the "House That Ruth Built," is the result of his service to baseball. The name Babe Ruth has become an American slogan. Like our nation's flag he has become a symbol of the American spirit. In his twenty-two years in the game, he was the idol of American boyhood and loved by the entire nation.

A left-hander in batting and throwing, he established a world record that even a future player will have difficulty in breaking. There never has been anybody like the Babe. A big man, 6 feet, 2 inches, weighing 215 pounds, he played in 2,503 games, 8,399 times at the bat, he made 2,873 hits, with .342 lifetime batting average.

Not only was he a great outfielder with an amazing record, but he was also a great pitcher. In the pitcher's box in 165 games, he won 92, lost 44, a .676 percentage record. But it was in the affection and adoration of the American people that we can truly say of him that he led all the rest!

Men with High Rating

We pass along to other "greats." Here is a tablet bearing the name: "George Harold Sisler, St. Louis-Washington A. L., Boston N. L., 1915-1930. Holds two American League records, making 257 hits in 1920 and batting .41979 in 1922. Retired with major league average of .341. Credited with being one of the best two fielding first basemen in history of game."

Again we find one of our old A's. "Tristram E. (Tris) Speaker, Boston (A) 1909-1916, Cleveland (A) 1916-1926, Washington (A) 1927, Philadelphia (A) 1928. Greatest centre fielder of his day. Lifetime major league batting average of .344. Manager in 1920 when Cleveland won its first pennant and world championship."

Tris Speaker, playing actively in the game twenty-two years

(1907-1928) is another six footer, weighing 193 pounds. He played in 2,789 games, more than any other man except Ty Cobb and Eddie Collins. His record at bat was 10,208 times, exceeded only by Ty Cobb and Hans Wagner. He made 3,515 hits, exceeded only by Ty Cobb. And his lifetime batting average is .344.

The name Spalding has always stood high in the game, the man with the highest percentage of pitcher's victories since the game began—.783. His tablet reads: "Albert Goodwill Spalding, organizational genius of baseball's pioneer days. Star pitcher of Forest City Club in late 1860's, 4-year champion Bostons 1871-1875 and manager-pitcher of champion Chicagos in National League's first year, Chicago president for 10 years. Organizer of Baseball's first Round-the-World Tour in 1888."

A name in baseball almost as famous as "Casey at the Bat." Here's his tablet: "Joseph B. Tinker, famous as a member of one of baseball's greatest double-play combinations—from Tinker to Evers to Chance—a big leaguer from 1902 through 1916 with the Chicago Cubs and Cincinnati Reds and the Chicago Feds. Manager Cincinnati 1913, and Chicago N. L. 1916. Shortstop of Cub's team that won pennants in 1906, 07, 08 and 1910."

"Pie" Traynor! A wizard in the game. His tablet reads: "Harold J. (Pie) Traynor, rated among the great third basemen of all time. Became a regular with the Pittsburgh N. L. team in 1922 and continued as a player until conclusion of 1937 season. Managed the Pirates from June 1934 through September 1939. Holds several fielding records and compiled a lifetime batting mark of .320. One of few players ever to make 200 or more hits during a season, collecting 208 in 1923."

"Rube" Waddell, another of my prize "boys." Read the tribute to him: "George Edward Waddell, 'Rube,' colorful left-handed pitcher who was in both leagues, but who gained fame as a member of the Philadelphia A. L. team. Won more than 20 games in first four seasons with that club and compiled more than 200 victories during major league career. Was noted for his strike-out achievements."

Who Can Beat the "Flying Dutchman"?

"Hans" Wagner, the "Flying Dutchman"! If you never saw him in action, you've missed something great in your life. Read what the tablet says about him: "Honus Wagner, Louisville, N. L., 1897-1899; Pittsburgh, N. L., 1900-1917. The greatest shortstop in baseball history. Born Carnegie, Pa., February 24, 1874. Known to fame as Honus, 'Hans,' and 'The Flying Dutchman.' Retired in 1917, having scored more runs, made more hits and stolen more bases than any other player in the history of his league."

That's tribute enough for any man. In his twenty-one years in the league, 1897-1917, Hans gave it many of its most thrilling moments. Five feet, 11 inches, weighing 200 pounds, he was, as his tablet states, the "greatest shortstop in baseball history." He played in 2,785 games and was at bat 10,427 times, more times than any other man except Ty Cobb. As a National Leaguer he made 3,430 hits, exceeded only by Ty Cobb and Tris Speaker. His record shows 101 home runs and a lifetime .329 batting average.

"Big Ed" Walsh came from Meriden, Connecticut, where I started out as a professional. His tablet reads: "Edward Arthur Walsh, 'Big Ed,' outstanding right-handed pitcher of Chicago A. L. from 1904 through 1916. Won 40 games in 1908 and won two games in the 1906 World Series. Twice pitched and won two games in one day, allowing only one run in double-header against Boston on September 1908. Finished big league pitching career with Boston N. L. in 1917."

Our last tablet pays tribute to the man who pitched more games than any other man in league history: "Denton T. (Cy) Young, Cleveland (N) 1890-1898, St. Louis (N) 1899-1900,

Boston (A) 1901-1908, Cleveland (A) 1909-1911, Boston (N) 1911. Only pitcher in first hundred years of baseball to win 500 games. Among his 511 victories were three no-hit shutouts. Pitched perfect game May 5, 1904, no opposing batsman reached first base."

Cy Young was the wonder of baseball, one of our pitching giants, 6 foot, 3 inches, weighing 210 pounds, a powerful right-hander. He set a standard that hasn't been surpassed. In twenty-two years in action, 1890-1911, he pitched the most games, 906, and won the most games, 511, with 73 shutouts. He lost 315 games and established a lifetime .619 percentage of victories. But his greatest glory was in pitching the perfect game.

Our Own Predictions

How do the baseball stars of today compare with the stars of yesterday? The records of our players today will determine whether they will win a place in the Hall of Fame.

It might be interesting to venture a few guesses as to future names of candidates. What players in action today do you believe will earn their way into this distinguished company of immortals?

The award to the "most valuable player" in the National League in 1949 was conferred on Jackie Robinson, of the Brooklyn Dodgers. The award in the American League went to Ted Williams, of the Boston Red Sox. Jackie Robinson received the Benny Leonard Good Sportsmanship Trophy for "courage, fair play and interest in humanity." He also was awarded the George Washington Carver Memorial Institute Gold Medal for "betterment of racial relations."

We must further take under consideration these decisive factors: Stan Musial, of the St. Louis Cardinals, has been given the Most Valuable Player Award in· the National League three times, 1943, 1946, 1948. This recognition also

has come to Joe DiMaggio three times in the American
League, 1939, 1941, 1947.

Ted Williams has received the award twice, 1946, 1949. Hal
Newhouser, of the Detroit Tigers, has been a two-time winner, 1944, 1945; also Hank Greenberg, of the Detroit Tigers,
1935, 1940. Jimmy Foxx, of the Philadelphia Athletics, won
it two successive years, 1932, 1933, and again with Boston in
1938. And among the star pitchers, what about Bob Feller's
great record?

It looks to me as if Joe DiMaggio, Ted Williams, and
Jackie Robinson stand a good chance to land in the Hall of
Fame if they keep up their good work in 1950 and succeeding
years.

CHAPTER 14

Baseball would never be what it is today if it were not for the women who have given it distinction. When I first started in baseball, the game was not so respectable as it is today, but the women have been a powerful moral influence in raising its tone.

It was a woman who made the sculptured bust of Christy Mathewson for the Hall of Fame. It is Grace Coolidge, the beloved wife of the former President, who has set the example of a First Lady of the Land to grace our game.

I had the honor to sit with Mrs. Coolidge at the World Series in 1949 in the Yankee Stadium, where former President Hoover was also in attendance. Every American woman can well follow Mrs. Coolidge's distinguished leadership.

During my long observations of the game I have found that the wives and mothers of the players have had a paramount effect on their lives. Babe's Ruth's wife was a strong factor in molding his life. Lou Gehrig's wife was his best companion. Casey Stengel's wife is his most ardent supporter. So it has been with most of our great players and managers.

Today our American women are the mainstay of baseball. "Ladies' Day" has now become a custom in all our ball parks. We can find no more enthusiastic supporters of the home teams than the women fans. Our grandstands and boxes are filled with them; they add color and charm to the scene.

It has become fashionable for women to go to ball games. In the old days of hoop skirts and bustles the fashions made it uncomfortable for their wearers to sit on hard benches. Huge broad-brimmed, flower-bedecked hats were a torment to the spectators. Today's fashions of comfortable dresses and bare heads are much more sensible.

The First Ladies' Baseball Club

Among the many curiosities in the National Baseball Hall of Fame and Museum is a picture of the Young Ladies' Baseball Club No. 1, season of 1890-1891. These girl players were: Effie Earl, shortstop; Edith Mayves, third base; Alice Lee, left field; Rose Mitchell, right field; Angie Parker, second base; May Howard, captain and pitcher; Annie Grant, center field; Kittie Grant, first base; Nellie Williams, catcher.

This first girls' team created a sensation, for their startling appearance caused considerable comment. Ministers preached sermons against both the players and their costumes. The press attacked them, but still crowds flocked to see their exhibition game with the New York Giants.

Our American women today hold substantial interests in baseball. My partner, Mrs. Thomas Shibe (as I have already mentioned), is one of the owners of the Philadelphia Athletics. Women have also inherited interests at various times in such clubs as the New York Yankees and the Brooklyn Dodgers.

The first woman to own a major league club and operate it was Mrs. Helene H. R. Bigsby, who was president and owner of the St. Louis Cardinals when she sold the club in 1918. Her uncle, Martin Stanley Robison, had left her a large percentage of the stock. He, with her father, the late Frank DeHass Robison, owned the Cleveland club when it was in the National League.

Mrs. Bigsby was an ardent fan throughout her life and was one of the first to propose "Ladies' Day" in our ball parks.

"Being a woman owner of a baseball club was difficult at

first," she once said. "I loved it, though, and regretted selling my club."

Among other women who have held large interests in ball teams are Mrs. Barney Dreyfuss and Mrs. Charles Comiskey.

From my observations at our baseball parks, I have been impressed with the fact that the women fans know baseball as expertly as do the men. Their judgment and perception are keen and accurate. They are quick to respond to good sportsmanship and they frequently lead the cheering. Their enthusiasm is unbounded; their wit is quick and sharp. I am grateful to them for their unwavering support. Their loyalty to the home team can always be depended on.

Questions Women Ask Me

I have received thousands of letters of encouragement from loyal women fans and also many questions. A few of these questions I should like to share with the reader, along with my reply.

Should I permit my son to become a professional ball player? Yes, it is a healthful and honorable profession.

Are the habits of ball players good or bad? They must be good, or the men wouldn't stay in the game long today. I should say that the habits of ball players are on as high a level as those of men in any other pursuit in life.

Do ball players make good husbands? I know hundreds of players who have the happiest kind of home life. The percentage of divorces is probably lower among baseball players than in any other profession.

What is the secret of your long life? I am not old enough yet to answer that. Ask me again when I am a hundred!

Do you drink? No! I have seen the abuse of alcohol do too much damage to otherwise great players. Moreover, as I told you in the beginning of this book, I made a promise to my mother to let intoxicants alone.

Do you smoke? I find enough interesting things to do without smoking. I have no objection to it, however. It is a matter of personal choice.

Do you swear? I see no sense in taking the name of God in vain. A profane vocabulary is the last resort of a man who has little command of the English language.

Do you dance? I did; until the years crept up on me. Now I conserve my energies.

Do you take exercise? Yes, moderately. I have lived a strenuous life and am learning in recent years to take it easy.

Do you play golf? I did at one time and enjoyed it. It's a great game. Many players take up golf after they have retired from baseball.

Do you go to the theater? I have seen most of the great plays, and I am quite a movie fan. I think that the stage and screen are fine forms of entertainment.

Do you go to the opera? There is nothing more inspiring than music. Personally, I have never been able to carry a tune other than some of the old popular songs.

Do you go to church? I certainly do! I consider the Church the greatest institution in the world. It is the fountainhead of civilization. Our first duty is to worship God with reverence. Religion is the most vital force in human life.

Do you believe in immortality? I believe that the great Creator who made this marvelous universe, who made mankind and endowed us with intelligence, has not failed to provide for our future.

Can you give us the secret of longevity? I wish I could. Every time I try to set up a formula somebody who is older than I am comes along and upsets it. I know men of ninety and ninety-five whose rugged constitutions have withstood all sorts of abuse. But I would not advise you to abuse yourself. Safety first and temperance in all things is the best security.

Can you give us any advice? I have never been a preacher or a reformer. I believe that every man or woman should live his or her life according to his or her own intelligence and the dictates of conscience.

Do you worry? I did until I learned better. I quit worrying about thirty years ago. I found it self-destructive. Worry and a bad temper are insidious diseases—the underlying causes of many of our illnesses.

What is the best safety valve for emotions? I have found nothing better than baseball. It gives one the opportunity to work off all excess energy in healthful bursts of enthusiasm. It is an exhaust valve for human emotions.

How do you make friends? The way to make a friend is to be a friend. You get what you give. I have treasured the friendship of many great personalities of our time. My friends have included persons of all creeds, nationalities and races. We are all brothers under the skin.

Do you enjoy family life? God has blessed me with a wonderful family. I am rich in love and devotion and am supremely happy.

CHAPTER 15

DON'T KILL THE UMPIRE!

THE MAN WHO roars "kill the umpire" would kill baseball. The umpire is the presiding judge. In my opinion it is "contempt of court" to attack his decisions violently. In my long life in baseball I have come to revere the umpire. It has been my life practice to refrain from being seriously disturbed when decisions went against me. Even the judges on our higher courts of justice make mistakes.

During my sixty-six years in the big leagues I have been in continuous contact with umpires. I know no group of men who are more fair or square. Under our league rules they are invested with great authority. If an umpire fails to abide by these rules, he is soon relieved of his responsibilities.

Remember that an umpire must be an expert in the game or he does not get the job. He must know all the rules and regulations; he must follow every move with keenest observation and be capable of making quick decisions.

His vision must be quick as a flash—many of his decisions are on hairbreadth actions. The fraction of a second, or a fraction of an inch makes a player "safe" or "out."

Every spectator sitting in the stands thinks he is the umpire! In his intense excitement he forgets that the umpire is right there on the spot. The fans rise in tumult if they do not agree with him. The umpire must patiently and calmly endure the shouting until some overt act is committed.

Partisan fans, rooting for their team, see everything favorable to them. It does not occur to them that in their excitement and favoritism their judgment cannot be as unbiased as that of the umpire.

Baseball is the most human of all games. It is humanity collectively. The crowds roar with freedom of speech and action. It is freedom of expression to the fullest measure, the American spirit personified.

We can well understand the tension of the players, for every nerve is strained to the utmost. Every decision is momentous, meaning either victory or defeat. When, like a stroke of lightning, a decision goes against a team, the breaking point is reached, and they "blow their tops." They firmly believe that a great injustice has been done to them.

Human Emotions in Action

We really should not be surprised at an outburst of the players and managers or the partisan fans; it is to be expected. Yes, it is a part of the game, the inevitable result of human emotions.

At times I have been criticized for remaining undisturbed in a crisis. My team frequently has received what it considered "raw decisions." It has been difficult for me to remain quietly and calmly on the bench, but I have had to restrain myself with the knowledge that the umpire is the judge. If his ruling is appealed, it must be in a judicial manner.

Getting into arguments with umpires is largely a matter of temperament. Fiery tempers, quick on the trigger, explode with spontaneous combustion when an umpire makes a split-second decision. Great strategists, such as John McGraw and "Lippy" Durocher, blow up like dynamite.

Although a display of vehemence usually puts the umpire on the spot, it generally delights the spectators. When they see the extra attraction of a good fight, they think they are getting their money's worth. Explosions of this kind get big headlines in the newspapers and bigger crowds at the box office.

League officials, endeavoring to maintain law and order. administer heavy penalties in fines, and banishment from the game for days or months. Then the incidents are soon forgotten until another one breaks out.

In the early days of baseball, when umpires wore high silk hats and dressed as if they were going to a wedding or funeral, they would turn to the spectators when close plays were made and ask their opinion. The crowd was usually as divided in opinion as the United Nations, but they felt complimented by the umpire's consideration of them. The umpire would then make his decision. This was a practical method of stopping wars at their point of inception.

The Turbulent Era in Baseball

It was in the '80's and '90's that the game passed through its turbulent era. Umpire-baiting became a popular pastime. As the crowds became tougher, the umpires became tougher. An umpire had to be at least a middleweight boxer to hold his own on the diamond. Fist fights were common occurrences. Barrages of bottles and cans showered the field. Some games developed into a free-for-all battle.

Again the league officials had to take over to protect the umpire and the game. When the American League entered the field at the turn of the century, it began to negotiate with the National League to establish peace in baseball.

The "peacemaker" was Ban Johnson. He issued edicts for the protection of umpires, players, and fans, and even began to bring club owners together for their mutual protection. The present system of base umpires to divide the responsibility, was also started, as the game had grown beyond the control of one man at the plate.

Ban Johnson opened a new era in baseball, and let it be known that no abuse would be tolerated. Although keen rivalry existed between the old and the new league, they eventually met amicably in the World Series and have since fought their "world wars" on diamonds as the decisive battlegrounds.

Umpires, once vested with authority, began to be given their proper dignity and compensation.

The first pay given to umpires was back in the 1870's. He got whatever he could get, probably a few dollars from the home team. It's been a long road from this pittance to the salaries we now pay our umpires.

Umpires in my early days in baseball in the 1880's were getting five dollars a game. It was not until the turn of the century that A. G. Spalding said that the pastime of slugging the umpire was over. It was no longer considered a part of the game.

Today an umpire enters the majors at $4,000 a season. He gets an annual raise of $500, which continues until a maximum of $12,000 a season is reached. If he is fortunate enough to be appointed to serve in the World Series, he receives an extra $2,500 for working about two hours a day for four to seven days. A pension system, which allows a man to retire, is also provided for.

What chances has a man to become a World Series umpire? It is a matter wholly of advancing from the minor leagues to the major leagues. The majority of umpires start in the lower brackets in high school and college games. The next step is into one of the more than fifty minor leagues. The pinnacle is reached in one of the major leagues, each league carrying fifteen active umpires and one supervisor, a total of thirty-two umpires in the big leagues.

The working hours each day in the big leagues are short, only two hours a day during the season. On the other hand, there are nearly 300 split decisions to be made at every game, on strikes and balls alone, or about 45,000 a season. In addition, there are thousands of decisions on fouls, base hits, and at the bags, so an umpire must possess extraordinary tact and alertness.

How Quick Thinking Averts Violence

One of the best stories I ever heard about tact and quick thinking in a game is told about Clarence Rowland. In a close play he called Babe Ruth out at second base. Babe, in a daring attempt to stretch a single into a two-bagger, slid in with a cloud of dust.

"Out!" shouted Umpire Rowland.

The Babe jumped to his feet in a rage. He glared at the umpire like a Bengal tiger.

The umpire, looking grieved, exclaimed sympathetically: "What a shame, Babe, I had to call you out when you made such a magnificent slide! It was the finest slide I ever saw."

Babe's frown turned into a smile; he brushed the dust from his uniform and silently trotted back to the dugout.

Umpires began to appear when matched teams began to meet for the first time in the 1860's. It was generally considered the right of the home team to select its own umpire. This immediately left him open for charges of bias and favoritism.

I've witnessed tense moments when it looked as if both teams were to turn the game into a war, with the fans leaping into the fray. There is a photograph showing a Brooklyn fan jumping on big six-foot George Magerkurth, an ex-football player who became an umpire. For an instant it looked as if the great Magerkurth had met his Waterloo.

There is the story of the umpire who shouted "Strike three!" Whereupon the batter gave him three strikes in the eye. Another about the base-runner who was called out. He knocked the umpire cold and then, towering triumphantly over him, growled, "Who's out now?"

Modern Knights in Armor

Some of our umpires look like knights of old going into jousting mêlée. Chest protectors to ward off dangerous balls; heavy steel plates to protect the feet from tornadoes of foul tips; steel-ribbed mask with heavy padding when standing behind the batter's box. Some carry six emergency balls in their pleated pockets, for they must be ready for whatever may happen.

Our dean of umpires is the grand Bill Klem. His voice has been sounding like a foghorn on our diamonds for nearly half a century. Bill's judgment has been almost infallible, and his decisions have been reversed on appeals in two cases only.

I have been tremendously impressed by his alertness, accuracy, and high sense of justice. I have watched with admiration his command over the players. When they become argumentative, Klem draws a line in the dirt with his foot.

"Put one foot over that line and you're out of the game!" is his stern command. The foolhardy player who tries it is in hard luck. The penalty is banishment.

Klem had a difficult decision to make in the 1934 World Series between the St. Louis Cardinals and the Detroit Tigers. In the final hotly contested game, Joe Medwick hit a three-bagger. When he was sliding into third, he collided with Tiger Marvin Owen, the third baseman.

It looked like a gladiatorial combat until Umpire Klem separated them. The grandstands then entered the mêlée. Detroit rooters began to bombard Medwick when he took his position in the field, with barrages of empty bottles, ripe fruit, and anything else they could lay hands on.

For five innings they kept up the attack, defiant of police or umpire's warnings. As it was the last game of the World Series, Klem decided to attempt to restore order and finish the game. Appeals were made to Commissioner Landis who was sitting in an official box. The Judge decided that to protect both Medwick and the game it would be better to send Medwick to safety in the clubhouse.

This created tumult in the Cardinal ranks, but when order was restored, Dizzy Dean got his revenge. He pitched fury at the Tigers and broke the series tie. The Cardinals came out World Champions, 4 games to 3.

The high esteem in which Bill Klem is held was attested when, in 1939, on the hundredth anniversary of the game, he was presented the first Award of Merit ever given to an umpire, by Ford Frick at a dinner given by the New York Baseball Writers.

Decisions on Spur of the Moment

Umpires have their own individual mannerisms. The first umpire to hold up his right hand when he called a strike was Charley (Cy) Rigler. The first to croon his decisions was Bill Byron, who became known as the "singing umpire." One of his famous decisions in rime is: "It cut the middle of the plate, you missed because you swung too late." Another: "You'll have to learn before you're older, you can't hit the ball with the bat on your shoulder."

The most sweeping action ever taken in a game was when Umpire Bill Summers and Umpire Red Jones banished fourteen Chicago players. This was in a game between the White Sox and the Red Sox in 1946 at Fenway Park, Boston. The umpires had constantly warned the hecklers in the dugout that their tumult must stop. Finally in the fifth inning they were banished from the field. The interesting observation is that Chicago was prepared for any emergency, and won by a score of 9-2.

What was the most difficult decision an umpire ever had to make? I should say it was in a game between the Giants and the Cubs on September 23, 1908. It was in the ninth inning, two out, and the score 2-2. The Giants were the last batters, with a man on third and first. Al Bridwell at the bat smashed out a single to center and McCormick scored from third.

Merkle, the runner on first, confident that the game was won, left the diamond and made no attempt to run to second.

Johnny Evers, seizing the chance of a lifetime, and gripping the ball madly, touched second and put the missing Merkle out.

The umpires were in the greatest dilemma they ever had faced. They went into a long huddle in the clubhouse. Did Merkle leave the game before it was officially over? Did Evers' quick action in touching second base put Merkle out, inasmuch as Al Bridwell, who had made the hit, was on first? Was McCormick's run thus nullified?

It was ten o'clock that night that Umpire O'Day made the official decision: "Tie game!" The play-off came on October 8. "Three Fingers" Brown beat Christy Mathewson and the Giants lost the pennant.

We Must Take Life in Perspective

Baseball historians dwell considerably upon the "days of violence." These days make exciting reading, but it should be considered in proper perspective, that during these same times there was violence everywhere; it was an age of violence. There was violence in the Wild West when it was being settled. There was violence in the upbuilding of the country. Political campaigns had their riots. Three Presidents were assassinated. Labor had its uprisings. Early baseball was characteristic of its times.

With the coming of Ban Johnson and the American League, and its eventual "peace treaties" with the older National League, the age of violence stopped. But the National League blazed the trail through the formative years when the road was hard. It deserves the credit of the pioneers.

The life of the umpire is no longer precarious. His person is held inviolate. His verdicts have become the law. He is a man of ability, respectability, dignity and power.

CHAPTER 16

GENTLEMEN OF THE PRESS

Sports writers are the power behind the tremendous growth of our national game. We managers of teams know that we would not be what we are today if it were not for our American newspapers.

How did baseball develop from the sand lots to the huge stadiums—from a few hundred spectators to the millions in attendance at professional games today?

My answer is: Through the gigantic force of publicity. Publicity has done for baseball what it has done and is doing for the industrial expansion of our nation. It made us "news." It put the force of public opinion behind us. It brought the customers to us. It built us into the "big business" that we are today.

When I use the term "made us news," I recognize the fact that the game and the players were the news that drew and held the constantly increasing customers, but it was the newspapers which spread the stories of players' exploits throughout the country that made them famous.

When I entered the game we first received only a few lines as news. These few lines expanded into columns and pages; in ratio the crowds in our ball parks grew and grew and grew. News, like advertising, is a powerful momentum behind any enterprise.

The sporting world was created and is being kept alive

by the services extended by the press. As a result of a national survey on this subject, it was estimated that the newspapers give to the world of sports *a million pages a year.* The value of this free space devoted to all sports by the newspapers would reach hundreds of millions of dollars a year.

The Power of the Press

It has been affirmed that tens of millions read the news on the sporting pages every day. From these come the vast crowds that witness these games.

The first newspaper to begin to print baseball as news was the New York *Sunday Mercury* in 1853. Ninety years ago athletics were practically unknown to the American people.

When newspapers discovered that sports could be made popular, the idea of reporting them grew by leaps and bounds. John Allen Krout and Charles J. Storey, authorities on this subject, have made many interesting observations. They claim that before this era of publicity sports had their players but not their fans. "It was difficult to resist the lure of pages upon pages of professional baseball, football, and prize fights when we have them before our eyes every morning and evening," said Mr. Storey.

It would be interesting to know who the first baseball sports writer was, but I believe no one has ever discovered this. The services these writers have performed for the game are beyond calculation. Likewise, the sports writer today is an important and highly esteemed factor in baseball.

My relations with the press have been very friendly, and many of the writers have been intimate friends. I consider it an honor to be associated with Grantland Rice, considered by many to be the dean of sports writers, on the governing committee of the Hall of Fame. I likewise have always considered it a privilege to be on a committee with Ford Frick. Among my friends of the press also have been such famous writers as the late Ring Lardner and Damon Runyon.

Masters of Human Interest

Sports writing has become a great literary art in itself. It has more originality, sparkle, brilliance, and humanity than any other branch of journalism, or so I've been told by some well-known literary critics.

I recall the days when it was the most picturesque form of writing in America, when imagination was permitted to run riot. Games in those early days were made to appear fantastic. Then it passed through its dramatic stages with rapid action and exciting climaxes.

The trend today in sports reporting is toward the factual, with less emphasis on the picturesque. Sports writing is now treated as everyday news. As the game has become more scientific, the press has presented it more concretely, giving readers detailed reports of the plays by innings.

The columnists, on the other hand, still preserve the old-time flavor. Such men as Bill Corum have become masters of "snappy" comment with emphasis on the human interest angle.

As a whole, I cannot complain about the treatment I have received from the press, as long as I do nothing to incur their wrath, but woe unto me if I make a move that does not meet with their approval. But they are working in the best interests of the game, so this stewardship over baseball is of great value. It helps to stir up controversy that in the long run revitalizes the game.

Exciting Tales of Famous Players

"My Greatest Day in Baseball" is the title of a series of articles that were published in the Chicago *Daily News* and later published in book form. John P. Carmichael, the sports editor, and other well-known sports writers interviewed forty-seven star players for the answers to this question. I related my Ehmke story, for I felt it justified the purpose of the subject. Others who told about their biggest moments on the diamond were Ty Cobb, Tris Speaker, Jimmy Dykes, Jimmy Foxx, Rogers Hornsby, Hans Wagner, Al Simmons, Cy Young, Carl Hubbell.

Among those who contributed to the series were some of my old friends: Big Ed Walsh, Johnny Evers, Clark Griffith, Mel Ott, Joe Tinker, Grover Alexander, Buck Weaver, Charlie Grimm, Hank Gowdy, Gabby Hartnett, George Sisler, Christy Mathewson, Walter Johnson, Enos Slaughter, Lefty Gomez, Bill Dickey.

Babe Ruth, Dizzy Dean, Martin Marion, Billy Southworth, Leo Durocher, Casey Stengel, Morton Cooper, Jimmy Wilson, Hippo Vaughan, Ray Schalk, Mordecai Brown, Muddy Ruel, Waite Hoyt, Frankie Frisch, Freddie Fitzsimmons, Babe Adams, Jimmy Archer, Satchel Paige, Pepper Martin, Johnny Vander Meer—all these famous stars had a forceful and exciting story to tell. I mention the players by name because you may have seen them all in action on the diamond and also because they all did a good job of reporting.

The sports editors and writers on our Philadelphia newspapers have been my never silent partners in the building of the game in this city, and I am grateful to them for their support and coöperation. Without them there would be no Philadelphia Athletics and no Phillies.

They praised us to the skies when we won our pennants and world championships, but they have been just as considerate of us when we have failed to win. I feel deeply indebted to them for what they have done for me personally and also for my team during the past fifty years.

"IRON MAN" McGINNITY gained his title by pitching and winning five games in six days during his first season with the Brooklyn club.
Wide World Photo

JACK BARRY, shortstop in Connie Mack's "$100,-000 infield," has coached his alma mater's baseball team for more than twenty-five years.
Wide World Photo

A pair of rookie sand-lot graduates get some hurling pointers from Chief Bender, considered by Connie Mack as the greatest one-game and the greatest money pitcher baseball has ever known.
International News Photo

Lou Gehrig, the "Iron Man," shown taking a healthy swing at a Washington pitch, came to the Yankees from Columbia University. His all-around ability helped win nine American League championships for New York and Most Valuable Player Award in '27 and '36.

Wide World Photo

A reunion of "Old Timers" talking shop before ceremonies honoring Connie Mack at Yankee Stadium on August 21, 1949. Yesterday's stars, all of them Mr. Mack's boys, include George "Mule" Haas, Jimmy Foxx, Bing Miller—and the veteran manager himself.

Wide World Photo

Umpire Babe Pinelli talks fast, furiously, and with gestures to shout down the game's foremost umpire-baiter. Leo (The Lip) Durocher (right), Brooklyn Dodgers' manager, loudly protests a strike called on Dodger Mickey Owen. Onlooker, Coach Red Corriden.
Wide World Photo

These old-time stars are pictured in 1939 attending the dedication of the Baseball Hall of Fame, Cooperstown, N. Y. All won election to Hall of Fame. Left to right: (front row) Eddie Collins, Babe Ruth, Connie Mack, Cy Young; (rear row) Hans Wagner, Grover Cleveland Alexander, Tris Speaker, Napoleon Lajoie, George Sisler, Walter Johnson.
Wide World Photo

MEL PARNELL—Boston Red Sox.   HAL NEWHOUSER—Detroit Tigers.

BOB LEMON—Cleveland Indians.   BOB FELLER—Cleveland Indians.
Photo by Arthur A. Somers

AMERICAN LEAGUE STAR PITCHERS

JOE DIMAGGIO—New York. *New York Yankees*   LARRY DOBY—Cleveland. *Photo by Arthur A. Somers*

TED WILLIAMS—Boston.   "HOOT" EVERS—Detroit.

AMERICAN LEAGUE HEAVY HITTERS

HOWARD POLLET—St. Louis Cardinals.
Press Association, Inc.

LARRY JANSEN—New York Giants.

DON NEWCOMBE—Brooklyn Dodgers.
Brooklyn National League Baseball Club, Inc.

EWELL BLACKWELL—Cincinnati Reds.
Cincinnati Baseball Club Co.

TOP-FLIGHT NATIONAL LEAGUE HURLERS

DEL ENNIS—Phillies outfielder.
Wide World Photo

JACKIE ROBINSON—Brooklyn infielder.
Brooklyn N.L. Baseball Club, Inc.

RALPH KINER—Pittsburgh outfielder.

ENOS SLAUGHTER—St. Louis Cardinals outfielder.
Photo by George Dorriall

STELLAR NATIONAL LEAGUE SLUGGERS

What happens when a great slugger like Joe DiMaggio faces a pitcher like Bob Feller? Fans saw a tight no-hit game between the New York Yankees and the Cleveland Indians in 1946.

International News Photo

STAN MUSIAL, spark plug of the St. Louis Cardinals, is one of the best hitters in the history of the National League. He took that League's Most Valuable Player Award in 1943, '46, '48.

International News Photo

MIGHTY BABE RUTH swats a mighty hit in 1926 World Series, New York vs. Pittsburgh.
International News Photo

TRIPLE STEAL. Dodger second baseman Jackie Robinson (right) scores from third as his team executes a triple steal against Cincinnati, July 16, 1949. Cincinnati catcher, Walker Cooper, handles the pitch while Dodger catcher Roy Campanella, who was at bat, ducks aside. Simultaneously, Gil Hodges advanced to third while Billy Cox advanced to second.
Wide World Photo

Connie Mack Day in New York City, August 19, 1949, found Mr. Mack and a baseball parade touring the crowded streets to acknowledge a wild tribute from millions of fans.
Wide World Photo

Mayor O'Dwyer, Joe DiMaggio, Joe DiMaggio, Jr., and Tommy Henrich smile as 86-year-old Connie Mack accepts the scroll of distinguished service from the City of New York.
Wide World Photo

As manager of the East team in the All-American Boys' Baseball Game (1944), Connie gives advice to four Southern boys from Nashville, Birmingham, Memphis, and Atlanta.

Press Association, Inc.

Managers Joe McCarthy of the Yankees and Connie Mack of the A's autograph baseballs for wounded servicemen (1946). They saw Bronx Bombers soundly whipped by A's, 7-1.

Press Association, Inc.

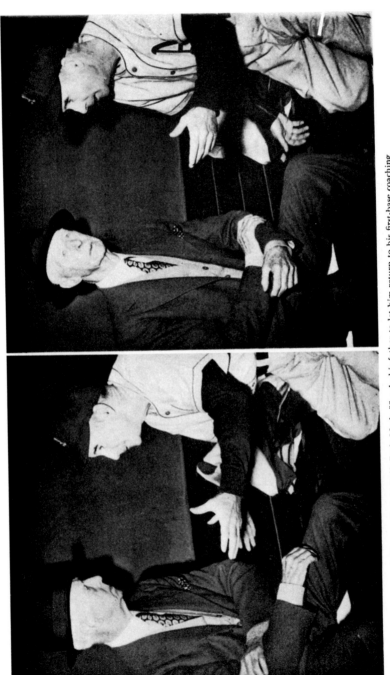

At Fenway Park in 1948, Earle Mack, 55, asks his father to let him return to his first-base coaching duties. Connie Mack said definitely "no" and stuck to it "because the boy is getting up in years."
Press Association, Inc.

"The Knot Hole Gang"—enthusiastic, critical, loyal. Today cheering the home-town A's —tomorrow, a lucky few will take to the field, themselves big league star performers.
Photo by Jack Snyder

"Ladies' Day" has introduced baseball to millions of American women. Gone are the days when men alone took over the ball park for an afternoon game! This female trio contribute more than their share of boisterous grandstand heckling and enthusiastic cheering.
Photo by Jack Snyder

GRAND OLD MAN OF BASEBALL directs traffic in a typical pose, gesturing with score card in the dugout. He has been pictured so often in this attitude that it is almost his personal trademark.

Wide World Photo

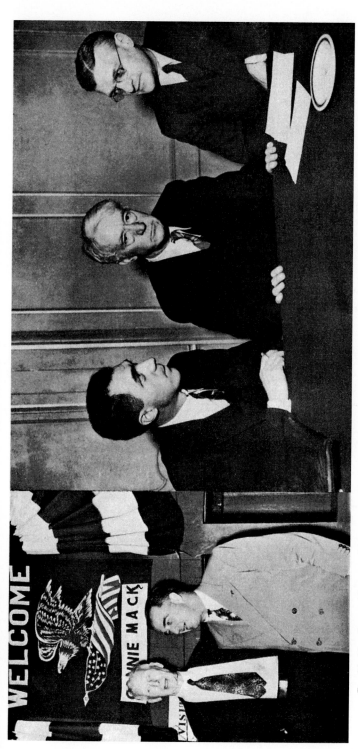

Few Meriden, Conn., citizens recall the summer of 1884 when Connie launched his career, but all claim him as an alumnus. Commissioner A. J. Chandler and Connie Mack enjoy Meriden's welcome. *Press Association, Inc.*

JUDGE KENESAW MOUNTAIN LANDIS rightly earned the title of baseball's "Czar." His personal integrity and insistence on good sportsmanship were largely responsible for building baseball into America's national game. Judge Landis is shown discussing business problems with Ford Frick and Will Harridge, League Presidents of National and American leagues in 1935. *Wide World Photo*

CHAPTER 17

THE CONTRIBUTION OF COLLEGES

COLLEGES, ACADEMIES, and high schools have been the mainstay of baseball. Before the organization of the baseball leagues, our educational institutions literally kept the game alive.

For fifty years I have been scouting our colleges and schools in search of new and promising material. It is a great satisfaction to me to be able to say that some of the greatest players both among my own "boys" and on our diamonds have come from our colleges.

The first intercollegiate meet between two competing teams was played on July 1, 1859, between Amherst and Williams. Amherst won 73-32. Today in the Amherst trophy room is this inscription: "The veritable balls used in the first intercollegiate game of Base Ball ever played."

In those days it was a chivalrous custom for the captain of the defeated team to hand to the victorious captain the ball with which the game had been won. These balls were kept in trophy cases, and in many colleges are preserved as highly valued Americana.

Our college libraries also contain historical records of their individual teams. These treasured records tell the whole story of college baseball in America. Our colleges claim they were the first to introduce the curve which revolutionized baseball and made baseball pitching the science it is today.

151

The First Curve Pitcher—a College Contribution

The first pitcher in professional baseball to create a sensation by using the curve was W. A. "Candy" Cummings.

My old friend Frank Blair has made an exhaustive research into the historical records in the effort to find where and how curve pitching started.

"Curve pitching was not of professional origin," this venerable baseball authority declares. "It came from a college diamond. And so did the first no-hit, no-run records."

The underhand throw was first permitted by rules of baseball in 1872, and it was this underhand throw that soon developed the curve. Curve pitching introduced science into the game and greatly cut down its length and scores. Before that time scores had been running into three figures.

"I saw a game played in 1870 between West Brookfield and Sturbridge, a few miles from Connie Mack's home," Mr. Blair recalls. "It was played on the old commons, all the afternoon into the edge of the evening. After the score was computed by candlelight the results read: Sturbridge 113—West Brookfield 30."

Curve-ball pitching soon swept through the country like wildfire. When Goldsmith and Corcoran pitched for Anson in Chicago in the early '80's, they shut out so many visiting teams that the fans had a name for it. If any team was defeated without scoring a single run in any place in the country, they said it had been *Chicagoed!*

"The first man to pitch a curve-ball game," Blair told me, "was Charles Hammond Avery, Yale 1871-75, popularly called Ham Avery," and the first curve-pitched college game was played between Yale and Harvard at Saratoga, New York, June 14, 1874, the week of the college boat races. Avery pitched for Yale and won by the score of 4-0, the first shutout ever scored against Harvard.

The next day Yale defeated Harvard by a score of 7-4, Avery again pitching for Yale. Some records state that Avery was the first Yale pitcher to beat Harvard. All records show that the cause of the victories was "balls that curved away from a right-hand batsman, pitched by Avery."

The fact that Avery was to perform this miracle was undoubtedly a secret known only to his team. For the next year it still remained a mystery. Very few newspapers even mentioned it. The first pitchers to fathom the Avery mystery were Mann of Princeton, Richmond of Brown, and Carter of Yale. In a very short time after that it was evident that something startling had happened in baseball.

"You can't call those old college pitchers 'forgotten men!' " exclaims Mr. Blair in presenting the above-mentioned facts. "It's a pretty good college contribution to our national game, isn't it?"

This old-timer states emphatically, however, although he began to use the curve in the big leagues, he would take none of the credit from "Candy" Cummings. "There is room for all," Blair says, "but credit should be given where credit is due, and I think Cummings and college baseball should have more than a fair share of the credit."

Documents at Princeton University

A volume in the Princeton University Library, entitled *Athletics at Princeton,* proves that colleges developed the first curve pitchers. This book gives box scores and some descriptive matter of every game played at Princeton from 1860 to 1901. It notes also that at the end of the baseball season in 1874, the same year that Avery began to pitch his curveball games at Yale, the professional Philadelphia team, with Arthur Cummings as pitcher, came to Princeton.

Many times while the batter was taking his stance, Cummings would leave the pitcher's mound and throw the ball to second base so that it would curve in its flight. This feat always amazed and delighted the spectators.

"He had been doing this for some time for the amusement

of the fans," states Mr. Blair. "It was considered a trick of magic, and he did not venture to get it under sufficient control to use it over the home plate from the pitcher's box until some years later."

The testimony of this veteran of academy and college baseball throws much light on the early days of the game. In his first year at Williston Academy, in 1873, one of Blair's chums was Charles Francis Carter, a left fielder who went to Yale in 1874, and the following year played on Avery's famous Yale team. Stories began to drift back to Williston that Avery was a wonder, for he had introduced something new into baseball—a curve ball that was puzzling batters and was proving very difficult to hit.

"But the college professors declared there could be no such thing as a 'curved ball,' it must be an optical illusion," Frank recalls with amusement.

One day in 1876, Blair was examining the condition of the diamond on the Academy campus. He spied Carter coming up the street from the station. Carter spotted Blair at the same moment, and vaulting the fence, shouted to him, "I can pitch curves! Avery taught me!"

"With that, Carter took a baseball from his pocket, laid aside his overcoat, and began to show me how the mystery was performed."

Carter, having passed on the instructions to Blair, picked up his overcoat and started for the train back to New Haven. He had seemingly accomplished his mission! Blair was eager to pass on the secret to the Williston pitcher. The result? Williston Academy placed on the diamond the first curve pitcher used in any prep school in the United States.

The standard ball in use by professional and college teams in those early days was a red ball. It was introduced into the game in the early '70's because it was believed that the fielders could see a red ball in the sunny skies better than they could spot a white one. In the latter part of the '70's the white ball

began to be used once more; and soon after 1880 the red
ball disappeared, never to return to baseball.

Amherst College a Baseball Shrine

Amherst established the first college baseball field in the
country. It was known as Blake Field, named after Lucien Ira
Blake, a senior from Taunton, who had raised the money from
the alumni to help construct it. Professional teams from the
New England cities, from Washington, and as far west as
Columbus, Ohio, came to play exhibition games on this field.

When Frank Blair went to Amherst along with John An-
drews, of Holliston, Massachusetts, who had learned curve
pitching at Williston with Blair, they took curve pitching
along with them.

The day Harvard came to Amherst in 1877 was a memorable occasion. Harvard was sartorially superb; the players
wore tan leather shoes that laced up around the ankle. It was
the first time leather had ever been used for baseball shoes.
The tan shoe era dates back to that Harvard-Amherst team.
The high canvas shoes that the players had formerly worn
began to disappear and give place to the low leather shoes
which players today wear.

Harvard's catcher, Tyng, appeared on the diamond that
day carrying a satchel of the same color and material as his
shoes. When the umpire called "Play Ball," Catcher Tyng
opened his satchel with much ceremony and took from it a
mask which he carefully placed over his face.

This was the first baseball mask. It was invented and pat-
ented by Fred W. Thayer, of Harvard, in 1876, another important college contribution to baseball.

Historic Battle: Yale vs. Harvard

One of the great games in early baseball history was played
at New Haven on May 26, 1877, when Carter of Yale pitched
his no-hit game against Harvard. One Harvard man reached

first on an error, but was immediately thrown out trying to steal second.

"This was the first game in baseball history where the members of a defeated team were put out in one-two-three order," Mr. Blair states. "It is true that Princeton defeated Yale at New Haven in a no-hit, no-run game on May 28, 1875 (3-0), but two Yale men reached first on errors, thus breaking up a one-two-three play. J. M. Mann pitched a great game for Princeton."

The first time Amherst defeated Yale was on June 13, 1877. The big news was wired from New Haven: "Amherst has beaten Yale." When the team returned to its home town near Northampton that night a considerable part of the population was waiting on the road. The horses were unhitched from the wagon that was waiting for the victorious team, and some of the students put themselves between the shafts and drew the students to the campus.

It was like an old-time election night. Bonfires were lighted and cheering crowds rallied round the fires, while wildly enthusiastic students carried the players on their shoulders. Round and round the bonfire they circled as the crowd broke into songs.

It was only when the flames died down that the excitement subsided and the crowds dispersed.

Richmond of Brown University

The first renowned left-handed curve pitcher to come over the baseball horizon, in 1879, was John Lee Richmond, of Brown University. Avery was the first right-hand curve pitcher. "Lefty" Richmond made the circuit of college teams, and defeated them all—no one was ever able to hit his curve pitching.

The next spring, 1880, Richmond started to repeat his amazing performances. The National League, then but four years old, determined to capture the new boy wonder. Worcester, then in the National League, signed him up on his graduation from Brown University.

On the day of his graduation, the Worcester team had a special train waiting for him at the Providence station. Richmond and his catcher, also a college man, Winslow, were taken aboard. That afternoon they were to face the hardhitting Cleveland team at Worcester.

Richmond's debut as a professional is one of the big events in the annals of baseball. In the forenoon he was only an amateur college pitcher; in the evening he was acclaimed as the most famous pitcher in the baseball world. Not a Cleveland man had been able to reach first base. The Worcester National League team had scored the first no-hit, no-run game in professional baseball history. That day the frantic search for good left-hand pitchers with curve under control started, and never has waned in all these years.

CHAPTER 18

THE AMERICAN LEGION AND BASEBALL

M̲Y̲ BASEBALL career has brought me into intimate contact and relationship with many national movements for civic and social betterment. One of the most important of these movements, in my estimation, is the American Legion, for which I am serving as a commissioner and adviser for the Pennsylvania group in its vast chain of nationwide Junior Baseball leagues.

Our American Legionnaires and the members of all our veterans' associations have helped to make our national game an exemplification of the true American spirit. The Army and Navy and Marine Corps in two wars have carried our truly American game with our own American flag to all the countries of the world.

The American Legion, which (with its American Legion Auxiliary) has over 4,000,000 members, is engaged in a program for molding the future of our American youth by utilizing baseball as a powerful factor in the social, moral, and economic development of the younger generation.

Inaugurating a campaign for good citizenship, the Legion has organized more than 500,000 boys into baseball clubs. In 1949 it had 15,912 American Legion Junior Baseball teams competing for the Junior World Series.

This good-citizenship organization operates clubs in all

the forty-eight states and in Hawaii. Established in towns and cities, the clubs form a network covering our entire nation.

The two major baseball leagues (American and National) extend full coöperation in promoting State Championship teams both as a civic betterment enterprise and in the development of new players for our national game.

The work of the American Legion has been so successful that 255 of its boys had graduated to the payrolls of the big leagues in 1949, and 3,672 more were with the minor leagues.

Code of Sportsmanship

The Code of Sportsmanship of the Junior Baseball Rules in the American Legion Department of the Pennsylvania Activities Committee is a significant one: .

KEEP—The Rules—Faith in your comrades—Your temper —Your self fit—A stout heart in defeat—Your pride under in victory—A sound soul—a clean mind—and a healthy body.

This Code of Sportsmanship must be memorized by every Junior club member and repeated in unison before each game. If a team permits an ineligible member to continue to play, the entire team is disqualified, and all games won or lost are not put on the records.

This high standard of character and conduct is maintained throughout the more advanced teams in the American Legion Junior Leagues, which firmly implant the ideals of *good sportsmanship, honesty, loyalty, courage, reverence,* and the qualities of *good citizenship* in the boys of every community.

American Legion Junior Baseball is an established national institution for boys in all sections of our country.

The National Americanism Commission of the American Legion operates this public service from its headquarters in Indianapolis. "The bringing together of thousands of boys into one gigantic, nationwide program and then getting them back home safe and sound, imbued with a more thorough understanding of American ideals and principles, is the problem the American Legion solves each year," states the Commission.

"Great responsibility rests upon the shoulders of the adults leading the teams. These men must emphasize the strict enforcement of all rules. The building of winning teams is of secondary importance to teaching the proper appreciation of good sportsmanship and good citizenship. Its primary purpose is to build *character* and not championship."

I am indebted to my colleague, George E. Bellis, Director of the Athletic Activities Committee of the American Legion Department of Pennsylvania, for making accessible to me the reports of the National Commission, and to him I extend my deepest gratitude.

Young America in Action

These official reports show that the first national competition was played off in 1926, with only fifteen states competing. The first Junior World Series was played in Philadelphia during the American Legion 1926 National Convention. Four champion teams were brought together: New York, Ohio, Kansas, and Idaho. The first championship was won by New York with its Yonkers team.

The program was officially completed in 1928 under the leadership of Dan Sowers, then National Director of the Americanism Commission. He placed the Legion program before a conference in Chicago, attended by High Commissioner Kenesaw Mountain Landis; Ernest Barnard, then president of the American League; and John A. Heydler, then president of the National League. They agreed to underwrite the national program up to $50,000. State championships were played off in forty-four states. The final competitors in the Junior World Series were California (representing the West) versus Massachusetts (representing the

East). The series was played in Chicago, where Massachusetts won (with its Worcester team) against California (with its Oakland team).

Every state in the Union entered the competition that year. In the Junior World Series the championship was won by New York (with its Buffalo team), against Louisiana (with its New Orleans team).

Civic organizations of all kinds, church groups, business groups, boys' clubs, Boy Scout troops, and the National Recreation group coöperated in 1930. Memphis, Tennessee, provided a real setting for Junior World Series, between Maryland (the Eastern champions) and Louisiana (representing the western half of the country). Judge Landis and many other big league notables were in the stands as the American Legion champions contested. Maryland won (Baltimore team), defeating the New Orleans team in a hard struggle.

The Junior World Series opened in Houston, Texas, in 1931. Played at night—in a brilliantly illuminated stadium, it had all the color and ceremony of a big World Series. Bands played, Legion drum and bugle corps paraded, and Commissioner Landis threw out the first ball. The game ended in a thrilling fourteen-inning finale with a score of 1-0, Illinois (with its Chicago team) the winner, against South Carolina (with its Columbia team). It is important to note that the American Legion pitcher for Columbia was Kirby Higbe, who ten years later became the National League's top pitcher.

Amid another spectacular setting in Manchester, New Hampshire, in 1932, Louisiana (with its New Orleans team) won the championship against Massachusetts (with its Springfield team) in a ten-inning climax with a score of 5-1.

The scene again shifted to the South in 1933, when New Orleans was the battleground for the game between the midwestern champions from Chicago, led by Philip Cavarretta, who later starred with the Chicago Cubs, against the New

Jersey champions from Trenton. The game was officially opened by the raising of the American flag and the playing of the national anthem by the Crescent City American Legion Post band. The splendid pitching of Cavarretta for the Chicago boys ended the hopes for Trenton with a final score of 7-6 in favor of Chicago.

Year by year the battles between the East and the West, the North and the South, have been fought. These annual championship tournaments have become national events.

In 1948 American Legion Junior Baseball soared to 14,531 clubs. For the second straight year Hawaii entered a contestant along with the forty-eight continental states.

National finals in the same year were held for the first time in Indianapolis, national headquarters of the American Legion. Games were played at Victory Field, home of the Indianapolis American Association Baseball Club. The Junior World Series attracted some of the biggest names in big league baseball: George Trautman, president of the National Association of Professional Baseball Leagues, High Commissioner Chandler, Rogers Hornsby, Bill Terry, Dizzy Dean, and a score of major league scouts.

The four states in the 1948 Junior Baseball World Series were: New Jersey (represented by Trenton), Florida (with the Edward C. DeSaussure Post No. 9 team), Nebraska (with Post No. 1 from Omaha), Illinois (with the George Hilgard Post No. 58 from Belleville). Trenton captured the national championship by beating Jacksonville in the final game 4-1.

Fifteen Thousand Teams Fight for Championship

The year 1949 came to a close with a total of 15,912 teams certified for competition in the American Legion national contests. The forty-eight states and Hawaii were again in line. This magnitude was reached through the coöperation of many civic organizations and business enterprises, with the nation's leading radio networks, newspapers, wire services, and magazines which put it in a prominent spot on the American sports scene. Thousands of volunteer coaches and managers, many of them ex-big league stars, lent an active hand.

The national finals staged in the new Municipal Stadium at Omaha, Nebraska, in 1949 were witnessed by 45,358 paid admissions. The eyes of the baseball world were focused on the battle between California (with its Captain Bill Erwin Post No. 337 team from Oakland) and Ohio (with its George W. Budde Post No. 507 from Cincinnati).

The two clubs engaged in three terrific battles. The Californians won in the final contest by the score of 8-6. A brilliant triple-play started by Ray Herrera, shortstop, was a contributing factor to the victory. Ferrera was named "American Legion Junior Baseball Player of the Year" and became the first of these junior players to be honored by the National Baseball Hall of Fame and Museum at Cooperstown. A committee of five, headed by Director Robert Quinn, conferred the honor.

The Hillerich and Bradsby batting trophy for 1949 was awarded to J. W. Porter, sixteen-year-old Oakland, California, catcher, who, with a batting average of .551 made 27 safe hits, batted in 22 runs, and scored 20 himself, in ten tourney games.

Pennsylvania's Notable Record

I am especially proud of Pennsylvania's contribution to this vast good-citizenship movement because, for the last ten years, I have been a commissioner for the Department of Pennsylvania in these athletic activities in association with my friend George E. Bellis as director.

It was my good fortune to meet Bellis first in 1912, when he started as a batboy for the Allentown Tri-State League team. I have known him ever since as a fine leader for American manhood. My predecessors as Pennsylvania Commis-

sioners were also old friends of mine: The late Honorable
John K. Tener; my revered partner, the late Thomas B.
Shibe; also the late Barney Dreyfuss and Gerry Nugent.

Leo Riordan, executive sports editor of *The Philadelphia
Inquirer,* to whom I am deeply indebted, arranged the first
"All Star" Junior American Legion baseball game that was
held at Shibe Park in 1944. Major league scouts, representing the sixteen big league teams, were present and selected
Joseph Fromuth, a third baseman of the Reading team, as
the most outstanding player of Pennsylvania. Fromuth later
signed a contract with the Boston American League Club.

Curt Simmons of Coplay, now a member of the Phillies,
was named the most valuable player in 1945. He received
the largest bonus ever paid at that time by a major league
club for signing his contract.

Others who have been selected are: Mike Kemp, shortstop of Reading, 1946, who later signed a contract with the
Detroit Tigers; Clarence Watson, of Manheim Township,
1947, now attending Villanova College. He too is considered
a fine major league prospect and, in all likelihood, will be
signed at the conclusion of his college career; Richard Strick-
ler, pitcher of Myerstown, 1948, was signed by the Boston
Braves; Robert Simononis of Girardville, 1949, and at present attending the Girardville High School. No doubt he too
will be signed up by a major league team at his graduation in
1950.

These "all star" games have increased from one in 1944 to
twenty-six in 1949, giving thousands of boys an opportunity
to perform before major league scouts. The success of the
program in Pennsylvania, we feel, has been due to these "all-
star" games, promoted and sponsored by *The Philadelphia
Inquirer,* the Athletics and the Phillies, in coöperation with
the American Legion.

Pennsylvania led the nation in the sponsorship of Junior
American Legion Baseball teams for the fifth consecutive

year, in 1949, with 1,743 teams and over 30,000 boys under the age of eighteen. Pennsylvania does not participate in the National Tournament because of this great number of teams.

We are proud of the fact that three of the great players in the World Series in 1949 were graduates of our Pennsylvania Junior American Legion Teams: Roy Campanella and Carl Furillo with Brooklyn, and Joe Page with the New York Yankees.

Campanella, a fine player in the National League and beloved with Jackie Robinson and Newcombe of the Dodgers—three wonderful Negro lads—is an honor to our national game. Campanella is now interested in organizing American Legion teams in Harlem. He is firmly convinced that this movement will help to solve the gang problem and reduce juvenile delinquency, for the most wholesome and healthful gangs in the world are the baseball gangs.

How Boys Learn Good Citizenship

Thousands of boys have learned the American way in sportsmanship and citizenship by playing on American Legion baseball teams.

Junior baseball was started in Pennsylvania in 1926, with only three teams competing: York, Lehighton and Manheim, under the direction of T. Walker Cleeland. The idea of this great youth project developed during a National Convention of the Legion in Philadelphia in 1926. At that time the Legion was holding its eighth convention.

As we mentioned before, Dan Sowers from Kentucky and West Virginia put on the first tournament. "It cost plenty," states George Bellis. "Help came to the Legion from such Pennsylvania leaders as Connie Mack, Thomas B. Shibe, Joseph K. Schmidt, Vincent A. Carroll, William Phillips and Vernon Heilman. These were the pioneers, along with T. Walker Cleeland and Ben H. Giffen, the Honorable John K. Tener, and Barney Dreyfuss."

The program faced further struggles in later years, but in 1934 Joseph K. Schmidt, then serving as Athletic Chairman, and Paul Griffith, Department Commander (now Assistant Secretary of National Defense), met with the Department Auxiliary Executive Committee and its President, Mrs. Jane H. Beadle. Out of this meeting came the announcement from Mrs. Beadle that the Auxiliary would underwrite the program. Since that time the Auxiliary has contributed over $50,000.

George Bellis was appointed Department Chairman in 1936. He persuaded me and Gerry Nugent, President of the Philadelphia National League Baseball Club, and William Benswanger, President of the Pittsburgh Pirates, to contribute toward the financial support of the great Pennsylvania program. Since that time both the Athletics and the Phillies, now under the leadership of Robert R. M. Carpenter, Jr., have been the financial backbone in helping to make the Pennsylvania program the success it is today.

This partnership between the American Legion and baseball has lasted more than a score of years. Boys who have played on the teams have learned more than baseball—they have learned the essentials of manhood.

Training School for Building Character

What makes Junior Baseball a great American movement is the realization by the public that it is first of all an activity for the building of character.

The American Legion in Pennsylvania has had the splendid support of all civic organizations, such as the Moose, Elks, Kiwanis Clubs, Rotary, Exchange Clubs, Lions, Optimists, local fire companies, the Pennsylvania Interscholastic Athletic Association, the Police Athletic League of Philadelphia and the Ford, Lincoln, and Mercury dealers of Pennsylvania. The organizations and groups who coöperate in this program have the welfare of America and its youth, at heart.

On the rosters of the 448 National Association clubs in 1949 were the names of 3,672 one-time American Legion Junior Baseball players.

Twenty-seven American Legion Junior Baseball graduates were among the fifty players certified by Commissioner Chandler as eligible for participation with the New York Yankees and the Brooklyn Dodgers in the 1949 World Series.

Twenty-nine of the fifty players selected for the 1949 Major League All-Star game played on July 12 at Ebbets Field, Brooklyn, were alumni of the American Legion Junior Baseball program. They must often think gratefully of the help given them through the American Legion Junior Baseball program in the days when they were struggling to become good baseball players and good Americans.

In all the states in the Union there are men such as we have in Pennsylvania who are giving of their time and energy to make this national project a success. The state has had some fine chairmen: T. Walker Cleeland, Ben H. Giffen, Joseph Schmidt, Thomas E. Williams, Alvin Maurer, George Bellis, Lewis Goldberg, Joseph McCracken—and our present chairman, Milton Moore, with Mr. Bellis as director of Athletic Activities.

The American Legion is assisting our youth up the ladder of success in towns and cities throughout our country. Two hundred and fifty-four players in our major leagues in 1949 came from Junior Baseball teams. I had fourteen of these boys with my Philadelphia Athletics.

The work that is being accomplished by this national movement is best told by the records beginning on page 226. There you will find a list of players in our big leagues who got their start through the American Legion Junior Clubs. Dale Miller is director of the National American Legion Junior Baseball program.

CHAPTER 19

HIGH SCHOOLS AND NATIONAL DEFENSE

Our schools are the bulwark of our nation; they are the training grounds for the manhood of the future. In the high schools throughout our country there are baseball teams that are helping the youth of our towns and cities to acquire strength and character through good sportsmanship.

I have been especially interested in these activities in Pennsylvania, where baseball is being played in nearly 500 high schools. Ten years ago the number of schools sponsoring the game was approximately three hundred. Commendation should be given to the school authorities, who are encouraging our youth to participate in this sport.

The Pennsylvania Interscholastic Athletic Association, with a membership of approximately 1,050 schools, has always promoted the uniformity of standards agreed to be necessary to regulate interscholastic athletic competition for public high schools. The policies maintained by the PIAA have encouraged school authorities to develop the commendable baseball program carried on in nearly one-half of its member schools. PIAA schoolmen definitely believe that the total benefits accruing from baseball warrant the total effort expended.

The extensive and efficiently directed summer baseball program of the Pennsylvania Department of the American

Legion provides an organized and controlled statewide opportunity for school-age baseball players to continue participation in the sport throughout the summer months. This opportunity has motivated the schoolboy to intensify his interest in the program of the school.

Another factor that has been instrumental in supporting the school's baseball program is the definite understanding regarding contractual negotiations now existing between professional baseball and our high schools. The agreement prohibits professional baseball representatives from signing students of any high school to a professional contract until after the student is graduated.

Because the player is not eligible for inducement into organized baseball until he has spent the required time in getting his secondary schooling, he looks toward the school's program for experience in baseball. This agreement has indirectly created a demand for more baseball in the schools and at the same time assures a supply of participants.

The Connie Mack Baseball School

The Connie Mack Baseball School is now located at the West Palm Beach International Airport, Florida. The annual sessions are conducted by a faculty of well-known baseball figures. In 1950 the session started February 20 and continued until March 4—thus giving the boys two weeks of intensive training and tryouts.

Athletics Farm Director, Arthur Ehlers, who knows players when he sees them, directs the school; Ira Thomas, long-time scout; Chief Bender, famous pitcher for the A's a number of years ago; and scouts, Bernie Guest, Tom Oliver, and John O'Rourke comprise the faculty.

The school produced notable results in 1950 and will continue in West Palm Beach until 1955, with yearly changes in player-instructors.

Story of a Courageous High-School Boy

While we are talking about schools, I'd like to tell you about a boy who is finding his place in the world through baseball. This story was brought to our attention by Director Bellis of the American Legion. Robert (Bobbie) Simononis has put the town of Girardville, a typical coal-mining town, in the spotlight.

Bobbie Simononis was a crippled lad who spent three years in the hospital and two and one-half years in a wheel chair. When he was seven years old, he was afflicted with a malignant leg ailment. While doctors despaired, Bobbie kept doggedly at his books, and his mother kept to her prayers. Bobbie just knew that he'd grow up to be a regular fellow, and his mother placed her faith in God that he would.

Bobbie's seemingly frustrated ambition in life was to become a baseball player. His parish pastor, The Reverend A. J. Nevers, bought him a baseball and a glove. The two played catch, with Bobbie burning them in from his wheel chair. As the years passed, Bobbie's leg grew stronger and stronger.

Father Nevers organized, managed and coached the new Girardville American Legion Baseball team. Practice was held in an alley. When he looked about for a pitcher, the best one he could find was his own invalid protégé. Bobbie Simononis, who was now up and around, was just itching to burn them in.

The rest is simple history. The erstwhile wheel-chair invalid, towering on the pitching mound with all his six-feet-four height, carried his team to the semi-finals of the Legion All-Star game, and he was also voted the outstanding player of the All-Eastern Pennsylvania and East-West All-Stars.

He overcame his handicap and became an All-Star pitcher. He is now eighteen, and will graduate from the local high school in 1950, where he has been an honor student for the past three years.

Albert (Chief) Bender coached the Eastern team and liked Bobbie's "live" fast one, so Bobbie is now pitching for the Girardville High Blue Aces. Most of the players are his seniors in age and experience, yet Bobbie is holding his own very capably.

Girardville has much to be proud of in Bobbie Simononis, for his record shows what courage and perseverance can achieve. As young as he is, his name can be mentioned along with other Girardville greats and near greats, such as Chick Fullis, who had played with the New York Giants, the Phillies and with the St. Louis Cardinals in the World Series. Then there were the Drulis brothers, Charles and Joe, who achieved fame and still retain a high place in the football world.

Baseball a Factor in Army Morale

Paul H. Griffith, Assistant Secretary of Defense in Washington, upholds baseball as a morale factor in our Army: Baseball has always been high on the popularity list of the American soldier, both as a spectator and a participant sport. During World War II, baseball was played in all corners of the world by the troops. Often the soldiers in combat areas would immediately start a baseball game after they had been pulled out of the lines for rest.

Even before the war ended, baseball was very popular in Europe: One war correspondent reported that whenever he came to a rest area for combat troops in Germany, he usually found the GI's playing ball, and whenever there was a game in progress, German children would approach as close as they dared, then sit and watch. At one spot three German women watched from the window of a near-by house. "I don't think," states the reporter, "that the kids understood what was going on, but it wouldn't surprise me if they started playing the game themselves before long."

In a poll taken during World War II to determine the

likes of the enlisted men for particular sports, baseball was one of the leaders on the list. The statistics showed that 72 per cent liked it as a spectator sport and 53 per cent liked it as a participant sport.

The men in the Pacific area were asked to name the sports or athletic games which they would like most to take part in during their off-duty time in the tropics. The report is interesting and lists the sports ranked in order of mention: (1) swimming; (2) softball; (3) baseball; (4) fishing; (5) volley ball; (6) ping-pong; (7) basketball; (8) horseshoes; (9) football; (10) boxing.

Baseball was a major consideration in the plans presented to the soldier in Europe for the biggest athletic program of all time—one that attracted well over one million participants during the summer. The program was designed by a committee of civilian athletic specialists, educators and military men, including Ford C. Frick, President of the National Baseball League; Avery Brundage, head of the U. S. A. Sports Federation; Professor P. O. Badger, of New York University; Colonel Henry "Eskie" W. Clark, War Department Athletic Director; Arthur Daley, sports columnist of *The New York Times;* Bill Slater, sports announcer, and many others.

A ten-million dollar purchasing order for special services equipment for Europe included 100,000 baseballs, 180,000 baseball bats, and 100,000 gloves. After all the planning, instruction, and leadership that was contributed to this program, it was necessary to have the proper playing equipment.

Baseball Follows the American Flag

Baseball in Europe, in the summer of 1945, drew about 1,000,000 spectators throughout the command. To culminate the active program, the Army scheduled a "GI World Series" between the Communication Zone and the Third Army, two top teams in Europe. This series was played in two cities,

Rheims (France) and Nürnberg (Germany), before crowds that averaged 40,000. Five games were played, with the Communication Zone, representing the Service Forces, winning three games to two.

An interesting sidelight on the European Theater Baseball Championship of 1945 was the democratic influence exercised by the Americans who played baseball in Germany. Nürnberg's modern athletic plant, renamed Soldier's Field, was once the shrine of Nazidom.

Large party rallies were held there, and on many occasions Hitler spoke from the rostrum in the center of the huge field.

The diamond on which the ETO championships were played was partially surfaced with red brick dust from the rubble of ruined Nürnberg.

The play-offs proved to be a reunion for several of the big-time players, including Pitcher Walt Hilcher, XVI Corps, formerly of the Cincinnati Reds; Second Baseman Benny Zientara, Third Army, also an ex-Redleg; Ken Heintzelman, pitcher; and Maurice Van Robays, outfielder, members of the Third Army and team mates at Pittsburgh; along with Service Forces' Russ Bauers, who hurled for the Pirates; Harry Walker, Third Army outfield, who was a regular for the St. Louis Cardinals before entering the Army; and Manager Sam Nahem of Service Forces, who twirled for the Cards, Dodgers and Pirates prior to the war.

Baseball is still actively participated in as a sport in Occupied Germany, where every major post and military community boasts of its own home team.

Although the list of young Army players today may not include the big names, it does include many potential stars for the major varsities and the professional leagues. At least one rookie professional—Clint Hartung of the New York Giants—found the Army a good place to gain polish for big league competition. He left the Army in 1947 to join the

Giants and open the season, with his Army experience as one of his qualifications.

Of particular interest to major league ball fans is an inside story on the 1949 All-Army baseball tournament. Hank Gowdy, star catcher on the Boston Braves' "Miracle Team" of 1914, and the first major leaguer to volunteer for service in World War I, was an honored guest at the All-Army baseball series. The eight-day tournament was played on Gowdy Field at Fort Benning, Georgia, named for Hank. The field, complete with concrete stands, was the first one ever built by soldier labor and soldier donations.

Baseball in Our National Defense

The importance of recreational athletics in building better soldiers was first acknowledged by General John J. Pershing, in his now famous General Order 241, 29 December, 1918. Prior to that time, the Army sports program had been largely one of training for combat—hand-to-hand fighting, calisthenics, and boxing. General Pershing's action marked the first time in the history of the Army that athletics were made the subject of a General Order.

Baseball was played in the Inter-Allied Games in Paris in 1919 with the Le Mans team of the American Expeditionary Forces League, representing the United States, taking first place in the competition against the Canadians. The Americans took the first, third, and fourth games; the Canadians won the second.

Wherever possible, throughout the occupation zones today, and in practically every area of the globe where the Army is stationed, available stadiums and amphitheaters are utilized. Meiji Shrine Park, in Japan, which was to have been the scene of the 1940 Olympic Games, has an elaborate network of athletic facilities, including a baseball stadium that seats 60,000. Lou Gehrig Stadium, used for Army baseball and football in Yokohama, holds 10,000. Other great stadiums that have been converted for the use of American soldiers of the Occupation Armies are the huge Olympic Stadium in Berlin, the Victory Stadium near Frankfurt, and the great Rizal Stadium in Manila. Seoul Stadium in Korea has also been used for baseball games by American soldiers.

Baseball is taught to youths in Germany by American soldiers as a part of the German Youth Program. The revival of baseball in Japan in postwar years has been due chiefly to the efforts of the American soldiers, who organized games, furnished equipment and gave the young Japanese guidance in what is now the national sport of the country.

Baseball as an Inspirational Force

Army sponsored baseball continues as a constructive force in the lives of soldiers everywhere by helping to insure the physical well-being of many soldiers and by inspiring the ideals of sportsmanship and the team spirit of competitive sports.

The United States Navy likewise encourages its men to play baseball. The boys aboard ship always listen attentively to radio broadcasts on the games being played in the big leagues back home. Baseball has been, and will continue to be a powerful morale factor. During the war, wherever crews landed and were not engaged in battle, the first thing they started to do was to play baseball.

In a report from Captain Tom Hamilton, U. S. N., retired, wartime director of the Naval Aviation Physical Fitness Program, and present Director of Athletics at the University of Pittsburgh, he says: "The excellent record of our troops in action was at least partially brought about by mass participation in baseball by the individuals in our armed forces. Many of the leading players of baseball were in the line-up of our Army, Navy, and Marine Corps in this last war.

"The list would run into thousands of names. I can only indicate a few with whom I came in personal contact: Ted Williams, Mickey Cochrane, Bob Feller, Johnny Mize, Charles Gehringer, John Pesky, Buddy Hassett, Ray Scarborough, Dusty Cooke, John Sain, Hugh Casey."

My desire in this chapter has been to show how our national game of baseball has been a powerful educational factor in our schools and in the development of the physical, mental, and moral well-being of the students, and what an important part it has played in building morale in our armed services.

CHAPTER 20

TODAY AND TOMORROW

A TEAM that walks away with the flag is a good team. A team that wins two years running is better than good. The great team is the one that gets on top and stays there for three years or more."

That, in his own words, is John McGraw's opinion of a winning team. The Philadelphia Athletics, I am proud to say, have been on top. There have been two periods in baseball history when the A's have dominated the baseball world for considerable stretches of time. And they will do it again!

Building a winning team is neither luck nor chance; it is dogged persistence. First, a manager must be able to collect the proper materials; then he must, by patience, experience, and judgment, develop these materials into an organized unit. Material and organization must work together with the precision of a machine.

But remember this is a human machine. Players must be treated both as individuals of importance and as members of a happy family. Each must not only do his job to the best of his ability but in complete coöperation with all the other players on his team.

The human equation and human relationships are of the utmost importance. I have always tried to be a father to my players—one to whom they could come with their problems and receive sympathetic attention.

Humanity is the keystone that holds nations and men together. When that collapses, the whole structure crumbles. This is as true of baseball teams as of any other pursuit in life.

I have never indulged in the habit of swearing at my "boys" when something went wrong, nor have I ever done anything to humiliate a player who had an off day. Since most of us have good days and bad days, we cannot live up to our fullest abilities every day.

Each individual has his own life to live and each has his own personal problems. We must take these factors into consideration whenever he shows any inclination for self-expression or self-indulgence. Man may be led, but he cannot be driven! The best advice I can give to managers is: Be human!

What to Expect in the Next Half-Century

As we look ahead from 1950, we may expect many unforeseen happenings. I believe that in the future, baseball will progress with the times.

I have lived through the days when our pitchers have done away with the emery ball and the saliva ball. Today a pitcher can call for a new ball any time he feels the ball isn't to his liking. At the present time we have what we call the "lively" ball. Years ago we played with a "deader" ball. Some of the players used to choke up their bats instead of trying to make home runs as they do today. The live ball has made the home-run record, and players who hit home runs are big-salaried men.

Since the days of Babe Ruth, all the clubs are on the lookout for another Babe. Have you heard the story about one I was supposed to have found in the Midwest? He was much bigger than Babe Ruth and could drive the ball right out of the park. However, he was using an iron bat. Since the rules allow only the use of a wooden bat, he got a wooden bat, which was just like a feather in his hands. When a fast ball came, he hit it so hard we couldn't find the ball. We looked everywhere for it. When we picked up the bat, there was the ball imbedded in it!

We have to know when there may be changes in the rules of the game. Over the years there have been many, but now the rules seem to be pretty well organized. However, changes come as the necessity arises, and baseball is no exception. Some people say let the rules alone so that they will know them.

Scouting System vs. Bonus System

Today we have the "bonus player"; he gets $50,000 just for signing a contract. Very few of them make good. The Phillies have any number of bonus players. We had one—I thought he was a pretty good hitter, but he turned out very bad for us. We paid him $30,000.

I was one of the very few who believed in the scouting system, but I felt that it wasn't the proper thing to establish the "chain stores" that we have in baseball today. Today, in addition to the majors, we have six classifications into which the minor leagues are divided. There are three AAA leagues, two AA leagues, four A leagues, and the remaining 50 leagues comprise the B, C, and D leagues. Every major league team is affiliated either by working agreements or outright ownership with several minor league clubs.

If I remember correctly, it was the St. Louis Cardinals under Branch Rickey who started the chain-store clubs. He is a good sportsman and a good businessman who has any number of players. We bought one of his players from Montreal, paid something like $25,000 for him. For some of his very best players he demands $100,000. He wants about $250,-000 for Jackie Robinson, but probably would not sell him even for that amount.

Before the days of the chain store we could go out and

bring in a player who would be satisfactory. The first few years I was in Philadelphia I could pick up a player who was good enough to join our Major League Club.

The last four years we have had a number of clubs, two in Class A and a working agreement with the clubs in B, and I don't know how many D clubs, maybe 7 or 8. We move up a Class A or B player to AAA club and give him a year in AAA, then bring him into the Major League club.

Perhaps I'm an old-timer, but I don't like the chain system. Judge Landis told me he did not like it either. We both believed it showed better sportsmanship to go out and find our players and develop them—and take pride in our discoveries. Competition has forced the A's into operating a farm system. And I certainly do not like the bonus system. It's too big a gamble.

We all know that governments have their Secret Service to give them inside information on the strength and weaknesses of other nations. Modern baseball, too, utilizes these same methods. When we are about to start a close pennant race, or about to enter a World Series, we send out our secret-service men (scouts) to keep us posted on the strength and weaknesses of the opposing players.

We Need Brains Plus Brawn

Baseball today is a game of brains as well as brawn. It is a game of strategy with its signals, codes, and intricate devices for instant communication with our players. You have probably heard that I use my score card to convey information. Since our opponents know this, they keep a close watch on every movement I make with my score card, but this is fortified with many other devices. Every move of my head, hands, feet, every turn of my body, every expression of my face, may convey its own special meaning.

The Signal Corps in our Army is no more alert than the

men who plan the strategy on our baseball diamonds. As I am the oldest strategist in the game, with the most years of experience, I have tried to develop it into a science. But like a good general, I must take the responsibility for my mistakes and give the credit for winning battles to the soldiers in the field. The thrills come when your strategy leads to victory; the disappointments when it leads to defeat.

My talent scout, Ira Thomas, once a great baseball player himself, wants to tell his own story: "I came to Connie Mack in 1909 and have been with him ever since. I had played for such great managers as Griffith, Jennings, and Dunn, and at first hesitated about going to Connie Mack's team of college boys.

"It has been marvelous to see how Connie Mack has built young men into great players and into fine characters. He has been a maker of men as well as a maker of players.

"I have seen him sitting in his clubhouse, or in the lobby of a hotel with every member of his team gathered around him. In a genial, fatherly conversation he molded his team into a unit—a united family. Every man knew what he was expected to do. Instead of going out as nine individuals, they went out as one.

"One of the greatest assets a manager can have is to know the disposition of his individual players. Connie handled his players, each and every one, separately as individuals and then merged them into a team. He always spoke kindly and never humiliated a man by reprimand in the presence of other players.

"For a time I was his captain and from him I learned the lessons of good sportsmanship and human relationships. I recall losing a game in Detroit when I was his catcher. I felt pretty blue about it. Mr. Mack popped up from nowhere.

" 'Hello, Ira,' he said. 'How do you feel?'

" 'I feel very badly; I helped lose that game today.'

" 'What are you talking about?' he said. 'Look at that great play you made in the first inning. That gave us a chance.'

"I went to bed all pepped up. The boss understood my mistakes. I woke up the next morning filled with confidence and determination. Mr. Mack was always on the spot to say something encouraging to the player who was down.

"Connie Mack was the first to introduce 'skull practice,' where we were all asked to talk out loud and express our opinions. Other managers soon copied that—what the Army calls 'bull sessions.'

"It was Mr. Mack who developed the plan of sending pitchers down to the 'bull pen.' It was years before anyone else did it for the same reasons he had in mind—always to have a pitcher ready and waiting to meet any emergency.

"When a game began, he would send a pitcher into the box. His strategy was to send another pitcher to the bull pen at the end of the third inning. In the seventh inning the whole staff frequently went down to the bull pen. This kept all the boys on their toes. This was Connie's method in the periods when he was building teams. When he had champions he would alter his strategy."

Thank you, again, Ira Thomas. Now I'll go to bat and bat out my own story.

In my estimation, pitchers are 80 per cent of the game. Some managers estimate batters as 80 per cent of the game. But I think that one pitcher in top form can break that down to zero.

Edison Considered Baseball a Science

Thomas A. Edison, the great inventor, was tremendously fascinated by baseball as a science. He used to come to our training grounds in Fort Myers, Florida, and have long talks with me. He would bring his friends with him—Henry Ford, Harvey Firestone, and grand old John Burroughs.

It was delightful to hear Henry Ford talk about his recollections of the early games and players. His knowledge of baseball records was a big surprise to me.

Another surprise I got was at a dinner in St. Louis, when Harry Truman was running for vice-president. I was the "man who came to dinner" as a guest of Dr. Woods. As I looked around, I noted that many of the guests were wearing Dewey buttons. To relieve the tension, our host decided to keep politics out of the conversation and, turning to me, said:

"Mr. Mack, won't you tell us something about baseball?"

Mr. Truman seemed to be as much interested in the results of the World Series as he was in the election returns.

I wish I had pages enough to talk with you about some of the fine men I have met in the baseball world. I would like to talk about the managers as well as the players—about the builders of baseball: Brush, Soden, Billings, Spalding, Freedman, Byrnes, Wright, Robinson, Joe McCarthy, Billy Southworth, and a host of others.

I'd like to have space to say more about our umpires also: Bill Klem, Billy Evans, Tom Connolly, Jack Sheridan, Tom Lynch (I recommended him to the National League in 1884), and all the other famous umpires. And I'd like to tell you more about our sports writers and their wonderful work and express my gratitude to the sports editors of our Philadelphia newspapers.

Frank Hough, of *The Philadelphia Inquirer,* gave us a tremendous boost when he started his column: "Don't Knock —But Boost." Then there was S. O. Grauley and Jimmy Isaminger, of the *Inquirer;* John Nolan, of *The Evening Bulletin;* Ed Pollock, of the *Ledger* and *Bulletin;* George Graham, of *The North American,* and Ray Ziegler, Stoney McLinn, Bill Brandt, Edgar Wolfe, Bill Weart, George Mason and many others—all good friends.

Joe McCarthy is another name in baseball that I'll always remember: I recall a dinner in Germantown at which I was one of the speakers. Joe had been manager of Louisville for

five years. I believed he had a great future and predicted
big things for him. Joe has made good in a big way. He went
to Chicago and won the championship; then went to New
York and won eight American League pennants and seven
world championships. He is the only manager in baseball who
has won four world championships in succession.

Tributes to Great Players of Today

Events happen so rapidly in baseball that it is difficult to
keep up with them. Any minute any day some player may
break a long-standing record. That's one of the fascinations
about the game—the unexpected surprises.

Who, for example, ever heard of Jackie Robinson until,
by his own merit, he leaped into fame? One night in 1950
more than 1,000 well-known Americans gathered at a banquet
in Hotel Astor, New York, to pay Jackie and other fellow
sportsmen high honors.

When *Sport Magazine* made its awards for the "top performers of the year in the sports world," Jackie Robinson
(Brooklyn Dodgers) and Tommy Henrich (Old Reliable of
the New York Yankees) received the honors in the baseball
world. Jackie was given a rousing ovation, and Tommy was
proclaimed the "Athlete of the Year" on his outstanding record in performance, leadership, and character during 1949.
Lou Boudreau, player-manager of Cleveland Indians, won
the first award in 1948.

Jackie Robinson modestly said: "I should break up my
trophy in thirty-two pieces and divide them among my team
mates because they deserve it as much as I." Tommy Henrich
expressed similar gratitude to his team mates: "I am lucky to
be on the Yankees and I am lucky to be picked from such a
great team and so many great players on all the teams."

Further honors were paid to Jackie Robinson in 1950
when a banquet was tendered him by the Uptown Chamber
of Commerce in New York in recognition of his "outstanding

work in the field of race relations." Colonel Leopold Philipp, president of the Chamber, declared Robinson to be "a glorious inspiration to youth everywhere who has won thousands of friends for the Negro race."

Honors were bestowed on Joe Page of the New York Yankees as one of the "top relief hurlers of all time," by the New York Chapter of the Baseball Writers of America, who presented to him the Babe Ruth Memorial Award as the outstanding player in the 1949 World Series. Page is the first recipient of this bronze plaque in memory of Babe Ruth.

At the annual dinner of the Baseball Writers, held in the Waldorf-Astoria, Manager Casey Stengel, of the New York Yankees, was presented with the William J. Slocum Award for "meritorious services to baseball over a long period of time." The Sid Mercer Memorial plaque was presented to Phil Rizzuto, brilliant shortstop of the Yankees, as "player of the year."

Great players and great teams come and go in rapid succession. Who will be the next?

The big question each year is: "Who will win the next World Series?"

CHAPTER 21

BASEBALL AND "BIG BUSINESS"

The RISE of baseball from its humble beginnings to one of the most important "industries" in this country is an American epic in itself. It is the real American story of individual initiative and free enterprise.

It is, morever, an exemplification of the courage of men who risk their labor and their capital to develop a new business which gives employment and enjoyment to great masses of people. It is not all profit to its organizers and administrators, for, as in all lines of enterprises, there are periods of depression.

When I entered the game, the gate receipts were almost insignificant. It has required more than a half-century to build them up to present proportions. Baseball is strictly a competitive business that must be conducted on sound business principles.

It is a more problematical business than most lines of industry, because recreation and enjoyment, rather than a material product, are being sold. For that reason it is much more speculative. Some economists say it is not a business at all, but a hybrid product of entertainment. I am inclined to think it is a combination of both.

The first economic survey of baseball as a business enterprise is now under way. This survey is being conducted by Peter S. Craig, of Oberlin College.

186

Mr. Craig has told me that it is a strictly educational project, and that he intends to submit his findings in a thesis to Oberlin College. This researcher is studying the attendance figures from 1900 to the present time, with computations on income and expenditures and capital investments.

Sixty-two Million Rooters

The gross attendance in 1949, in major and minor leagues, reached, as we have noted, the amazing figure of 62,000,000, about 20,000,000 of these in the major leagues and the remaining 42,000,000 in the minor leagues.

The economic health of organized baseball can almost be measured through the years by the number of minor leagues in the field. They show the public "consumption."

Mr. Craig gives out these figures: Starting in 1900 there were but 13 minor leagues. These increased steadily through the first decade until they had reached 46 in 1910. From 1911 to 1914 an average of 40 minor leagues started each season. Then, during World War I, there was a sharp decline. Slumps in attendance and shortages of players reduced the minors to 9 by 1918, and most managers, even in the majors, were forced to retrench and to sell their players.

After the war the majors experienced a quick revival and rose to hitherto unprecedented heights. But the minors did not share in this boom, for only about 22 to 31 of them existed throughout the 1920's.

During the worst years of the depression the number of operating minors fell to 14. Then they began to climb again until there were 37 minors in the field in 1937. After a temporary recession a new peak was reached, and in 1940 there were 43 minors.

From what Mr. Craig told me, it is important to note that from 1933 to 1941 inclusive, not a single league is recorded as failing. The attendance in 1939 was estimated to have been 18,500,000.

Fifty-nine Minor Leagues in 1949

With the outbreak of World War II, the falling off of attendance and the loss of players to the Army and the Navy caused another recession. In 1942, 31 minor leagues started, but 5 of them failed. This number was sharply reduced to 10 in 1943 and 1944. Just before the Japanese surrender, in 1945, 12 entered the field.

Then the upward movement started and for the next four years there was a steady increase: 42 in 1946; 52 in 1947; 58 in 1948; and 59 in 1949. The paid attendance in the minor leagues for the season of 1949 reached 41,872,762, an astounding figure, over two-thirds of the grand total.

The major league attendance records in the beginning of this century were around the million mark. They too had their ups and downs, which lasted through two world wars and a depression. In the last ten years they have about doubled their attendance, however. The combined attendance of the American and National Leagues was about 10,000,000 in 1940, 1941; below 9,000,000 in 1942-1943-1944; over 11,000,000 in 1945; over 18,000,000 in 1946; about 20,000,000 in 1947; approximately 21,000,000 in 1948, and about 20,000,000 in 1949.

At this rate of increase, considering the increase in population and the expansion of the ball parks, it should reach 30,000,000 by 1960. If that is true, then the grand total of major and minor leagues would reach 80,000,000 by that time.

The capital investment in baseball is difficult to determine, as it depends on book values, resale values, replacements, and property investments. Balance sheets do not reveal selling prices of players, nor what clubs would want for their franchises.

Sports, a Billion-Dollar Industry

It has been conservatively estimated that at least $100-000,000 has been invested in baseball. With the present value

of real estate, baseball parks, equipment, and other properties, and prices of teams, players, and franchises, it would
require roughly $200,000,000 to purchase all the baseball
properties in the United States.

The manufacturing of baseball goods, uniforms, balls, bats,
supplies; all the concessions at baseball games, costs of operation, traveling and hotel expenses, salaries, sporting goods
stores, the turnover of wages of all employees engaged in all
phases of the game make baseball an industry of tremendous
economic value.

Statistics show that nearly $100,000,000 worth of sporting
goods are manufactured every year to meet the demand that
has been created by the game. These manufacturers maintain a payroll of over $20,000,000 a year. These figures give
some idea of the tremendous contribution sports make to
our national production.

The property values created in real estate alone reach into
scores of millions of dollars. Sports in general are becoming a
billion-dollar industry.

In the two big leagues the plant investments reach high
figures: In the American League the Cleveland Indians play
at Municipal Stadium with a seating capacity of 80,000; New
York Yankees play at Yankee Stadium, seating capacity 73,000;
Detroit Tigers at Briggs Stadium, seating capacity 58,000;
Chicago White Sox at Comiskey Park, seating capacity 47,000;
Boston Red Sox at Fenway Park, seating capacity 34,000; St.
Louis Browns at Sportsman's Park, seating capacity 34,000;
Philadelphia Athletics at Shibe Park, seating capacity 33,000;
Washington Senators at Griffith Stadium, seating capacity
32,000.

The National League investment is heavy, as it includes:
New York Giants at Polo Grounds, seating capacity 55,000;
Boston Braves at Braves Field, seating capacity 41,000; Chicago Cubs at Wrigley Field, seating capacity 38,000; Pittsburgh Pirates at Forbes Field, seating capacity 36,000; Brook-

lyn Dodgers at Ebbets Field, seating capacity 35,000; the St. Louis Cardinals share Sportsman's Park with the St. Louis Browns (A); the Philadelphia Phillies share Shibe Park with the Philadelphia Athletics (A); Cincinnati Reds at Crosley Field, seating capacity 30,000.

The attendance records at these parks far exceed the seating capacity. The total seating capacity of all of them is 693,000. The record single-day attendance for each club's park totals close to 800,000.

Large Incomes from Concessions

Many business concessions operating in baseball parks create a large annual income. It is said that Harry M. Stevens, the first big concessionaire, "parlayed a bag of peanuts into a million dollars." As a boy he started selling peanuts at Comiskey Park when Cap Anson and his Chicagoes were beginning to draw the crowds to that stadium.

Today the Stevens sons and grandsons continue the business as the largest concessionaires in the United States; in fact, they are probably the largest in the world.

"We operate in major and minor league parks and on six race tracks," they state. "Our biggest customers are the fans which crowd into the home games of the Yankees, Giants, Brooklyn Dodgers, Boston Braves, and the Red Sox.

"These baseball fans consume in an average year in a big ball park nearly 700,000 bottles of pop, about 600,000 hot dogs, over 500,000 slabs of ice cream, about 400,000 bags of peanuts. We also print last-minute score cards on our own presses right in the park, and the sale of these runs into millions of dollars."

There are 400 star players in the two big leagues—the elite "400" of baseball's most exclusive society. There are 7,000 more on the way up in teams of the more than fifty minor leagues. It has been estimated that in the nonprofessional groups, such as college teams, school teams, small town teams, American Legion teams, there are 6,000,000 more players.

Wage Scales and Salaries

The wage sheets in the professional leagues are private property, and therefore only an estimate of the salaries paid can be made, but it probably is somewhere around $10,000,000 to players for the season.

How this scale of salaries has been raised through the years is shown by the earnings of Babe Ruth: He received in Baltimore (1914) $600. Boston (A) paid him (1914) $1,300; (1915) $3,500; (1916) $3,500 (1917) $5,000; (1918) $7,000; (1919) $10,000. New York Yankees (A) paid him (1920) $20,000; (1921) $30,000; (1922) $52,000; (1923) $52,000; (1924) $52,000; (1925) $52,000; (1926) $52,000; (1927) $70,000; (1928) $70,000; (1929) $70,000; (1930) $80,000; (1931) $80,000; (1932) $75,000; (1933) $50,000; (1934) $35,000; (1935) with Boston (N) $40,000; (1938) with Brooklyn (N) $15,000.

Added together, these salaries made a grand total of $925,900 paid to the Babe. His share in ten World Series was $41,445 additional. It is estimated that in barnstorming tours, movies, radio, and endorsements, he made an additional $1,000,000. This means that his baseball career paid him an average of nearly $100,000 a year.

Joe DiMaggio's salary record during eleven previous seasons has reached $445,750, with an additional $46,693 for World Series. Its progressive steps have been: (1936) $7,500; (1937) $15,000; (1938) $25,000; (1939) $27,500; (1940) $32,000; (1941) $37,500; (1942) $43,750; (period out during World War II); (1946) $43,750; (1947) $43,750; (1948) $70,000; (1949) $100,000; (1950) $100,000.

DiMaggio has also engaged in other business transactions during the winter seasons, which bring his earnings up to about $1,000,000, thus practically equaling Ruth's earnings. Since his career is only about one-half as long as Babe Ruth's, DiMaggio has practically equaled Ruth's earnings in that time.

Cost of Spring Training Camps

The first spring training camps were started in 1886. In that year Cap Anson established headquarters in Hot Springs, Arkansas, for his Chicago Nationals. At the same time, Harry Wright went to Charleston, South Carolina, with his Philadelphia Phillies. This custom of spring training has remained in operation since that time. Teams go to Florida, California, Cuba, Arizona, and other Southern climates to limber up and to get into condition for the coming season.

Exhibition games to help defray expenses are usually played on the way home from training. During this training period the deficit to the owner of each team is from $30,000 to $50,000 each year. This means a total cost of $500,000 to $750,000 for pre-season workouts.

This loss, however, can be charged against the material gains. Managers not only put their players in good physical condition, but they have an opportunity at the training camps to size up their players and ascertain the potential strength of their teams.

Sports writers and photographers accompany the teams to each camp, so interest in baseball and the events of the approaching season are kept on the sports pages of our newspapers. This advance publicity is of inestimable value both to managers and to players.

Each manager usually takes about 40 players to training camp. This is further reduced to 25 players after May 15—the maximum number the leagues permit a team to carry during the remainder of the playing season.

The baseball school system is a heavy cost that eventually

develops valuable players as the years go on. The policy of
these schools is to give potential players a chance to prove
their worth.

The Philadelphia Athletics maintain the only school that
teaches the fundamentals of major league baseball. All other
schools are for tryouts only. At our school we select the best
material, and with a loud-speaker and coach, we put the boys
through a training course. It costs us nearly $1,000 a week,
or about $10,000 a summer, to run this school, but we con-
sider it money well spent.

The hiring of players in this vast chain of leagues, the
maintenance of ball parks, the supervision of payrolls, record
keeping of every play, and the business administration involved, constitute a highly organized business and an outlay
of a tremendous amount of capital.

Under "Baseball High Lights," beginning on page 213 you
will find the complete organization of the vast chain of professional leagues and the towns and cities in which they
operate.

Our national game has grown to such stupendous dimensions that the government is classifying it with big business,
and regularly conducts investigations to protect it from becoming a monopoly.

Radio vs. Baseball

A case has been pending in the antitrust division to elim-
inate any monopolistic practices. Ford C. Frick, of the National League; William Harridge, of the American League,
have urged strict compliance with all Government regulations. Club owners have believed that the case is "unjust"
and undermines their heavy investments.

The complaint was entered by a number of radio stations
against the major leagues in a dispute over rights to radio
and telecast games. Club owners prohibit broadcasting or

telecasting of major league games without the consent of all clubs within a fifty-mile radius of the city where the game is being played.

After protracted negotiations between the Government and High Commissioner Chandler, an agreement was reached to modify the rule to permit outside broadcasts except when the home team was playing. The radio stations assailed the suggested compromise. Club owners protested that they must protect their attendance and box-office receipts and not permit radio to cut them down. They further claim that the complaint against the baseball owners comes from radio magnates, who are themselves a monopoly.

CHAPTER 22

MY SELECTIONS OF ALL-STAR TEAMS

Down through the years I have been asked on many occasions to make a selection of those players whom I considered would make the greatest baseball team of all time.

I realize that in compiling such a selection probably no two big league managers would name the same players. In the following list, which I have made as my choice of the greatest team of all time, I have endeavored to give my reasons for having selected each one.

CANDIDATES FOR MY ALL-TIME TEAM

Pitchers

Christy Mathewson: The greatest pitcher who ever lived. He shut out our club three straight games in the 1905 World Series. Smart as a whip and the most clever pitcher. No batter ever got the best of Matty.

Lefty Grove: One of the greatest of left-handers. He won 31 games for us in 1931 and lost only 4. He took his time pitching, but he sure was fast with the ball. Gabby Hartnett, the Cub's catcher, said this about Lefty: "How can you hit the guy when you can't see him?" And Hartnett fanned every time at bat.

Walter Johnson: Fastest right-hander that ever lived. With any other club, Walter would have had even a greater record. He was past his peak when the Senators finally got into the World Series; but he was the best right-hander for a good 10 years.

195

Cy Young: Pitched more games than any other pitcher. He was in the game for 23 years and always good. He didn't have a great curve ball but certainly made the most of what he had.

Catchers

Mickey Cochrane: Mickey was fiery and fearless. Great receiver and batter. He could instill fighting spirit into others. He gets the call over Bill Dickey because of his terrific urge to win.

Bill Dickey: Bill was not only a great receiver but a great clutch hitter. He was adept at knocking in runs when they counted the most.

First Base

Lou Gehrig: Lou combined two sterling qualities and combined them well. He was a superb fielder and a great hitter, one of the greatest hitters who ever lived. Lou can't be kept off any all-star team.

Second Base

Eddie Collins: The greatest second baseman who ever lived. His fighting spirit was contagious. Eddie was a great base runner as well as one of the topnotch hitters. He played baseball as it should be played, making the tough ones look easy. Eddie would be my team captain.

Shortstop

Honus Wagner: I was never fortunate enough to see much of "Hans." He was in the National League, but I did see him one year at Louisville. John McGraw said he was the greatest short-stop he ever saw and I'll take McGraw's word for that.

Third Base

Jimmy Collins: Jimmy was another Lajoie, slick and fast. He had a great knack of coming up with the ball between hops. He also was a great base runner and a timely hitter.

Left Field

Babe Ruth: Babe was truly a great slugger, and we may never again see his equal. He was also a great fielder, which sometimes is overlooked in view of his tremendous hitting. There's something else about Ruth that few people realize, but to me he could run from first to third on a hit-and-run play faster than any man I ever saw.

Center Field

Tris Speaker: Great fielder and great hitter. There never was anybody who could play a hitter like Tris, coming in or running back and pivoting like a true athlete.

Right Field

Ty Cobb: Greatest base runner baseball ever saw. In value to a team alone, Ty was the greatest player who ever lived. He won the American League batting title nine straight years, lost it one year and then won it again for the next three. Ty once said, "The baseline belongs to me," and he meant it. A fearless runner who cared nothing for his own safety.

At the end of each season sports writers and fans speculate as to the outstanding players in each club. There is, of course, a wide variety of choices. In my opinion it is rather difficult to select an all-star team covering one season only, as a more fair selection should cover several seasons. The following list of players that I have chosen as today's all-star team has been based on each player's record during the past five years.

CANDIDATES FOR TODAY'S ALL-STAR TEAM
Pitchers

Bob Lemon: Bob won 53 games in three years. He was converted from a good third baseman to a great pitcher. He has great control and a fast ball. He has struck out 285 batters the last two years.

Hal Newhouser: Hal is the best left-hander in the American League, winning 136 games in the last six years. Hal uses his head when he pitches, always trying to outsmart the batter. His control is fine to watch.

Ellis Kinder: This fellow led the American League last year with an amazing winning percentage of .793, winning 23 games and losing only 6. Kinder deserves a rating with the best.

Harry Brecheen: Harry is called "The Cat" and for good reason. He is quick and alert and a great left-hander. He has won 96 games in the last six years.

Howie Pollet: Although I haven't seen Pollet, I can't omit him from any present-day team. He is one of the game's smartest left-handers, winning 33 games the last two years and 53 the last four seasons for the Cardinals.

Joe Page: Because of his great record, Joe Page should be nominated as a relief hurler. He is the best I ever saw. Relief pitching, as such, was late coming into baseball, and Fred Marberry of Washington was the first one of note in my memory. Another was Fireman John Murphy of the Yankees.

Catchers

Birdie Tebbetts: Great receiver and thrower. He is a good hitter and a clever handler of young pitchers. He is equal, if not superior, to any catcher in the game today.

Roy Campanella: Although this fellow has been in the big leagues only two years, really only one full year, he cannot be left off any present-day team. He is one of the greatest young catchers I have ever watched. He's got a great head on his shoulders and works behind the plate like a veteran. He hit .287 for Brooklyn last year and batted in 82 runs.

First Base

Stan Musial: Stan has done such fine work with the bat and around the bag for the Cardinals that he deserves a high place on this all-star team. Truly, he is one of the great batsmen in baseball history.

Second Base

Bobby Doerr: For the last few years Joe Gordon of Cleveland and Doerr of Boston have been the leading second basemen, but at this time I pick Doerr because he's younger, faster and drives in more runs. Doerr is an excellent double-play man. In the last four years, Doerr has batted in 431 runs, averaging more than 100 each year.

Shortstop

Vernon Stephens: Picked over any other shortstop, such as Boudreau, because of his hitting and fielding prowess. This combination makes him the standout. He tied with Ted Williams in runs batted in for last year, each driving home 159 runs.

Third Base

Robert Elliott: This fellow has a great throwing arm and that quality plus his hitting gives him this recognition. Our own Bob Dillinger is a close second.

Left Field

Ted Williams: One of baseball's great hitters and also a crack fielder, a fact that is overlooked too often. Since he joined Boston in 1939, Ted has batted in more than 100 runs each year. In fact, his total for eight major league seasons is 1,038 runs batted in.

Center Field

Joe DiMaggio: This fellow is everything that everybody says about him. And Joe's true value to his team is his ability to inspire his team mates. A great leader and competitor. He ranks with the great Babe Ruth in the ability to draw people into the ball parks. His wonderful throwing arm makes him a threat on defense as well as offense.

Right Field

Ralph Kiner: If any man today is capable of breaking Ruth's home-run record of 60 in one season, it is Ralph Kiner. He is the leading home-run hitter right now and also a mighty good fielder. Kiner hit 54 homers in 1949; 40 in 1948; 51 in 1947.

CHAPTER 23

STORIES AND ANECDOTES

AMERICAN STORY-TELLERS, poets, and song writers have not neglected our national game. Ring Lardner, Damon Runyon, and many others were masters of characters and plots such as we see every day in our grandstands.

Some of the characters who follow the game would do justice to anything O. Henry ever wrote. Mark Twain understood the love for baseball in every Tom Sawyer and Huckleberry Finn in our country.

Will Rogers a Great Baseball Fan

Will Rogers, one of our most beloved baseball fans, was an after-dinner speaker at the Friars Club in New York when Judge Kenesaw Mountain Landis was an honored guest. Will always made a home run when he was batting at a banquet.

"Take this man Landis," he said. "Well, he comes from the bench—he is the only man in the history of the world that ever jumped from the bench into the grandstand.

"I happened to be here one day when the sun was shining on a certain afternoon over Coogan's Bluff," continued Will, referring to a Giant-Yankee World Series game he had witnessed in 1922 at the Polo Grounds. "I thought at that time when those people were howling around his [Judge Landis] box that his next jump would be from the box to the scaffold."

Rogers was referring to the second game of that series,

which was called by the chief umpire because of darkness, although nearly half an hour of daylight remained. Indignant fans booed Judge Landis under the impression that he had advised the umpires to call the game. Soon after the game the Judge ordered the receipts turned over to New York charities.

On another occasion Will Rogers appeared with Fred Stone, a baseball fan like our friend George M. Cohan, at the civic banquet in Los Angeles, which turned out to be a sort of baseball rally. Its purpose was to arouse the Californians to fever heat over the national game.

For an hour the diners were held spellbound by Rogers and Stone. Rogers imitated Stone's dances, and Stone did Rogers' rope stuff. When Will returned to his chair at the table, he found it occupied by another man.

"You're in the wrong seat," Will grinned.

The stranger wanted to argue.

"I'm playin' this base," exclaimed Will with his infectious grin. "You're out in center field." The obstinate gentleman soon found himself out in the center of the floor, much to the delight of the banqueters.

"I guess I made a hit," Rogers whispered to the others at the table, "but that other feller's makin' a home run."

A Political Secret Revealed

I am going to tell you a political secret: I'll let "the cat out of the bag." When Branch Rickey was about to leave the St. Louis Cardinals to go to the Brooklyn Dodgers, the political insiders in St. Louis tried to get him to stay in Missouri and run for governor. Rickey, on the other hand, decided to stay with baseball.

Here's a historic "if": If Branch Rickey had accepted the opportunity to run for governor of Missouri, he would have been overwhelmingly elected. "If" he had been governor of Missouri during the time President Roosevelt was looking for a vice-presidential running mate, Robert Hannegan, the campaign manager, would probably have backed "Governor Rickey." Rickey would have won with Roosevelt.

What does all this sum up to? Just this: Vice President Rickey would have become President of the United States upon the death of Franklin Roosevelt.

My prediction, from my long years of intimate acquaintance with Rickey and knowing his great ability, is this: Branch Rickey would have made good in the White House and been elected by the people in 1948, and thus would be President of the United States during 1948 to 1952.

I'm not going to predict who might be our President from 1952-1956 because I do not know whether my friend, Branch Rickey, would have accepted a second nomination. But "if" he did, on his record, I believe he would win the pennant again.

Branch Rickey, in his modesty, may deny this, but he cannot stop me from saying that he is a man of great administrative ability, unimpeachable character, and an honor not only to our national game but to the nation. He is in every sense an upright American!

Presidents Ardent Baseball Fans

Many of our Presidents have been baseball fans. The first one I recall was Grover Cleveland, when I was playing with the Washington Senators in 1886. President Harrison, who followed Cleveland's first term, was a loyal fan. Then came President McKinley and that great sportsman, the beloved Teddy Roosevelt. President Taft threw out the first ball to open the season, and every President since then has continued the custom.

Presidents Wilson, Coolidge and Hoover have been loyal supporters of our national game. President Franklin D. Roosevelt, through the difficult years of depression and World War II, and even in the greatest crises, always wanted to know:

"What's the score?" President Truman is also an ardent supporter of our national game.

Among the tens of thousands of old-time fans who were my friends was Al Smith. He was one of the most loyal rooters that our national game has known. Brought up as a kid playing baseball on the sidewalks of New York, he entered into the game of politics with the same fervid American spirit with which he played baseball.

Rising to the governorship of New York State, Al entered the national series for President of the United States. His opponent, Herbert Hoover, was another baseball fan. Fan Hoover fanned Al out. And that's my story and I'll stick to it.

Good Sportsmanship Among Players

At a recent testimonial dinner to Bill Corum, the famous sports writer who has taken over the Kentucky Derby, Manager Burt Shotton, of the Brooklyn Dodgers, found himself at the same table with Manager Casey Stengel, of the champion Yankees. Shotton extended his hand cordially to the man who had beaten him in the World Series.

"Burt," exclaimed the genial Stengel, "I love you in the winter as I love you in the spring—but that doesn't go for the fall."

Good sportsmanship is an American characteristic. This story by Leonard Lyons is a typical example of the American spirit. Commissioner Chandler was guest of honor at the City Athletic Club in New York and introduced the sports notables. When he came to Leo Durocher, whom he once suspended for a full season, the guests broke into resounding cheers.

"This proves the truth contained in the Bible," Commissioner Chandler remarked when the ovation subsided. "There's more rejoicing over the one that was lost and returned than over the other ninety and nine."

A well-known American author has sent me these two limericks:

> There was a male Babe by the name of Ruth,
> A famous Babe born without a tooth;
>   He'd catch a ball on the hoof
>   And with a big poof
> Blow the sphere right over the roof!

* * *

> There was a tall man by the name of Mack,
> He was so slim he could crawl through a crack;
>   When he made an attack
>   His foe he'd shellack
> As the Pennant flag to the "A's" came back!

Ambitions of School Children

A schoolteacher in Philadelphia asked each of her pupils to stand up and answer the question: "What do you want most in the world?"

One enterprising boy said, "An atomic bomb." Another said, "The biggest airplane ever made." Still another wanted "world peace."

A little girl wanted "a daddy—I lost mine in the war." Another replied, "I want my sick mother to get well."

So it went, down the line until the last little boy was reached. He had had more time to think. Throwing his shoulders back manfully, he exclaimed, "What I want most in the world is to see the Philadelphia Athletics win another pennant."

What Our British Cousins Think of Us

America's national game is a mystery to the Englishman. To him it is more confusing than a jigsaw puzzle, even more confusing than hearing an American "try to talk the English language."

A group of Britishers were gathered in a London club, discussing the future of the British Empire, America, and the world in general.

"If these bally Americans would take time off from their bloody national game and learn to play cricket, we might be able to understand them," remarked an English statesman.

"Baseball!" bawled an old Tory. "It is sheer madness. A huge crowd gathers to watch some men in their underwear chase each other around to take a ball away from each other. What's the ball worth anyway after they get it? Not more than a few shillings. It is the greatest nonsense since the Americans issued their Declaration of Independence!"

King George of England, Winston Churchill, and the Duke of Windsor, I am told, get real enjoyment in witnessing our national game. The Canadians likewise are enthusiastically baseball-minded. All nations and their leaders who admire individual initiative like baseball.

Earth's Last Ball Game

Walter Pulitzer produced a parody on Kipling's poem "L'Envoi," when he wrote the following lines:

> When earth's last ball game is finished,
>   And the crowd has passed from the stand,
> When the youngest fan has subsided
>   And gone to the Promised Land
> We shall rest—and gosh!—we shall need it,
>   Knock off for a season or two,
> Till the greatest of all the Series
>   Shall set us to root anew.
>
> Then all the fans shall be happy,
>   They shall sit in a shady stand,
> They shall smoke their clear Havanas
>   And list to the heavenly band;
> They shall see real stars in the diamond,
>   And watch them swat the ball,
> They shall cheer for an age at a sitting
>   And never grow tired at all.

And no one shall be a knocker,
    And none of the fans shall blame,
For no one shall make an error
    And no one shall call out "Shame!"
"You thief!" "You robber!" "You lobster!"
    But each in his cushioned seat
Shall call it a just decision
    And know that his team will beat!

"All Men Die—But the Record Lives"

Grantland Rice, the dean of sports writers, wrote this poem entitled "The Record"[1] and recorded in the *Fanthology:*

When the game is done and the players creep
One by one to the League of Sleep,
Deep in the night they may not know
The way of the fight, the fate of the foe.
The cheer that passed, and applauding hands,
Are stilled at last—but the Record stands.

The errors made, and the base hits wrought;
Here the race was run! There the fight was fought!
Yet the game is done when the sun sinks low
And one by one from the field they go;
Their day has passed through the Twilight Gates,
But the Scroll is cast—and the Record waits.

So take, my lad, what the Great Game gives,
For all men die—but the Record lives.

---

[1] Used by permission.

CHAPTER 24

WHAT WILL THE FUTURE BRING?

T̲HE DOOR to a baseball career is wide open to any young man who wants to make it his profession. As you will realize after you have read about my long career in baseball, it was my lifelong desire to follow the game. Even as a small boy, I knew I wanted to become a professional and, as I grew up, my ambition was to become a big league player.

Perseverance, industry, courage, and indomitable will are the motive power of ambition. Integrity and uprightness are the foundations of every successful lifework. No matter which profession a man follows, he should possess these qualities.

Baseball, like every other pursuit in life, must have ambition and ability back of it. The young aspirant to it generally begins to play on the sand lots near his home. Even the sand-lot teams today play off a national championship contest at the end of each season.

The next step from the sand-lot team is a public-school team, then the high-school team. A player under eighteen years of age may join the American Legion Junior Baseball club in his home town, where he has an opportunity to get into a nationwide Junior World Series.

If a young player has the stuff in him, it won't take the scouts long to discover him. Once they are aware of him, he may jump directly into the big leagues as many other stars have done, or he may come up through the minor leagues.

Physically, mentally, and morally, baseball affords great opportunities for a boy's future. Economically, it is also a good vocation to follow, for there is many a young man getting anywhere from $5,000 to $100,000 for working only seven months of the year.

But a young man must realize that his success depends entirely on his own ability, as it does in every other vocation. Every player now in the big leagues had to prove his own value before he reached the higher salary brackets. Every one of them started from the bottom, and made the grade on his own merits.

High-School Boy Gets $100,000

In 1950 the Pittsburgh Pirates paid a record $100,000 for an eighteen-year-old southpaw pitcher right out of high school —Paul Pettit, a strapping 6 foot 2 inch, 205 pounder. This is believed to be the highest price ever paid a rookie untried in pro baseball.

This unprecedented price for a schoolboy rookie focuses on Pettit the spotlight of the baseball world. He first commanded attention by his amazing pitching record for his high-school team and for the American Legion Junior team in Los Angeles and Long Beach. He pitched six no-hitters, and has won seventy-three games. In the last three years he has lost but fifteen.

Pettit is the son of a night watchman in Long Beach, California. The Pirates' general manager, Roy Hamey, states that they are very happy to land the boy. "Our scouts," Roy says, "have watched him closely for a long time. We rate him highly, and believe he has a chance to become an outstanding pitcher in the majors. He will be given an opportunity in New Orleans during 1950, and will be brought up to the Pirates in 1951."

The terms of payment for this lad are very interesting:

Under the original contract held by a motion-picture agent, he was bought for both pictures and baseball for $85,000. The Pirates then bought out this contract, assuming the obligations and adding $15,000 to the deal, thus making the total price $100,000.

The payments provide $10,000 on signing of contract; a bonus of $50,000; a three-year salary of $18,000; $5,000 for his father; $1,500 for his attorney; ten per cent of screen profits; and $750 for honeymoon expenses if and when he marries! Out of this amount, however, must come his agent's commission. Inasmuch as Paul is still a minor, the transaction was made through his father.

"What are you going to do with all that money?" young Pettit was asked.

"Nothing," he replied. "I can't touch it until I'm twenty-one."

Sports Authority Assails Bonus Orgy

Arthur Daley, in his column, "Sports of the Times" in *The New York Times,* stated a short time ago that the bonus system of gambling on rookies results in some incongruous situations, and I am inclined to agree with him. "Three baseball players will each be paid approximately $100,000 this year," he says. "They are Joe DiMaggio, who is one of the great outfielders of all time; Ted Williams, who is the finest natural hitter of this generation, and Paul Pettit, who is eighteen years old." Here we have Pettit stepping right into the top group with DiMaggio and Williams a few days after he is graduated from high school!

"DiMaggio will more than earn his salary. So will Williams. But Pettit will pitch for New Orleans and then will join the Pittsburgh Pirates, for better or worse, in 1951," continued Mr. Daley.

Everyone will certainly wish young Pettit the best of good

luck. Now that he has been given the opportunity of a life-time, it is sincerely hoped that he will make good. But I personally do think it is dangerous to start a boy off in the top brackets before he has proved his worth.

The man who has proved his value as the greatest gate attraction since Babe Ruth is Jackie Robinson, and his salary for 1950 is $35,000. Tommy Henrich, another great ball player, is getting around $40,000. Ralph Kiner, one of the best players ever with the Pittsburgh Pirates, is making about $50,000. Pee Wee Reese, of the Brooklyn Dodgers, and one of the greatest shortstops in baseball, is earning about $30,000.

Big players should get as high salaries as a team can afford; but I do not believe in drawing lottery tickets out of a hat through the bonus system. The Boston Braves tried this in 1948 when they paid Johnny Antonelli, a left-handed schoolboy, $75,000, and he pitched only four innings in an entire season. He bettered that record a year later when he pitched ninety-six innings and won three and lost seven games. It is possible he may yet work his way to stardom.

Another of these $75,000 bonus lads is Frank House, catcher with the Detroit Tigers, who is still in his apprenticeship. Dick Wakefield, who was given a $52,000 bonus by the Tigers, bogged down after a brilliant flash and was sold to the Yankees, where he is now being given his opportunity to demonstrate his value.

About thirty-five years ago an eighteen-year-old southpaw was being signed by Jack Dunn, manager of the Baltimore Orioles.

"I'll pay you $600 for the season," Manager Dunn said.

"Do you mean I'm gonna be *paid* to play baseball?" the amazed youngster asked.

That eighteen-year-old kid was Babe Ruth! Eighteen-year-old Pettit will get, for his first year in organized baseball, $99,400 more than the "King of Swat" received at the start of his career.

Big Rewards for Good Service

All the great players started at the bottom and worked their way up. It is gratifying to me to know that I gave some of them their first chance. As they showed progress, many of them got into the high brackets on a basis of the services they performed.

There are worth-while opportunities in baseball for boys who are willing to prove their talents. The big leagues are looking for such boys every day. The need for new players is so great and the competition so strong that big rewards are offered.

Within a few years all the star players now in the big leagues will have passed their years of usefulness in baseball and will retire to other lines of business. Replacements will have to be made and new jobs will be available for those who show promise.

Starting wages in baseball are larger than those in most occupations, and likewise the advance is much more rapid. This is one of the great advantages in our individual initiative and free enterprise system. It gives every person an incentive to do his best and get the largest rewards for his labors.

The old saying, "Competition is the life of trade," is truer today than ever before. It is the fairest system ever devised by the minds of men. Systems that abolish the incentive motive are robbing men of both incentive and opportunity to improve their condition; they rob one of hope, enterprise, determination and courage which are the propelling force behind human progress.

Incentive is power! Without it we become laggards and beasts of burden, mere cogs in a machine with no possibility of freeing ourselves from economic serfdom.

We are entering upon the last half of a century of tremendous possibilities. Discoveries and inventions can remake the world. We can use them to solve our problems or to destroy ourselves and the world in which we live.

We Americans and our fellow Canadians are proud of our heritage. We are not going to throw away our freedom and opportunities and rights for self-development. We shall have our problems and we shall solve them.

What will the future bring? The future will be just what we make it. I have implicit faith, for I know whatever temporary digressions we may make, the destiny of man is onward and upward—always toward the goal.

Firsts in Baseball

There are so many interesting "firsts" in the history of baseball that these facts have been compiled in chronological order to show the origin and development of our national game.

1830—"Town ball," an Americanized version of the old "rounders," became a popular pastime in New England.

1834—Photograph of boys playing the game on Boston Commons was printed in the *Book of Sports*.

1839—Game established by Abner Doubleday on the basic principles of our present national game, took place in Cooperstown, New York. Now the seat of the Baseball Hall of Fame and Museum and known as the "Birthplace of Baseball."

1845—Rules of play establishing the foundation for modern baseball were made by Alexander Cartwright, known as the "Father of Baseball," with nine men on a team and bases ninety feet apart.

1846—Game between two organized rival teams was played under the Cartwright rules at Hoboken, New Jersey. Competing teams were the Knickerbockers vs. New York.

1848—Games in Boston and Philadelphia played under their own rules, which differed from those known as the New York Game.

1849—Baseball uniforms were worn by the Knickerbockers: white polo shirts and blue trousers.

1856—Team in Chicago, known as the Unions, adopted the rules of the New York Game.

1857—Baseball association was organized in New York as the National Association of Baseball Players. Representing twenty-five amateur teams, they adopted the nine-inning game which abolished the plan whereby the game ended when one of the teams had scored twenty-one runs.

1859—Intercollegiate game played between Amherst and Williams. Amherst won 73-32.

1861—Game was first played by soldiers in Army camps during the Civil War. This introduced the game to men from all the states.

1863—Box scoring system was established by Henry Chadwick. This required the runner to touch each base as he passed around the diamond.

1864—Rule requiring a fly ball to be caught on the fly and not on the bound as hitherto played was adopted. Foul flies could still be caught on the bound as outs.

1867—Experiments made with curve balls, William (Candy) Cummings of Brooklyn giving exhibitions as tricks in magic, but these did not appear in baseball games until some years later.

1869—First professional baseball team, the Cincinnati Red Stockings. It was the first to wear the knee-length uniform. Played fifty-seven games without being defeated.

1871—First professional league was the National Association of Professional Baseball Players with clubs in ten cities.

1872—Adoption of an official baseball, specifying the weight and circumference used today.

1873—First pitcher and first player to be acclaimed as a hero in the streets was Albert G. Spalding, who later founded the first great sporting-goods house.

1874—First pitcher to use the curve in a college game was Charles Hammond Avery, of Yale, in a Yale-Harvard game at Saratoga, New York. First shutout ever scored in a college game, 4-0. Claims have been made that this antedated William Cummings' first use of the curve in a professional game.

1874—Tour by ball teams to a foreign country when Al Spalding took the Bostons and the Athletics to England for exhibitions to introduce America's national game.

1875—First no-hit game recorded was between Philadelphia and Chicago. Joseph Borden pitched for Philadelphia and won, 4-0.

1876—National League was organized with eight clubs and a league schedule of seventy games for each club.

1876—First teams in the new National League were Hartford, Louisville, Cincinnati, New York Mutuals, Chicago, Old Athletics of Philadelphia, Boston, St. Louis.

1876—National League pennant winner, Chicago, under the management of Albert G. Spalding.

1876—National League batting champion, Barnes of Chicago, with a .403 season's record.

1877—First minor league, called the International Association, was organized.

1880—First no-hit, no-run game in professional history was played between Worcester and Cleveland, when John Lee Richmond, of Brown University, a curve pitcher, appeared for the first time with Worcester. Not a Cleveland man reached first base.

1881—Important change in pitching was made when the box was moved back from forty-five feet to a distance of fifty feet. This was the first time that pitchers were allowed to throw sidearm as well as underhand.

1884—First time the pitchers were allowed to use the overhand delivery. These changes in rules, with the introduction of the curve, revolutionized pitching and made it a science.

1885—Use of chest protectors by catchers.

1886—Rule that stopped the old custom of a batsman being allowed to call for a high or low ball.

1888—Round-the-world tour of America's national game. It was made by the Chicago White Stockings and a picked team from seven National League clubs under direction of Albert G. Spalding.

1893—Adoption of the sixty-feet-six-inch pitching distance. This was necessitated by the new fast technique developed by pitchers.

1895—First time the foul tip was ruled a strike. This tended to shorten the length of the game.

1896—The schedule of the National League was extended to 154 games, thus lengthening the season.

1901—First American League came into action. Pennant won by Chicago under the management of Clark C. Griffith. Second pennant the next year was won by the Philadelphia Athletics under Connie Mack.

1901—American League batting champion, Napoleon Lajoie, of the Philadelphia Athletics, .405.

1903—First World Series between National and American Leagues won by Boston (AL) 5 to Pittsburgh (NL) 3. Not under the Brush rules.

1904—First Junior World Series between the International League and the American Association was won by Buffalo of the Internationals against St. Paul (AA) 2-1.

1905—First postseason play-off between the rival leagues permanently establishing the present-day World Series for World Championship. The Boston Americans won five games to three against the Pittsburgh Nationals.

1907—Announcement of the Mills Commission that Cooperstown, New York, was the birthplace of baseball in 1839.

1910—First use of the "live" ball. The old dead ball went out of existence when the cork-center ball appeared. This was the beginning of the new era in home runs. Ball used today has a core 13/16″ in diameter made of cork composition containing a minute percentage of rubber.

1910—First President to throw out the first baseball, opening the season, was William Howard Taft.

1921—High Commissioner in Baseball appointed by the major leagues with absolute authority to protect the game. Judge Kenesaw Mountain Landis was appointed.

1933—First all-star game was played in Chicago with picked teams from the National and the American Leagues.

1935—First night game in the major leagues was played in Cincinnati. Night games under powerful electric lights have greatly increased the yearly attendance.

1939—Establishment of a Baseball Hall of Fame and Museum.

1945—Change in the High Commission of Baseball. Upon the death of Judge Landis, who had served brilliantly for twenty-four years, United States Senator Albert Chandler, of Kentucky, was appointed as successor.

1950—Jubilee Year of our national game: Seventy-fifth (Diamond) Anniversary of the National League; Fiftieth (Golden) Anniversary of the American League; Fiftieth (Golden) Anniversary of the National Association of Baseball Players representing the minor leagues; Fiftieth (Golden) Anniversary of Connie Mack as manager of the Philadelphia Athletics.

Major League All-Time Records

First in number of games played, Ty Cobb, 3,033.
First in number of times at bat, Ty Cobb, 11,429.
First in single base hits, Ty Cobb, 3,052.
First in batting average for ten or more years, Ty Cobb, .367.
First in safe hits, Ty Cobb, 4,191.
First in total bases, Ty Cobb, 5,863.
First in total number of runs, Ty Cobb, 2,244.
First in total stolen bases, Ty Cobb, 892.
First in stolen bases for one season (1915), Ty Cobb, 96.
First in home runs, Babe Ruth, 714.
First in home runs in one season, Babe Ruth, 60.
First in runs batted in, Babe Ruth, 2,209.
First in number of base on balls, Babe Rube, 2,056.
First in bases on balls in one season, Babe Ruth, 170.
First in total bases for one season (1921), Babe Ruth, 457.
First in long hits (other than home runs), Babe Ruth, 506, two-baggers; 136 three-baggers.

First in length of service as player, Eddie Collins, 25 years.

First in consecutive games played, Lou Gehrig, 2,130.

First in home runs in one game, Lou Gehrig, New York Yankees, 4 in 1932; Lowe, Boston Nationals, 4 in 1894; Delahanty, Philadelphia Nationals, 4 in 1896; Klein, Philadelphia Nationals, 4 (10 innings) in 1936; Seerey, Chicago Americans, 4 (11 innings) in 1948.

First in consecutive games batted safely, Joe DiMaggio, 56 in 1941.

First in consecutive hits in one game, Wilbert Robinson, Baltimore, 7 hits in one game in 1892.

First in hits in succession, Frank Higgins, Boston Americans, 12 successive hits in 1938.

First in hits for one season, George Sisler, St. Louis Americans, 257 hits in 1920.

First in 3-base hits, Sam Crawford, Cincinnati Nationals and Detroit Americans, 312.

First in 3-base hits in one season, J. Owen Wilson, Pittsburgh Nationals, 36 in 1912.

First in 2-base hits, Tris Speaker, Boston, Cleveland, Washington, Philadelphia Americans, 793.

First in 2-base hits in one season, Earl Webb, Boston Americans, 67 in 1931.

First in bases on balls in one game, Jimmy Foxx, Boston Americans, 6 in 1936.

First in fewest strike-outs in one season in 150 or more games, Joe Sewell, Cleveland Americans, struck out only 4 times in 1925 and 1929.

First in singles in one season, Lloyd Waner, Pittsburgh Nationals, 198 in 1927.

First in runs batted in during one season, Hack Wilson, Chicago Nationals, 190 in 1930.

First in runs batted in during one game, James Bottomley, St. Louis Nationals, 12 in game against Brooklyn Dodgers in 1924.

First in consecutive years as manager of one club, Connie Mack, 50 years with the Philadelphia Athletics.

First in total bases in one game, Bobby Lowe, Boston Nationals, 17 in 1894—Ed Delahanty, Philadelphia Nationals, 17 in 1896. Each got four home runs and one single.

First in batting average for one season in nineteenth century, Hugh Duffy, Boston Nationals, batted .438 in 1894.

First in batting average for one season in twentieth century, Rogers Hornsby, St. Louis Nationals, .424 in 1924.

First in times at bat in one season, Forrest Jensen, Pittsburgh Nationals, 696 times in 1936.

First in hitting into double plays in one season, Ernie Lombardi, Cincinnati Nationals, 30 in 1938.

First in hitting into double plays in one game, Goose Goslin, Detroit Americans, 4 in one game in 1934.

First in Natonal League home runs, Mel Ott, New York Giants for 22 years, 2,876 hits and 511 home runs.

First in home run record for one season, New York Giants in 1947, with 221 home runs; Johnny Mize, high man with 51 home runs; Willard Marshall, 36; Walter Cooper, 35; Bobby Thomson, 29.

First to break records with longest throw, Sheldon Lejeune, who threw a baseball 426 feet 9½ inches in Cincinnati in 1910.

First in number of games pitched is Cy Young, with a total of 906 (516 in National League and 390 in American League).

First in number of games won is Cy Young, 511.

First in highest percentage of victories in modern baseball is Lefty Grove, .680.

First in percentage of victories in old-time baseball is Al Spalding, .790.

First in number of shutouts is Walter Johnson, Washington pitcher, 113.

First in number of strike-outs is Walter Johnson, 3,497.

First in consecutive shutout innings, Walter Johnson, 56 in 1913.

First in shutout games in one season is Grover Alexander, 16 in 1916.

First in number of innings pitched in one season, Ed Walsh, Chicago Americans, 464 in 1908.

First in games won in one season, Jack Chesbro, New York Yankees, 41 in 1904.

First in strike-outs in one season, Bob Feller, Cleveland Americans, 348 in 1946.

First in strike-outs in one 9-inning game, Bob Feller, 18 in one
game in 1938.

First in consecutive games won, Rube Marquard, New York
Giants, 19 straight in 1912; Tim O'Keefe, New York Nationals,
19 straight in 1888.

First in number of games pitched in one season, Ace Adams, New
York Giants, 70 in 1943.

First in pitching complete games in one season, Jack Chesbro,
New York Yankees, 48 in 1904.

First in pitching two consecutive no-hit games, Johnny Vander
Meer, Cincinnati Nationals, two straight no-hit victories in
1938.

First to pitch eight one-hit games, Bob Feller, Cleveland.

First no-hit game pitched in 1875 by Joe Borden.

First pitchers to hurl a no-hit game against each other, were Fred
Toney and Jim Vaughn in 1917. The tie was broken in tenth
inning when Toney's team got a hit.

First pitcher with only one arm to hurl a no-hit game was Hugh
Daily in 1883. He won 72 games during his career. He struck out
19 men in one game.

First one-legged player to pitch a game was Bert Shepard, for the
Washington Senators in 1945. (Note: There have been several
one-eyed players and a large number who wore spectacles.)

Which pitcher had the greatest speed? This controversy may be
settled by the record tests. Bob Feller holds a record of 145 feet
a second. This means the ball would pass the 60 feet from pitcher's box to batter's plate in less than half a second—a flash of the
eye. It further means that the ball is traveling at the rate of 98.6
miles an hour. This test was made in the Washington baseball
park in 1946, with an Army measuring device sensitive enough to
record the speed of a shot from a rifle.

Feller's 145 feet a second beat all previous records. Atley Donald, a pitcher for the New York Yankees, threw a baseball 139
feet a second at the Cleveland Stadium in 1939. Dee Miles, with
the Philadelphia Athletics, earlier made a record of 136 feet a
second. The record of Christy Mathewson, when he was with the
New York Giants, was 134 feet a second.

I have been looking over the records of 28 no-hit games, in which pitchers have starred from two to three times. There is a much longer list of one-time no-hit pitchers.

Heading the three no-hitter list, we find Cy Young, of Cleveland and Boston in the American League, and Larry Corcoran, of Chicago in the National League.

The two no-hitter champions are Christy Mathewson, of the New York Nationals; Bob Feller, of the Cleveland Americans; John Vander Meer, of the Cincinnati Nationals; Hub Leonard, of the Boston Americans; Thomas Hughes, of New York Americans and Boston Nationals; Addie Joss, of the Cleveland Americans; Frank Smith, of the Chicago Americans.

When we go back to some of the old-timers of the last century, we find among two-game no-hitters: James Galvin, of the Buffalo Nationals; Albert Atkinson, of the old Philadelphia AA; William Terry, of the old Brooklyn AA, and Theodore Breitenstein, of St. Louis and Cincinnati.

NATIONAL BASEBALL HALL OF FAME

Candidates for the Hall of Fame are chosen on the basis of playing ability, integrity, sportsmanship, character, and their contribution to the team on which they played and to baseball in general. To be elected to this honor, a player must receive at least seventy-five per cent of the votes cast. The electors are members of the Baseball Writers' Association in America of at least ten years' standing. Only players are eligible who must be (1) retired as an active player for at least a year; (2) playing career must fall within the previous twenty-five-year span. The election of the old-time players and the creation of the Honor Rolls is made direct by the Baseball Hall of Fame Committee.

IMMORTALS

ALEXANDER, Grover C.

ANSON (Cap), Adrian C.

BRESNAHAN, Roger

BROUTHERS, Dan

BROWN, Mordecai Peter

BULKELEY, Morgan G.

BURKETT, Jesse

CARTWRIGHT, Alexander J., Jr.

CHADWICK, Henry

CHANCE, Frank

CHESBRO, John

CLARKE, Fred

COBB, Tyrus R.

COCHRANE (Mickey), Gordon S.

COLLINS, Edward T.

COLLINS, James

COMISKEY, Charles A.

CUMMINGS (Candy), W. A.

DELAHANTY, Ed

DUFFY, Hugh

EVERS, John J.

EWING (Buck), William B.

FRISCH, Frank

GEHRIG, Lou

GEHRINGER, Charles

GRIFFITH, Clark

GROVE (Lefty), Robert M.

HORNSBY, Rogers

HUBBELL, Carl

JENNINGS, Hugh

JOHNSON, Byron Bancroft

JOHNSON, Walter

KEELER (Wee),Willie

KELLY (King), Mike

LAJOIE, Napoleon

LANDIS, Kenesaw Mountain

MACK, Connie

MATHEWSON, Christy

McCARTHY, Tom

McGINNITY, Joseph

McGRAW, John J.

NICHOLS (Kid), Charles A.

O'ROURKE, James

PENNOCK, Herbert J.

PLANK, Edward

RADBOURNE (Old Hoss), Charlie

ROBINSON, Wilbert

RUTH (Babe), George Herman

SISLER, George

SPALDING, Albert G.

SPEAKER, Tris

TINKER, Joseph

TRAYNOR (Pie), Harold J.

WADDELL (Rube), Edward

WAGNER, Honus

WALSH, Edward

WRIGHT, George

YOUNG (Cy), Denton T.

HONOR MEN

Managers

Carrigan, William	Huggins, Miller J.	Ward, John M.
Hanlon, Edward	Selee, Frank	

Executives

Barnard, E. S.	Dreyfuss, Barney	Quinn (Bob), J. A.
Barrow, Edward G.	Ebbets, Charles	Soden, Arthur
Bruce, John J.	Herrmann, August	Young, Nicholas
Brush, John T.	Heydler, John A.	

Umpires

Connolly, Thomas	Gaffney, John	Lynch, Thomas
Dinneen, William	Hurst, Timothy	O'Loughlin (Silk),
Emslie, Robert	Klem, William	Francis
Evans, William	Kelly, Honest John	Sheridan, Jack

Writers

Barnes, Walter Boston	Mercer, Sid New York	Slocum, William New York
Cross, Harry E. New York	Murnane, Tim Boston	Tidden, George New York
Hanna, William New York	Richter, Francis C.	Vila, Joe New York
Hough, Frank Philadelphia	Sanborn (Cy), Irving E.—Chicago	
	Sheridan, John B.	

ORGANIZATION OF AMERICA'S NATIONAL GAME

The structure of professional baseball government is a vast organization covering all our states and cities. It is of such magnitude that it maintains "capitals" or headquarters in various parts of the country. The headquarters of the High Commissioner, with former United States Senator Albert B. Chandler presiding over the major National League and American League, and the minor National Association, are in Cincinnati, Ohio.

Ford C. Frick, president of the National League, maintains headquarters in New York. The headquarters of the American League, with William Harridge as its president, are in Chicago. The headquarters of the National Association of Minor Leagues is in Columbus, Ohio, with George M. Trautman as president.

A chain of leagues unites our country into a great baseball democracy. The two major leagues have sixteen teams. The minor leagues had more than four hundred clubs in 1949.

National League (in order of their standing as they entered the 1950 season): Brooklyn, St. Louis, Philadelphia, Boston, New York, Pittsburgh, Cincinnati, Chicago.

American League (in order of their standing as they entered the 1950 season): New York, Boston, Cleveland, Detroit, Philadelphia, Chicago, St. Louis, Washington.

The leading minor leagues (in order of their standing as they entered the 1950 season) are:

American Association (AAA): St. Paul, Indianapolis, Milwaukee, Minneapolis, Kansas City, Columbus, Louisville, Toledo.

International League (AAA): Buffalo, Rochester, Montreal, Jersey City, Toronto, Syracuse, Baltimore, Springfield. The Newark franchise was sold in 1950 by the New York Yankees to the Chicago Cubs and transferred to Springfield, Massachusetts.

Pacific Coast League (AAA): Hollywood, Oakland, Sacramento, San Diego, Seattle, Portland, San Francisco, Los Angeles.

Southern Association (AA): Nashville, Birmingham, Mobile, New Orleans, Atlanta, Little Rock, Memphis, Chattanooga.

Texas League (AA): Fort Worth, Tulsa, Oklahoma City, Shreveport, Dallas, San Antonio, Houston, Beaumont.

Eastern League (A): Albany, Scranton, Wilkes-Barre, Binghamton, Hartford, Williamsport, Elmira, Utica.

South Atlantic League (A): Macon, Savannah, Greenville, Columbus, Jacksonville, Augusta, Charleston, Columbia.

Western League (A): Lincoln, Pueblo, Denver, Des Moines, Omaha, Sioux City.

Central League (A): Dayton, Flint, Grand Rapids, Charleston, Muskegon, Saginaw.

The minor league system, which is also in the nature of farms, is the greatest of all training schools. It is graduated in classes. The 1949 setup:

Class AAA: American Association, with headquarters in St. Paul; International League, with headquarters in Buffalo; Pacific Coast League, headquarters in Hollywood.

Class AA: Southern Association (Nashville); Texas League (Fort Worth).

Class A: Central League (Dayton, Ohio); Eastern League (Albany); South Atlantic League (Macon, Georgia); Western League (Lincoln, Nebraska).

Class B: Big State League (Wichita Falls, Texas); Carolina League (Danville, Virginia); Colonial League (Bristol, Conn.); Florida International (Havana, Cuba); Inter-State League (Allentown, Pa.); New England League (Pawtucket, R. I.); Piedmont League (Lynchburg, Va.); Southeastern League (Pensacola, Fla.); Three-I League (Evanston, Ind.); Tri-State League (Florence, S. C.); Western International (Yakima, Wash.).

Class C: Arizona-Texas League (Phoenix, Ariz.); Border League (Geneva, N. Y.); California League (Bakersville); Canadian American (Quebec); Central Association (Burlington, Iowa); Cotton States (Greenwood, Miss.); East Texas League (Longview); Evangeline League (Houma, La.); Middle Atlantic (First Half, Johnstown, Pa.); Middle Atlantic (Second Half, Erie, Pa.); Northern League (Eau Claire, Wis.); Pioneer League (Twin Falls, Idaho); Sunset League (Las Vegas, Nev.); Western Association (St. Joseph, Mo.); West Texas-North Mexico (Albuquerque).

Class D: Alabama State League (Greenville); Appalachian League (Bluefield, W. Va.); Blue Ridge League (Mt. Airy, N. C.); Eastern Shore League (Easton, Md.); Far West League (Pittsburg, Calif.); Florida State (Gainesville); Georgia; Alabama League (Newnan, Ga.); Georgia-Florida League (Albany, Ga.); Georgia State (Eastman); Kansas-Oklahoma-Missouri League (Independence, Kan.); Kitty League (Owensboro, Ky.); Longhorn League (Big Spring, Tex.); Mississippi-Ohio Valley (Central, Ill.); Mountain States League (Harlan, Ky.); North Atlantic League (Stroudsburg, Pa.); North Carolina State (Thomasville); Ohio-Indiana League (Portsmouth, Ohio); Pony League (Bradford, Pa.); Rio Grande Valley League (Corpus Christi, Texas); Sooner State League (Pauls Valley, Okla.); Tobacco State League (Dunn-Erwin, N. C.); Virginia State League (Franklin); Western Carolina League (Newton-Conover); Wisconsin State League (Oshkosh).

AMERICAN LEGION ROLL OF HONOR

In 1949 there were 3,672 players who had worked their way up from the American Legion Junior teams to the major and minor leagues to the two big leagues.

136 American Legion Players in the American League

New York Yankees—20 Players

Player	Home State	Player	Home State
Bauer, Hank	Illinois	Lindell, Johnny	California
Berra, Yogi	Missouri	Lopat, Ed	Arkansas
Brown, Bobby	California	Mapes, Cliff	California
Casey, Hugh	Georgia	Marshall, Clarence	Wash'gton
Coleman, Gerry	California	Niarhos, Gus	Alabama
Delsing, Jim	Wisconsin	Page, Joe	Pennsylvania
Hiller, Frank	New Jersey	Pillette, Duane	California
Houk, Ralph	Kansas	Raschi, Vic	Massachusetts
Johnson, Bill	Georgia	Sanford, Fred	Utah
Keller, Charlie	Maryland	Silvera, Charlie	California

Cleveland Indians—17 Players

Player	Home State	Player	Home State
Bearden, Gene	Arkansas	Lemon, Bob	California
Boone, Ray	California	Papish, Frank	Colorado
Boudreau, Lou	Illinois	Peck, Hal	Wisconsin
Feller, Bob	Iowa	Rosen, Al	Florida
Gordon, Joe	Oregon	Tresh, Mike	Michigan
Gromek, Steve	Michigan	Tucker, Thurman	Texas
Hegan, Jim	Massachusetts	Vernon, Mickey	Pennsylvania
Keltner, Ken	Wisconsin	Wynn, Early	Alabama
Kennedy, Bob	Illinois		

Boston Red Sox—20 Players

Player	Home State	Player	Home State
Batts, Matt	Texas	O'Brien, Tommy	Alabama
Combs, Merrill	California	Parnell, Mel	Louisiana
DiMaggio, Dom	California	Pesky, Johnny	Oregon
Dobson, Joe	Oklahoma	Quinn, Frank	Connecticut
Doerr, Bobby	California	Stephens, Vern	California
Dorish, Harry	Pennsylvania	Stobbs, Chuck	Virginia
Johnson, Earl	Washington	Tebbetts, Birdie	N. H'pshire
Kramer, Jack	Louisiana	Williams, Ted	California
Martin, Boris	Missouri	Wright, Tom	No. Carolina
Masterson, Walt.	Pennsylvania	Zarilla, Al	California

St. Louis Browns—17 Players

Player	Home State	Player	Home State
Anderson, Andy	Washington	Ostrowski, Joe	Illinois
Dillinger, Bob	California	Platt, Whitey	Florida
Drews, Karl	New York	Priddy, Gerry	California
Garver, Ned	Ohio	Raney, Bob	Michigan
Graham, Jack	California	Schultz, Joe	Missouri
Lehner, Paul	Alabama	Sievers, Roy	Missouri
Lollar, Sherman	Arkansas	Wilson, Jim	Oregon
Lund, Don	Michigan	Wood, Kenneth	No. Carolina
Moss, Les	Oklahoma		

Detroit Tigers—22 Players

Player	Home State	Player	Home State
Bero, Johnny	Michigan	Mullin, Pat	Pennsylvania
Berry, Neil	Michigan	Newhouser, Hal	Michigan
Campbell, Paul	No. Carolina	Overmire, Frank	Michigan
Gray, Ted	Michigan	Riebe, Harvey	Ohio
Houtteman, Art	Michigan	Swift, Bob	Kansas
Hutchinson, Fred	Wash'gton	Stuart, Marlin	Arkansas
Kell, George	Arkansas	Trout, Dizzy	Indiana
Kolloway, Don	Illinois	Trucks, Virgil	Alabama
Kretlow, Louis	Oklahoma	Wakefield, Dick	Illinois
Lake, Eddie	California	Wertz, Vic	Pennsylvania
Lipon, John	Michigan	White, Hal	New York

Philadelphia Athletics—14 Players

Player	Home State	Player	Home State
Brissie, Lou	So. Carolina	McCahan, Bill	Pennsylvania
Chapman, Sam	California	McCoskey, Barney	Michigan
Fain, Ferris	California	Rosar, Buddy	New York
Galan, Augie	California	Scheib, Carl	Pennsylvania
Joost, Eddie	California	Suder, Pete	Pennsylvania
Hausmann, Clem	Texas	Valo, Elmer	Pennsylvania
Majeski, Hank	New York	White, Don	Washington

Chicago White Sox—14 Players

Player	Home State	Player	Home State
Adams, Herbert	Illinois	Kuzava, Bob	Michigan
Baumer, Jim	Oklahoma	Michaels, Cass	Michigan
Cain, Bob	Kansas	Ostrowski, John	Illinois
Grove, Orval	Kansas	Rhawn, Robert	Pennsylvania
Gumpert, Randy	Penna.	Seerey, Pat	Arkansas
Higdon, Bill	Alabama	Tresh, Mike	Michigan
Judson, Howard	Illinois	Wheeler, Don	Minnesota

Washington Senators—12 Players

Player	Home State	Player	Home State
Candini, Milo	California	Lewis, Buddy	North Carolina
Christman, Mark	Missouri	Okrie, Len	Michigan
Coan, Gil	North Carolina	Scarborough, Ray	N. Carolina
Harrist, Earl	Louisiana	Thompson, Forest	N. Carolina
Hudson, Sid	Tennessee	Vollmer, Clyde	Ohio
Haynes, Joe	Georgia	Weigel, Ralph	Ohio

117 American Legion Players in National League

Brooklyn Dodgers—12 Players

Player	Home State	Player	Home State
Barney, Rex	Nebraska	Hodges, Gil	Indiana
Campanella, Roy	Penna.	Martin, Morris	Missouri
Cox, Billy	Pennsylvania	McCormick, Mike	California
Edwards, Bruce	California	Roe, Preacher	Arkansas
Erskine, Carl	Indiana	Reese, Pee Wee	Kentucky
Furillo, Carl	Pennsylvania	Whitman, Dick	Oregon
Hatten, Joe	Iowa		

Boston Braves—19 Players

Player	Home State	Player	Home State
Antonelli, John	New York	Reiser, Pete	Missouri
Barrett, Red	California	Ryan, Connie	Louisiana
Conatser, Clint	California	Salkeld, Bill	California
Crandall, Del	California	Sanders, Ray	Missouri
Dark, Alvin	Louisiana	Sisti, Sibby	New York
Elliott, Glenn	Oregon	Spahn, Warren	New York
Hall, Bob	Michigan	Thompson, Don	N. Carolina
Heath, Jeff	Washington	Torgeson, Earl	Washington
Hogue, Bobby	Florida	Voiselle, Bill	South Carolina
Livingston, Mickey	S. Carolina		

New York Giants—18 Players

Player	Home State	Player	Home State
Ayers, Bill	Georgia	Kerr, Buddy	New York
Culler, Dick	North Carolina	Layton, Lester	Kansas
Franks, Herman	Utah	Lockman, Whitey	N. Carolina
Gordon, Sid	New York	Marshall, Willard	Virginia
Hansen, Andy	Florida	Mueller, Don	Missouri
Higbe, Kirby	South Carolina	Rigney, Bill	California
Hofman, Bobby	Missouri	Thomson, Bob	New York
Jansen, Larry	Oregon	Webb, Sam	Washington, D. C.
Jones, Sheldon	Nebraska	Westrum, Wes	Minnesota

Pittsburgh Pirates—17 Players

Player	Home State	Player	Home State
Bockman, Eddie	California	Masi, Phil	Illinois
Bonham, Ernie*	California	McCullough, Clyde	Tennessee
Chambers, Cliff	Washington	Poat, Ray	Illinois
Dickson, Murry	Kansas	Restelli, Dino	California
Fleming, Les	Texas	Rojek, Stan	New York
Hopp, Johnny	Nebraska	Stevens, Eddie	Texas
Judnich, Walt	California	Werle, Bill	California
Kiner, Ralph	California	Westlake, Wally	California
Main, Forrest	California	* Deceased.	

St. Louis Cardinals—14 Players

Player	Home State	Player	Home State
Brecheen, Harry	Oklahoma	Marion, Marty	Georgia
Diering, Chuck	Missouri	Munger, George	Texas
Garagiola, Joe	Missouri	Musial, Stan	Pennsylvania
Hearn, Jim	Georgia	Nelson, Glenn	Ohio
Jones, Nippy	California	Pollet, Howie	Louisiana
Klein, Lou	Louisiana	Rice, Del	Ohio
Kurowski, Whitey	Penna.	Yuhas, John	Ohio

Cincinnati Reds—14 Players

Player	Home State	Player	Home State
Adams, Bob	California	Merriman, Lloyd	California
Corbitt, Claude	N. Carolina	Peterson, Kent	Utah
Erautt, Eddie	Oregon	Raffensberger, Ken	Penna.
Hatton, Grady	Texas	Stallcup, Virgil	S. Carolina
Lively, Everett	Alabama	Vander Meer, Johnny	N. J.
Lowrey, Harry	California	Walker, Harry	Alabama
Meeks, Sam	South Carolina	Wehmeier, Herman	Ohio

Philadelphia Phillies—12 Players

Player	Home State	Player	Home State
Ashburn, Richie	Nebraska	Hamner, Granville	Virginia
Blatnik, Johnny	Ohio	Konstanty, Jim	New York
Blattner, Bobby	Missouri	Lopata, Stan	Michigan
Caballero, Ralph	Louisiana	Miller, Bob	Michigan
Donnelly, Blix	Minnesota	Simmons, Curt	Pennsylvania
Ennis, Del	Pennsylvania	Trinkle, Ken	Indiana

Chicago Cubs—12 Players

Player	Home State	Player	Home State
Burgess, Forrest	N. Carolina	McCall, Dutch	Tennessee
Cavarretta, Phil	Illinois	Mauch, Gene	California
Hamner, Ralph	Arkansas	Muncrief, Bob	Oklahoma
Jeffcoat, Hal	N. Carolina	McLish, Cal	Oklahoma
Johnson, Don	California	Rush, Bob	Indiana
Lade, Doyle	Nebraska	Schmitz, Johnny	Wisconsin

ACKNOWLEDGMENTS

The author wishes to express his gratitude to the following:

Dr. FRANCIS TREVELYAN MILLER of Historical Foundations

J. A. ROBERT QUINN, Director National Baseball Hall of Fame
and Museum

ERNEST J. LANIGAN, Historian National Baseball Hall of Fame
and Museum

The Honorable ALBERT B. CHANDLER, Commissioner of
Baseball

WILLIAM HARRIDGE, President of the American League

FORD C. FRICK, President of the National League

GEORGE M. TRAUTMAN, President of the National Association
of Professional Baseball Leagues

STEPHEN C. CLARK, President of the National Baseball Hall
of Fame and Museum

GEORGE E. BELLIS, Athletic Activities Committee, The American Legion, Dept. of Penna.

PETER C. CRAIG, Oberlin College

FRANK W. BLAIR, Princeton, N. J.

ANN WOODWARD MILLER and Attorney H. S. TUNICK of New
York

INDEX

235